INDIAN HIGHER EDUCATION

A Conglomerate of Concepts, Facts and Practices

ABOUT THE AUTHOR

Professor K.B. Powar is Secretary General of the Association of Indian Universities. Earlier he was Vice Chancellor of Shivaji University, Kolhapur and before that Professor of Geology at the University of Poona, Pune. A well known earth scientist, who has been the President of the Geology and Geography Section of the Indian Science Congress and President of Wadia Institute of Himalayan Geology, Dehradun, he is a Fellow of the National Academy of Sciences, India.

In recent years Professor Powar has made significant contributions to research and policy planning related to higher education, especially in the areas of quality assurance and economics of education. He is the author of three books including *Accreditation in Higher Education - An Indian Perspective, International Students in Indian Universities* and *Performance Indicators for Distance Higher Education*. He has also edited 12 volumes on higher education including *University Administration and Management, Higher Education in India - In Search of Quality, State Funding of Higher Education, Higher Education for Human Development*, and *Internationalisation of Indian Higher Education*.

INDIAN HIGHER EDUCATION

A Conglomerate of Concepts, Facts and Practices

K.B. Powar

Secretary General
Association of Indian Universities
New Delhi 110 002

and

former Vice Chancellor
Shivaji University
Kolhapur - 416 004

Concept Publishing Company, New Delhi 110 059

ISBN 81-7022-940-5

First Published 2002

Published and Printed by
Ashok Kumar Mittal
Concept Publishing Company
A/15-16, Commercial Block, Mohan Garden
New Delhi-110059 (India)

Phones: 5648039, 5649024
Fax: 091-(11)-5648053
E-mail: publishing@conceptpub.com

Foreword

The system of higher education in the Indian subcontinent is one of the largest in the world, comprising about 260 universities and more than 11,000 colleges, about 8 million students and 0.35 million teachers. The evolution of the system from the ancient seats of higher learning at Nalanda and Takshashila to the modern international class professional education offered by reputed universities and higher education institutions has passed through many strides, and innovations and change. A selected few Indian universities are second to none in the international scenario, and a large majority of Indian graduates, especially in the field of information technology, have excelled, at times dominated the international competition. We have well initiated reforms in the form of vigourated university management, autonomous colleges, excellent scientific research, academic staff colleges, vocationalisation of education, academic restructuring, modular curriculum and credit system, open university education, private initiatives in education, internationalisation of education, to name a few.

In spite of such desirable changes, we have a system of higher education which has been best described as having 'islands of excellence in a sea of mediocrity'. When we examine the system along such parameters as access and equity, relevance, and quality, we obtain a mixed bag. The academia, the institutional leaders and the policy makers have debated issues concerning autonomy and accountability, educational reforms and restructuring, curriculum development, financing and resource mobilisation, private universities, institutional and programme evaluation, quality assurance and accreditation, joint degree programmes, state support to education, and such other issues from time to time in the context of both conventional and open distance education. Several important educational policy documents and commission reports are already in place. What is lacking is action - action which is concrete, acceptable, viable, effective and reformative. The present book by Professor Powar should be handy on this count.

Prof. Powar, whose experience as a teacher and educational administrator exceeds four decades, has written extensively on different aspects of higher education. This book is a collection of his papers published during the last five years. In these papers Prof. Powar has analysed the issues in higher education in a historical perspective, and more realistically within the context that the system functions. He has given useful suggestions, guidelines and directions for the consideration of the policy makers, institutional leaders, teachers, and government and non-government organisations to orient national higher education system towards development and creation of informed citizens who can set agenda for the future.

H.P. Dikshit
Vice Chancellor
Indira Gandhi National Open University &
President
Association of Indian Universities

New Delhi
July 26, 2001

Contents

Preface

The modern Indian higher education system, established in 1857 with the founding of universities in Calcutta (Kolkatta), Bombay (Mumbai) and Madras (Chennai), has expanded beyond all expectations and is today the second largest in the world. It has been compared to a monolith with a large core of mediocrity surrounded by a thin and discontinuous rim of excellence. For a country having an ancient and glorious past, and great expectations from the future, the large core of mediocrity is a matter of deep concern and the rim of excellence a matter of pride and hope. There is also the realisation that like the dinosaurs of the past the system has become very sluggish, and like them (and Garguntua) consumes enormous resources. One hopes that the system will not crawl to extinction (as the dinosaurs did), because of ineptitude, thereby fulfilling management *guru* Peter Drucker's prophesy that universities will not survive in the face of modern technological developments.

I have had the privilege of being associated with the Indian higher education system for well nigh fifty years, first as student, later as a teacher, and then as an administrator. It has not been easy to accept the transition from Nehru's idealism, to Mayor's pragmatism to today's crass commercialisation. Nor, to understand why a person entering the university fraternity is expected to perform (and that to competently) such varied functions as teaching and research and service and administration. Nor, appreciate the unwillingness of people in the profession to pair autonomy (which they fiercely want) with accountability (which at least a few consider irrelevant). Admittedly, for the major part of the five decades I have been a mute witness, and an uncomplaining acceptor, of all that is happening. However, during the last decade I have availed of the opportunities provided to pen (and re-pen) my thoughts on different aspects of higher education. I have frequently toyed with the idea of compiling my articles on higher education in a single volume, and a couple of promptings from friends have been sufficient to convert thoughts into practice. Hence, this volume for all that it is worth.

It may be necessary to say a few words about the title. My choice has been influenced by the fact that I have been a student and teacher of Geology. For the layman a conglomerate is that which is made up of parts of varying kind. However, in geological parlance a conglomerate is a rock-unit constituted of well-rounded pieces of rocks, of different composition, cemented together by a matrix of any material. The rounded nature of the rock pieces is the result of constant rolling — or re-working. I have attempted to draw an analogy, in which the higher education system is a rock-unit, the pieces of rocks of different types are the papers (chapters) on different aspects of higher education, and the cementing matrix is a commonly shared concern for higher education. Like the rounded pieces of rocks some of the papers have been 'reworked' from earlier versions. Those included in this volume were published during the last five years and present the state of education at the time of writing. No major effort has been put in to up-date the information (or change tense), for this could be an unending process. In fact the difference in statistics can itself be revealing. For example, the difference in the data given in papers 2 and 5 provides an idea of the growth of higher education in India between 1996 and 2000. As the papers were prepared for different occasions there is a certain amount of duplication and this has been retained as it enables the reading of a paper as a whole, without having to make cross-reference.

The papers in the first section of the book essentially examine the basic concepts of higher education, in the context of the Indian scenario, and look at the development of higher education in India. Those in the second section are India-centric dealing with the status of different areas and issues in higher education in India. The third section contains papers relating to financing of higher education, the fourth section includes papers related to quality of higher education, and the fifth section those concerning distance and flexible education. Hopefully, the book in its entirety justifies its title by being not only a conglomerate of papers on various aspects of higher education but also a conglomerate of concepts, facts, practices and (dare I say) thoughts.

I gratefully acknowledge the support extended by the Association of Indian Universities through its successive Presidents and member Vice Chancellors, who have encouraged me to write on different aspects of higher education. The present President Prof. H.P. Dikshit has been especially helpful. Many of the papers included in this volume first appeared in publications of the Association. Paper 16 is a modified version of a chapter in a previous book published by Viva Books, New Delhi.

The thoughts and ideas incorporated in this volume are by no means original. They have their roots in interaction with a host of stakeholders of higher education — too numerous to name. However, I must express my indebtedness to my closest co-travellers on the road of higher education namely, Prof. R.G.Takwale, Prof. A. Gnanam, Dr. M. Anandakrishnan and Prof. S. Ventakeswaran. And also to my colleagues in the Association of Indian Universities, and to my family, for the unwavering faith and unstinted support.

New Delhi,
June 1, 2001.

K.B. Powar
Secretary General
Association of Indian Universities

Concepts and Development

- The Changing Role and Functions of Universities
- Higher Education in India since Independence: The First Fifty Years
- Reforms and Innovations in Higher Education: The Relevance and Role of Research
- Higher Education in the Twenty-first Century
- Indian Higher Education in the Knowledge Era: The Challenges Within

1

The Changing Role and Functions of Universities*

Introduction

The term 'university' is derived from the Latin word *universitas* meaning an organised body of individuals (community), or a corporation. The first two European institutions of higher learning, at Bologna and Paris, were corporations respectively of students (*universitas scholarium)* and of masters (*universitas magistrorum*). There was no fixed place for study and *universitas* meant, not a campus where classes were conducted, but a fraternity of scholars (Lockmiller, 1969). Interestingly, the term university, as then used, did not include the concept of universality — a concept which is today considered to be fundamental to the idea of a university. However, as 'university' is phonetically close to 'universe' (which connotes both spatial and temporal vastness) an intrinsic relationship between the two is often presumed. Understandably, therefore, the common perception is that a university consists of a community of people, of superior intellect, engaged in critically or holistically examining all aspects of human life and activity. The examination involves discourse, discussion and debate; the work is essentially that of preservation, transmission and generation of knowledge; and the main actors are the teachers and students. If this perception is valid then the university, as an institution, can be traced back to ancient times. India can claim to be the home of the prototypes for, in the first millennium AD, centres of learning, having the attributes of a university described above, existed at Takshashila in the north, Nalanda and Vikramshila in the east, Vallabhi in the west and Kanchipuram in the south.

Historical Review

Jha (1991) provides details about the Indian institutions of higher learning that flourished between the first and eighth century AD. At

* Paper prepared for the International Seminar on '*Higher Education for Human Development*' organised by the Association of Indian Universities, New Delhi on February 22-24, 2000.

Takshashila, the most ancient of the institutions, students admitted at about the age of 16, could study the three basic subjects of *vedas*, grammar and philosophy, or learn some 17 crafts including medicine, surgery, astronomy, agriculture, commerce, dancing and painting. Nalanda had, at its zenith, about 1,500 teachers and 8,500 students. Admission was based on strict entrance examinations at which only about 20 per cent of the students, averaging 20 years of age, were successful. The curriculum of the university included a wide range of subjects, both brahmanical and buddhist. Vikramshila had six colleges each with 108 teachers. Vallabhi, with about 6000 priests, was a rival to Nalanda and promoted all branches of religious learning as well as medicine. Kanchipuram was a centre of learning that attracted scholars from all over the country. The number, though not specifically known, was large and the scholars devoted themselves to the study of sacred lore, especially the four *vedas* and the *vedangas*.

The forerunner of modern institutions of higher learning in Europe was a medical school, at Salerno in southern Italy, which was established in the ninth century AD. The first European university was established in Bologna in the eleventh century (1088 AD to be precise) and was followed by those at Paris and Oxford in the twelfth century. These were founded as centres for travelling teachers and scholars and their main objective was to propagate the intellectual currents of the time (Ben-David, 1968). The subsequent universities are descendants of these early universities. There have, of course, been changes in composition, approach and activities depending upon the needs of the time. In the thirteenth century the European universities developed into educational centres of the states, oriented to meet the demand for civil servants, especially priests and lawyers (Bertilsson, 1992). The universities of the Middle Ages were essentially centres for teaching and training.

The importance of research in universities was first recognised by Wilhelm von Humboldt, the German thinker on higher education. Realising the need to integrate teaching with research he formulated the concept of a research university which was put into practice with the founding of the Berlin University in 1810. The idea found fulfilment in the United States in the form of research universities like those of John Hopkins, Stanford and Berkeley (Bertilsson, *op. cit.*). In the late nineteenth and the twentieth centuries the need for trained manpower, and an educated labour force, ensured that science and technology became important in the universities.

Traditionally, the universities have been the preserve of the well-to-do. At the beginning of the twentieth century there was a social awakening that slowly transformed the universities from elite centres for the privileged to egalitarian institutions, responsible to society and mindful of its needs. By the end of World War II most universities had become strongly committed to the welfare of their societies and soon 'extension', or service to the community, became a recognised function of universities — at least in principle. Thus today a traditional university is charged with the responsibility of undertaking teaching, research and extension activities. As Daillant (1990) points out, the vigorous growth of socially committed universities reflects a confidence in higher education as a major instrument of social and economic progress.

The political, scientific and economic developments of the 1990's, especially the breakdown of political barriers, the emergence of free-market economy and the stupendous progress in information technology, have highlighted the need for a 'globalisation of education'. A paradigm shift towards learner-centred, lifelong education has opened up new and exciting possibilities for open and distance learning. These impose new demands on the universities, and if they are slow in responding to the challenge of distance education there is the possibility of their becoming dispensable.

Changing Perspectives

The modern concept of a university was presented by Cardinal John Henry Newman, the founder of the Catholic University of Dublin, in 1852, in a series of discourses on the '*Scope and Nature of University Education'*. These were later published under the title '*The Idea of a University' (cf. Ker, 1976).* Newman firmly believed that it was necessary to separate the search of knowledge from the cares of mankind. A university he, therefore, believed that a university should be dedicated to the pursuit of knowledge for its own sake. He visualised it to be *"the high protecting power of all knowledge and science, of fact and principle, of inquiry and discovery, of experiment and speculation"*. Newman believed universities should be ivory towers, far separated from the cares and the influence of society, where scholars could indulge in the pursuit of knowledge, in whatever area they chose, without being accountable to anyone.

Newman's vision of a university was in accordance with the traditional belief, which had prevailed since the establishment of the universities at Bologna, Paris and Oxford, that universities had the freedom of thought and action. This privilege was based on the maxim that there should be no hindrance to the search for truth. Since then academics have considered their freedom to think and to act to be unlimited, so much so that Sidney Smith (1988) suggested that it included *"the right to differ, and the most precious right of all, the right to be wrong".*

The traditional views regarding the mission, goals and role of a university continued to hold sway till the middle of the twentieth century though the utilitarian aspects became increasingly important. In India, because of its ancient heritage and traditions, great emphasis was placed on values. India's first Prime Minister Jawaharlal Nehru (1947), in his oft-cited convocation address to the University of Allahabad, asked the universities to lay stress on *"those standards of thoughts and action which make an individual and a nation".* He eloquently stated, *"A university stands for humanism, for tolerance, for reason, for progress, for the adventure of ideas and for the search for truth. It stands for the onward march of the human race towards even higher objectives".* Nehru's exhortations were in keeping with his idealism but did not have much to offer as regards the mundane expectation of the multitude who were more concerned with the wherewithal for a better standard of living.

As universities became more egalitarian in character the emphasis shifted from *values* to *utility.* In most of the western world the period between the two World Wars saw the introduction of vocational and utilitarian programmes. In the developing countries, including India, this is being done today. After World War II administrators have repeatedly stated that universities must interact with society and be useful to it. Fredrico Mayor, Director-General of UNESCO, in an address delivered at a seminar on Institutional Development of Higher Education in Africa (Mayor, 1991) laid emphasis on 'service to society'. He advocated a university *'forging numerous connections with society,....creating links with other forms of study...., developing outreach programmes....., and networking of all kinds".* He stated, *"I should like to see the university cultivate closer relations with the worlds of business, commerce, industry, agriculture, journalism and administration. Research links... need to be forged with all these sectors; greater efforts should be made to seek out consultancy and service work".*

The utilitarian perspective has sometimes created dissension within academia. Teachers of science, business and technology faculties have largely been able to adjust to the new environment. However, those from arts and humanities, and to a lesser extent from the social sciences, often feel left out. The frustration of the traditionalists is manifested in the best-seller *The Closing of the American Mind* by Allan Bloom (1987). Making a plea for the restoration of liberal education to the centre of university teaching he asks for an atmosphere of free enquiry where one could contemplate on *"questions that ought to be addressed by everyone but are not asked in everyday life"*. Disapproving of the involvement of a university with the problems of society he suggests that *"it need not concern itself with providing its students with experiences that are available in democratic society. They will have them in any event. It must provide them with experience they cannot have there"*.

The protestations of Bloom, apart there is a general acceptance of the fact that there has to be a close linkage between university and society, and that at least some of the programmes offered by a university should be useful to the student from the point of securing employment. While the transition from the traditional to a utilitarian outlook is consistent with the demands of an egalitarian society, what is worrisome is the increasing dominance of a commercial outlook. With the onslaught of free-market economy, and the increasing reluctance of governments to support higher education, the commercialisation of education by some universities is a matter of fact. Today, education is being subjected to the competitive laws of the market. Governments are encouraging universities to develop an entrepreneurial, if not commercial, approach. There is a mad rush to internationalise education, not because of its social, cultural and diplomatic benefits, but in order to generate additional income. The Times Higher Education Supplement, London, in its issue dated September 19, 1997, concluded in its column 'Opinion': *"Higher education is an international business and universities cannot afford to become parochial.... They (the universities) are par-excellence an industry in a cut-throat global market"*. The stake-holders of universities — students, teachers, academic administrators, government, potential employers and the society-at-large — need to take note of this development.

The Functions of a University

In the 900 and odd years following the establishment of the first European university at Bologna, the university system has periodically accepted additional responsibilities. Today, a university has multiple functions. It is expected:

First, to foster a spirit of free enquiry, and promote independent and critical thinking;

Second, to be a repository of knowledge, responsible for its transmission through teaching and extra-mural programmes;

Third, to be the place for the pursuit, generation and application of new knowledge, and for the 'search for truth';

Fourth, to be the training ground for competent professionals, including doctors, engineers, business managers and administrators;

Fifth, to render service to society, anticipating its needs and assisting in the fulfilment of social and economic objectives;

Sixth, to facilitate the formulation, development and implementation of national policies and programmes; and

Seventh, to promote values and assist in the preservation of culture and traditions.

A report of the International Commission on Education for the Twenty First Century (*Delors Report*), entitled *'Learning: The Treasure Within'* (UNESCO, 1996), visualises four functions for the universities:

First, to prepare students for research and training

Second, to provide training courses oriented to the needs of society

Third, to be open to all to foster lifelong learning in its broadest sense, and

Fourth, to strive for international cooperation.

Today, society has high expectations from the universities. By assigning to them a variety of functions it has reposed great faith in our academic institutions. This faith is based more on expectations than on firm evidence of the capabilities of the universities. Academics themselves are more cautious in this regard and also a little reluctant about venturing into areas other than research and teaching. There is a feeling that many universities are unable to perform up to expectations because they have been asked to do too much. Livingstone (1974) has drawn attention to the fact that *'as universities in the twentieth century have grown, countless new functions have been grafted on with little regard for how this growth of one function will affect the operation of the other"*. This is especially true of India where government functionaries tend to pass on every newly visualised programme to the universities — starting from adult literacy to environmental awareness to eco-restoration to protection of human rights. As a consequence the same set of people are expected to competently discharge functions that require disparate qualities and expertise. On the other hand, not unnaturally, most universities tend to concentrate their resources and energy on teaching and research, but not necessarily in that order. Agricultural universities have in-built extension programmes, and technical universities undertake consultancy services, and interact with industry. The extent of interaction varies considerably. In the United States, for example, the interaction is very close and mutually very satisfactory. The relationship between Stanford University and Silicon Valley is an outstanding example. In

India it is barely visible, except in the case of some elite institutions. In the traditional universities in India the 'service to society' aspect (extension) is in most universities largely on paper, as is the responsibility of promoting values and preserving culture and tradition. Not that this is unique to this country. Livingstone (*op. cit.*), while reacting to the recommendations of the Robbins Committee stated *"the idea of the university transmitting a common culture and common standards of citizenship has probably attracted most scorn. Manifestly it is a goal hardly even aspired to, outside a handful of smaller or collegiate universities"*.

Primary Focus: Teaching or Research?

Since the time Wilhelm von Homboldt introduced the concept of the 'research university' there has been an unending debate on whether a university should concentrate on teaching or on research, or undertake both teaching and research. Newman was quite categorical in stating that teaching and research were two distinct functions — the first belonged to the universities, the second to the (research) academies. In his 'discourse' he stated, *"To discover and to teach are two distinct functions; they are also distinct gifts, and are not commonly found united in the same person. He too who spends his time in dispensing his existing knowledge to all comers is unlikely to have either leisure or energy to acquire new. .... The greatest thinkers have been too interested in their subject to admit of interruption.... And have more or less shunned the lecture room and the public school."* (*cf.* Ker, 1976).

The consensus amongst educationists has, however, been that universities must perform both the duties, apparently because they are mutually beneficial. Thus, we have opinions, such as: *"The combination of research and teaching is the lofty... basic principle of the university."* (Jaspers, 1965); *"There would be widespread agreement with the view that the fundamental characteristic (of a university) is the combination of research with teaching."* (Brook, 1965); and *"I shall treat a university as though it has two major sub-systems: one for the discovery of knowledge — research; the other for the dissemination of knowledge — teaching."* (Rice, 1970). Perhaps, the 'mutually beneficial' aspect is being over-stressed. It is possible that attempts to achieve excellence in one aspect may distract from efforts in the other.

A study on the academic profession in 14 countries, undertaken by the Carnegie Foundation for the Advancement of Teaching (Boyer *et al.*, 1994), shows that contrary to popular belief academics in Russia and the United States give higher priority to teaching than to research. However, in Germany, Sweden, the Netherlands and Japan the primary commitment seems to be research. In other countries it is closer to half and half. The data presented in the study show that in Russia the interest of 68 per cent of the teachers is primarily in, or leaning towards, teaching. The remaining 32 per cent have interest primarily in, or leaning towards, research. The corresponding figures for the United States are 63 per cent and 37 per cent; for Brazil 62 per cent and 38 per cent; for Australia 48 per cent and 52 per cent; for England 44 per cent and 56 per cent; for Sweden 33 per cent and 67 per cent; for Japan 28 per cent and 72 per cent; and for the Netherlands 25 per cent and 75 per cent. In the United States 27 per cent are primarily interested in teaching while in Japan this is the case with only 4 per cent. In Sweden 23 per cent are primarily interested in research while in Russia the number is only 3 per cent. These figures reflect not only the variability in interest but also the difficulty of governments and grant-giving bodies in deciding which activity — teaching or research — to support more liberally.

In India, the term 'university' is often used in the broader sense, and includes the large number of colleges that are affiliated to the universities. The colleges cater primarily to undergraduate students and hence their main responsibility is teaching. The duality of function and interest arises only in the case of teachers on university campuses who are directly recruited by the universities. The teachers are expected to do both teaching and research in approximately equal measure. However, while assessing a teacher for promotion the main yardstick is his or her contribution in research. The teachers, therefore, have an inclination to pay greater attention to research and in the process, not infrequently, neglect teaching. Unfortunately, the research contribution is often not significant, for most university departments lack facilities in terms of laboratory and library support. Under the circumstances it is necessary to examine the question of priority of functions. It is time to de-emphasise research, except in the case of universities having excellent facilities, and ask the teachers to concentrate on teaching. It should be possible to distinguish, on the basis of past performance, the research-oriented departments (if not universities) from those that would be better-off concentrating on teaching. The separation of the (few) research universities from the conventional teaching universities appears to be a pragmatic (if undesirable) alternative.

The Nature of Research

There has been an ongoing debate on different aspects of research being conducted in the universities. The ongoing discussions are on such issues as basic research versus applied research, quantitative research versus qualitative research, discipline specific research versus inter-disciplinary or multi-disciplinary research, voluntary research versus contract research, and creative research versus research for circulation (Ferrer, 1999). Some of these issues need to be addressed.

Research is basically of two types:

- Basic (or fundamental) research undertaken in a free state of enquiry solely to acquire knowledge.
- Applied (or developmental) research undertaken to acquire knowledge or resource that has practical application to problems of society.

Basic research is pursued in practically all disciplines, and especially so in the departments belonging to the faculties of arts, humanities and natural sciences. It contributes to the intellectual development of the faculty and students though there may not be any immediate benefits. In basic research the initiative is generally taken by individuals or research groups, not by the institution. The nature of the research undertaken, and its quality, is based on tradition, ability of the faculty and available facilities. Applied research is undertaken largely in the laboratory-based science and technology departments, some social science departments, and the professional academic institutions (including those for science and technology, agriculture and medicine). The type of research reflects the needs of society. While funding for basic research generally comes from the university and government agencies, applied research may also receive money from industry and business (Young, 1988).

During the nineteenth century, and the greater part of the twentieth century, research was concentrated within disciplines, and to specialised areas within the disciplines. This led to the development of knowledge but also resulted in its segmentation. However, there has been a blurring of boundaries between different subjects, and with the need to examine problems from different viewpoints, the emphasis is now shifting to multi-disciplinary and interdisciplinary approaches. Research topics are increasingly being determined by the issues affecting society, like those relating to environment, energy and population. These, and many other areas, do not fall within the purview of a single discipline and hence an interdisciplinary approach is increasingly being adopted.

Research in science, technology, medicine and agriculture requires substantial financial support which government and other public agencies often cannot provide. Hence universities are looking to industry for support through contract research. The industry-sponsored research is usually for specific purposes, oriented towards production, and is therefore in many cases confidential. This is contrary to the traditions of universities and of academics who have always believed in publishing the results of their work as soon as possible. It is, therefore, natural that academics prefer to work in areas of their own liking with government support, and undertake contractual work only when it becomes necessary because of the funds it provides.

Bennich-Bjorkman (1997), in a critical study on the organisation of innovative research in universities, points out that research contributions need to be creative; and in order to be so classified, they should provide new concepts and theories that result in fresh interpretation of society and nature, or provide new solutions to old problems, or pose new questions, or rephrase problems in new terms. He points out that several scholars have suggested that to merit the label 'creative' the contributions should be, amongst other things novel and relevant (valuable). Based on a combination of these two requirements research contributions can be classified as:

- *Creative* for contributions that are both novel and relevant
- *Original* for contributions that are novel but not relevant
- *Cumulative* for contributions that are relevant but not novel
- *Replication* for contributions that are neither relevant nor novel

Bennich-Bjorkman (*op. cit.*) states, *"Progress, then, is made by research contributions of either a creative or cumulative kind. However, original work which is bereft of the quality of relevance does not constitute genuine progress"*. In defence of originality one can, however, say that what is not relevant today may become relevant in the near future. Original contributions, thus, have the potential of becoming creative. Contributions from universities are generally cumulative or replications. Original contributions are few and creative ones still less. The research contributions of many Indian universities are replications and a product of what is indigenously known as 'parallel research'. No wonder that many theses lie unpublished on the shelves of university libraries with the findings never seeing the light of day. The requirement of basic research, namely excellent infrastructure, highly qualified and motivated academic personnel and administrative support are available in only a few Indian universities. By and large, they would be better off if they concentrate on applied research.

Creative research is usually produced by universities and departments that have a tradition and culture of productivity. In this respect Bennich-Bjorkman's study provides two important conclusions. First, that for a department to become excellent in research it must develop a culture which encourages intellectual and scholarly exchange, forges social bonds and nurtures a genuine sharing of interest. Second, that such a culture has to develop spontaneously and cannot be bureaucratically imposed. The quality of scholarship that exists and the relations that are already in place play a definitive role in promoting the spirit of excellence.

While striving for excellence in research in the universities one may examine two contrasting models — the German and the American. In Germany, research was introduced as an important activity of the universities in the early nineteenth century. Research schools were built around a professor and his research interest. The student worked on his mentor's project and on his own dissertation simultaneously. In this system the individual's effort is the dominating factor with the supervisor playing a facilitator's role by providing the guidance. Talent is (or was) developed individually and independently. Research is an activity for a selected few. In contrast in the United States coursework is an important part of a doctoral programme. There are many interactions in the form of discussions and seminars. The professional dimension of research is emphasised, and one is 'trained for' and not 'born into' research. Which model is to be followed is for each institution to decide depending on its traditions and culture. However, in an era in which there is intense specialisation, yet in which a holistic approach is being advocated (partnership and networking are the key words), the American system promises to be more productive.

Responsibilities to Society

The transition of higher education from an elite system to an egalitarian one was accompanied by an acceptance of the idea that universities had a responsibility to the societies they serve. As pointed out earlier, by the end of World War II most universities were committed to the welfare of their respective societies, and at a Conference of Representatives of Universities, convened by UNESCO, at Utrecht, Netherlands, in 1948, the social responsibilities of universities were seen as extending much further than the mere welfare of intellectuals (Diallant, 1990). The universities can help their communities in various ways — by actually participating in development work, by developing teaching and training programmes relevant to the needs of its constituents, and by undertaking research-based studies on problems relevant to planning and development. Kumar (1988) has voiced the expectations of society thus: "*The universities must bring the academic talents of their faculties and the idealism of their youthful students to bear on the problems of the common people of the land, and not allow themselves to be elitist organisations, deaf to the groanings of the deprived".*

In India, the University Grants Commission adopted, in 1977, extension as the third dimension of higher education in addition to the two accepted functions of teaching and research. The policy statement issued at that time said: *"If the university system has to discharge adequately its responsibilities to the entire educational system, and to the society as a whole it must assume extension as the third important responsibility and give it the same status as teaching and research".* It added *"All universities and colleges should develop close relationships, of mutual services and support, with their local communities, and all students and teachers must be involved in such programmes as an integral part of their education"* (University Grants Commission, 1987). Since then extension programmes are being undertaken, through the National Service Scheme (NSS) and the Departments of Adult and Continuing Education and, to a lesser extent, through the National Cadet Corps (NCC). The college students have participated in rural development projects and have played an important part in programmes of eradication of illiteracy and adult (and continuing) education, and those related to the technology missions. The universities have also developed a wide variety of short-term training programmes for the benefit of under-privileged classes. Because of financial constraints, and possibly because of lack of conviction amongst faculty and students, in many cases the results have fallen far short of expectation.

Even if there are shortcomings in the formal mechanisms through which the universities can be of assistance to society they can be useful in other ways. They can be critics, helpers and advisers of the different constituents of society. Universities should have no difficulty in playing the role of critic of its own community. Their main function would be to analyse the economic, social, political and cultural development of their region; a role not alien to the teaching faculty and research scholars. The universities can help their community through the research they do and the information they disseminate. Faculty members can, and do, work on problems the results of which are useful in agriculture, business, management and social welfare. Assisting industry is something that is often talked about and even in India there are examples of active university-industry interaction and cooperation. The university has also the responsibility of advising government, industry and society in general on matters that concern the daily life of citizens; on environmental issues, for example. However, it must be emphasised that universities will be able to discharge their obligations adequately only if government, industry and other potential beneficiaries repose confidence in them. It is first necessary to accept the fact that the universities are pools of talent, knowledge and expertise willing to be tapped by government and industry; and that they have the potential to provide solutions to problems in key sectors like, agriculture, industry and development.

Relationship with the 'World of Work'

In recent years there has been a growing realisation that there has to be a symbiotic relationship between the 'world of knowledge' and the 'world of work'. Industry and business realise that with the expansion in higher education the information base has grown almost exponentially and new knowledge is a key factor in productivity. Likewise, academics accept that practical experience is a necessary component of the learning process and this can be provided only through the cooperation of the world of work. Silicon Valley provides a unique example of what can be achieved if the 'world of knowledge' and the 'world of work' act in unison. Casper (1998) points out that today Silicon Valley is a metaphor the world over for productive relationship between a university and the surrounding region. It is, therefore, instructive to review the characteristics of the two partners. Stanford University is a 'research-intensive university'. It fulfils three important criteria: it selects its students, it is primarily dedicated to the search for knowledge, and it fosters the spirit of critical inquiry. Casper (*op. cit.*) emphasises the fact that the university has a fundamental commitment to the building of 'steeples of excellence' in research, teaching and learning; believes in the combination of teaching and research; encourages freedom in setting agendas; seeks industry partnerships; maintains porous boundaries; and is open to chance and serendipity in research. To complement this Silicon Valley has a regional, network-based industrial system that promotes collective learning and flexible adjustments. There is horizontal communication between firms with the functional boundaries separating them being porous. And so is the boundary between university and industry. The partnership between the two is facilitated and brought to fulfilment through Stanford's Centre for Integrated Systems whose stated objective is the integration of hardware and software systems. It may be difficult to duplicate the ethos and environment of Silicon Valley but it is an example to be emulated and replicated.

For meaningful and fruitful cooperation between universities and industry there has to be a conducive environment. In India interaction between academe and industry has been rather restricted possibly because of difference in values and attitudes, lack of appreciation of each other's abilities, skills and needs, and the absence of economic compulsions. The traditional value system in the universities has placed stress on ethical behaviour and the disinterested pursuit of knowledge. In contrast many have perceived the main objective of industry to be production of more goods, at lower cost, and the exploitation of markets even if it means inappropriate practices (Taskar and Packham, 1993). However, in recent years the ground situation has changed. Academe has become more materialistic and industry has shown an awareness of society's problems. The styles of management are also converging. Under these circumstances it should be possible for academics to cast aside the shackles of traditionalism and establish a meaningful relationship with industry and business. Special efforts, like the establishment of liaison cells for university-industry interaction (*cf.* Association of Indian Universities, 1995) and promotional drives, need to be made. There is no reason why technology parks should not be successful.

University, Multiversity, Open University and Specialised Institutions

Newman, in his 'discourses' defined a university in simple terms as *'a place for teaching universal knowledge'*. He specifically stated that the object was intellectual not moral, and that the main purpose was the diffusion and extension of knowledge rather than its advancement. He thus excluded research from the purview of his university (Ker, 1976). More than a century later Ross (1976) wrote: *"The concept of the university, that emerged over the centuries, and that prevailed up to World War II, thus was that of a selective small, autonomous, self-contained community devoted to the preservation and advancement of knowledge, exercising something like pastoral care over its students, focusing on the great humanistic issues in life, and providing a place for the more prestigious professions in its midst. This was the 'idealised university' — or college. There was little disagreement about its purpose or form and none about its virtues"*.

The developments in the years immediately following World War II shattered this cosy image of the university. There was rapid growth in the number of students, the areas of study and the number of institutions. Students joined because they wanted to acquire knowledge or skills that would get them a job. The university found it fruitful to develop relationship with society, and especially with industry. The utilitarian aspect became important. Clark Kerr, President of the University of California, in his widely acclaimed Godkin Lectures of 1963 (Kerr, 1963) described the large post-war university as a multiversity. Characteristically it was large and growing, had multiple-campuses mostly composed of a number of separate and largely unrelated communities, was multifunctional, and was service-oriented offering programmes and activities that were influenced by social needs. In his characteristic way Kerr described education as a *"knowledge industry"* and added *"the university as a producer, wholesaler and retailer of knowledge cannot escape service. Knowledge today is for everybody's sake"*. So much for Newman's views on the university. One may add that the concept of a multiversity is based on the principle that a place must be provided in a university for any person who is willing and able to benefit from it.

The University of California, with its seven campuses, operations at more than a hundred locations, employees numbering several tens of thousands, 400,000 students, over 10,000 courses and billion-dollar budget, is a good example of a multiversity. The larger Indian universities, with over 200 affiliated colleges and student strengths of over two hundred thousand, in a sense, also qualify as multiversities.

Another post-World War II development of immense significance is the emergence of the open university that offers education through the distance mode. The development of distance education was facilitated by the extraordinary advances in communication technology and the globalisation of education. The open universities have provided access to a large number of students living in remote areas and those in employment. The need for re-training, and the acceptance by society of the concept of lifelong education, have been other contributing factors to the development and growth of open universities. The growth of the Indira Gandhi National Open University and some of the state open universities is a pointer in this regard. However, there are many academics who believe that open education cannot be an equal alternative to the formal system of education; at best it can be a supplement or a substitute of lesser dimension.

The second half of the twentieth century saw the emergence of two types of 'knowledge factories' — one academically legitimate, the other not entirely so. The first is the highly specialised type of university-level institution, especially in professional education. This type includes universities for engineering and technology, agriculture, medical sciences and management. For the larger part these are excellent training institutes for their respective professions, have good infrastructure and have a competent professional faculty. They maintain close links with industry. Indian examples are the Indian Institutes of Technology, the Indian Institutes of Management, the agricultural universities and the post-graduate medical institutes at New Delhi and Chandigarh. The Birla Institute of Technology and Science, Pilani maintains a close and symbiotic relationship with industry through its 'practice school'.

The second type of 'knowledge factory' is the privately-financed, high-fee charging, training and service-oriented institution operated to meet the immediate demands of society. It is a part of a parallel system that has sprung up in many countries to meet the needs of ambitious but less talented students who cannot find entry into formal universities. Such an institution has been referred to as a non-university, a pseudo-university and even anti-university.

Models of Universities

The character of a university depends upon a number of factors including tradition, social milieu and its mission or purpose. It may appropriately be said that there are 'universities and universities'. A number of 'models' have been recognised in the European and North American scene (Husen, 1994). Models that are represented in India include:

- *The Humboldtian Research University Model* in which there is emphasis on graduate teaching and research, and on close interaction between the two functions for their mutual enrichment. Typical examples are the Berlin University in Germany and, amongst others, Stanford and John Hopkins in the United States. In India university-level institutions that approach this model include the Indian Institute of Science, Bangalore and the University of Hyderabad, Hyderabad.
- *The British Residential University Model* or *the 'Oxbridge' Model* that stresses close formal and informal contact between teachers and students, through classroom lectures, tutorials, seminars and other forms of personal contacts. The British examples are Oxford and Cambridge Universities. In India these ideals are being sought to be met in the one-campus universities like Jawaharlal Nehru University, New Delhi and the Banaras Hindu University, Varanasi.
- *The French Grandes Ecoles Model* imparting elitist, professional education, mainly in science and technology, to the most talented, and intellectually select, students. The Indian counterparts are the Indian Institutes of Technology and the Indian Institutes of Management.

- *The Chicago Liberal Education Model,* launched by Hutchins at the University of Chicago, which has a strong liberal arts orientation that places emphasis on the development of independent and critical thinking. A few Indian institutions like the Banasthali Vidyapeeth in Rajasthan, and the St. Stephens College in Delhi, probably replicate this model.
- *The Affiliating University Model,* based on the University of London of the nineteenth century, wherein there is a central campus for post-graduate studies and research with a number of affiliated colleges spread over the university area. In spite of an overt central control the standard of education imparted by the colleges varies considerably. There are about 120 universities in India that are based on this model.
- *The Agricultural University Model,* developed on the lines of the land-grant colleges of the United States, that concentrate on agricultural studies, including forestry, horticulture and veterinary sciences. The utilitarian approach is exemplified by a strong emphasis on extension services. There are presently 35 agricultural universities in India based on this model.
- *The Professional University Model* that provides for higher education in one of the professional areas like engineering, and medicine and health services. This is a new trend that seeks to separate education in the professional subjects from the mainstream of higher education. Examples are the universities for science and technology, for law, and for medicine and health services, established in some states of India.
- *The 'Deemed University' Model,* by which institutions noted for their noteworthy contributions in specialised subjects or disciplines, are granted the status of universities. As of today there are 32 such institutions in India. Examples are the Deccan College Post-Graduate and Research Institute, Pune, the Birla Institute of Technology and Science, Pilani and the Manipal Academy of Higher Education, Manipal.
- *The Open University Model*, that provides education through the distance mode, to those denied access; and promotes the concept of lifelong education for all. Typical examples are the UK Open University, Milton Keynes and the Indira Gandhi National Open University, New Delhi.

The Future of Universities

The modern university has survived as an institution for over nine hundred years — longer than many a nation-state. This has been possible because it has adapted itself to the changing needs and demands of its clientele. The fact that in the past the numbers were restricted, the academic community was relatively homogenous, and the rate of change was slow, has perhaps helped. The situation today is different. Academic institutions are bursting at the seams and the multiversity has become a reality. The clientele is heterogeneous including almost the entire spectrum of society. In an information age developments in communication technology have taken education to the living rooms of students. Distance education is, to a certain extent, obviating the need for formal education. And in many a youth the urge to climb the social ladder is so strong that utilitarian programmes offered by the 'anti-universities' are preferred to the value-oriented learning provided by the universities. And above all there have been two major paradigm shifts, the world over, in the field of education. First, the prevailing model of higher education, that requires *selective learning over a specified period of time* is being replaced by a model that favours *lifelong learning for all.* This is because the changing nature of jobs, and much shorter obsolescence periods for equipment, necessitates continuous updating of knowledge and skills. Second, there has been an evident shift from the *teacher-centred model* that requires attendance at an academic institution, to a *learner-centred model* that is based on student initiative and access to learning resources. Additionally, with the extensive development of information technology, distance education has emerged as an effective and viable medium for imparting knowledge.

Traditions have a very important place in society and one cannot disregard them, or our cultural heritage. Pragmatism makes it necessary to examine the extent to which we can bind ourselves to the past keeping in view the fact that most universities are modelled on the medieval universities of Europe. As Husen (1994) points out these were elitist, had an 'ivory tower' existence, sharply differentiated between theory and practice, and placed a premium on aloofness and autonomy. In keeping with these ideas universities have adopted the role of preparing students for traditional professions within the self-imposed boundaries of an 'ivory tower' understanding (Teicher, 1999). However, the survey by Boyer *et al.* (1994), referred to earlier, showed that academics consider preparing students for work and helping resolve their basic social problems being as important as promoting scholarship and research, and protecting free intellectual inquiry (Altbach, 1996). It is, therefore, necessary to see how the great universities – Oxford, Cambridge, Paris, Harvard, Peking and Banaras Hindu to name a few – are adapting themselves to the changed demands. It is relevant that these citadels of learning are striving to maintain the traditional concept while making changes to meet the new demands. Harvard, for example, is striving to sustain the traditions of liberal education. It expects its students to study broadly across several different subjects in addition to intensively pursuing the subject, or discipline, in which they major. The university has a commitment to research at the most fundamental level. It is trying to look at problems that have international dimensions, and require collaborative efforts, and is thus emphasising the inter-disciplinary and multi-disciplinary spirits. The university has taken up the challenge of ensuring openness and inclusiveness of university communities (Rudenstine, 1998).

There has been much discussion on the nature of universities in the 21st century; and in view of the very rapid changes that are taking place in all spheres one cannot predict anything for the years beyond the first quarter of the new millennium. And to talk of developments that can possibly take place during this period one must review the present functions of the universities. For much of the 20th century these have been teaching, research and service. However, as Brighton (1998) points out there have been perceptible changes in the manner these functions are being performed. Teaching, as mentioned earlier, is moving away from the teacher-centred lecture mode to the student-centred self-learning mode. The emphasis on research is moving (except in research intensive universities) from fundamental research to research that is relevant to societal needs. And in service (extension) the approach is shifting from service to community to addressing industry and people's issues in a manner that promotes the generation of funds and improves the quality of life.

It is evident that the universities of the 21st century will have to function under the all-pervading influence of the electronic communication revolution which has underwritten world economy, globalised knowledge, accelerated innovation and facilitated the individual access to information and skills (Lucus, 1998a). The universities will have to teach the students how to cope with the vast amount of information that keeps pouring in; to discriminate between what is useful and what needs to be confined to the trash bin. An important function will be to teach students how to analyse information competently and thereby convert it into knowledge. Importantly, the universities will have to function in a period when people, in a large measure, already possess skill as also the power to innovate. They will come from a variety of backgrounds and have different levels of achievement. The basic requirement will be to add to skills or teach new skills (Lucus, *op. cit.*). Additionally with increased student mobility and the advent of virtual classrooms the university will have to globalise both in terms of curricula and quality. There would be the need to internationalise curricula so that the learner can think globally even if he has to act at a national or local level. And quality will have to be ensured so that the education imparted is internationally competitive. Finally, a disconcerting feature of the later part of the twentieth century has been to view education in terms of economic needs, and in the last decade, in terms of global economy (Lucus, 1998b) or international relationships (Niland, 1998). There is an imperative need to restore values as a key factor in education. We cannot afford to separate education from ethics and morality.

Lucus (1998b), summarising the views presented by a galaxy of Presidents and Vice Chancellors, at a conference on 'Universities of the 21st Century' held at Peking University, concluded that in the near future there would be two main types of universities — the research intensive universities and the principally teaching universities. The former are likely to remain relatively small, and in keeping with the characteristic of research intensive universities, have a highly selective type of entry, with quality teaching and staff that is active in research. The second type would cater to the demands of mass higher education, would seek different forms of delivery, and therefore of relationship between teacher and taught. In this group, at one end would be the virtual universities, delivering education through the internet; and at the other end multi-campus universities with a consortia of (affiliated) colleges. Whatever the form, the feeling of the conference was that the future of universities lies in networks.

The essential question posed at the Peking Conference was: What is a university for? While attempting to provide an answer, Lucus (*op.cit.*) states: "*Certainly, it is for transmitting skills in their broadest definition. However, it is more for unlocking minds, endowing them with awareness of their capabilities, and empowering their creativity. Information without meaning serves little purpose. The work of universities is to endow information with meaning that is to say to create and transmit knowledge. Therefore, knowledge is a matter of values...*". Significantly, the Glion Colloquium, in which senior academics from USA and Europe participated, in its declaration (Glion Colloquium, 1998) affirmed "*teaching is a moral vocation involving the balanced development of the whole person*" and recognised "*the ancient values upon which the academy is established*". In the ultimate analysis this means a return to the traditional concept.

Impoverished as they are, and desperately trying to meet the challenges posed by the problems of access and quality, Indian universities face an unenviable task.

In the first decade of the new millennium they must address a number of issues that can no longer be glossed over. These are:

- How to meet the increasing demand for higher education, especially from the less-privileged sections of society, without compromising on the quality of education?
- How to reconcile the perception of academics and intellectuals, that liberal education is necessary for an individual's development, with the popular demand for specialised (utilitarian) education?
- How to improve the quality of education so that it can meet the demands of society and be internationally competitive?
- How to provide adequate funding to academic institutions without resorting to blatant 'privatisation' (read commercialisation) of education?
- How to reorganise our higher education system so as to make it autonomous, flexible and innovative?
- How to promote/preserve nationalism (*swadeshi* culture) while accepting the need to internationalise our education in keeping with the needs of a global society?

Clearly there is a need for greater commitment; for infusion of large amounts of money required for improving infrastructure; for increased participation of society (especially industry); for introduction of flexibility in academic structure; for ensuring quality enhancement; and for encouraging networking and partnerships. The last would require a convergence of the conventional and open universities, and a pragmatic partnership with the 'training industry'.

The University of the Future

What does one seek in a university of the new millennium? As visualised by Rhodes (1999) the New American University would be one possessing institutional autonomy and academic freedom but with strong impartial public governance; increasingly privately supported but publicly accountable and socially committed; campus-rooted but internationally oriented; academically independent but constructively partnered; knowledge-based but student-centred; research-driven but learning focussed; technologically sophisticated but community-dependent; quality-obsessed but procedurally efficient; and professionally attuned but humanely informed. In the Indian context one may add the new university would be open to all who desire to enrol but ensure a close teacher-student relationship, be development-oriented yet laying stress on values.

In a UNESCO policy paper for change and development in higher education (UNESCO, 1995) the concept of a proactive university has been put forward. Such a university would be:

- "a place where high quality training would be provided…,
- a place in which entry will only depend on the intellectual merit of the individual…,
- a community fully devoted to the search, creation and dissemination of knowledge, and to the progress of science...,
- a learning environment only founded in quality and knowledge…,
- a place where updating and continuous improvement of knowledge is promoted…,
- a community in which cooperation with industry and the service sectors (is) encouraged and actively supported….,
- a place where the most relevant local, regional, national and international problems and solutions are identified, analysed and discussed within an environment of critical learning...,
- a place where governments and other public institutions can address the search for reliable scientific information….,
- a community whose members, committing fully themselves to the principles of academic freedom, devote themselves to the search for truth, to the defence and promotion of human rights, to democracy, social justice and tolerance within their own community and all over the world…, and
- a well placed institution in the world context, adapted to the pace of contemporary life, to the different characteristics of every region and of every country".

At the present moment universities as visualised above may seem to be utopian, but they provide ideals to be striven for.

Conclusion

In the nine hundred odd years since the first modern university was established in Bologna there has been an evolution in the role and functions of universities. The rate of change, which was slow till the second half of the nineteenth century, quickened as the universities acquired an egalitarian character about the beginning of the twentieth century. To the basic functions of teaching and research, 'service to community' was added as the third dimension. With rapid developments in communication technology we have now entered a period of 'accelerating change' and an argument has been put forward that the universities are failing in their ability to keep pace with society's (read industry's) demands (Neave, 2000). However, it has to be kept in mind that higher education is not an industry in the sense, say, computer technology is. Production of knowledge is not its sole concern. Preservation, transmission and application of knowledge is equally, if not more, important. Hence, higher education must move at a pace that is most useful to society as a whole not to industry alone. Having said this, it is necessary to add that, functioning under the shadow of the communication revolution, higher education has to make the best use of it. Information, and with it knowledge, is likely to double every five years, and universities will have to find ways of coping with this development. There is no option to making academic structures flexible, and to regularly updating curricula. We will also have to re-evaluate our perceptions relating to teaching-learning methodologies and the nature of research to be undertaken by the universities. As many see it, with distance and continuing education becoming increasingly important, there is a need for the convergence of the formal and non-formal streams of higher education; and the non-formal stream may well include the non-university organisations. With the setting-in of globalisation, quality, benchmarking and networking will need to be areas of priority. And, as was emphasised in the World Declaration on Higher Education adopted at Paris in 1998 (UNESCO, 1998), partnerships at national and international levels, based on common interest, mutual respect and credibility, should be a prime matrix for renewal of higher education.

References

Altbach, P., (1996), *The International Academic Profession: Portraits of Fourteen Countries*, Carnegie Foundation for the Advancement of Teaching, Princeton, N.J.

Association of Indian Universities, (1995), *Liaison Cells for University-Industry Interaction*, AIU, New Delhi.

Ben-David, J., (1968), Universities in Sill, D. (Editor), *Encyclopaedia of Social Sciences*, 16, 191-199.

Bennich-Bjorkman, Li, (1997), *Organising Innovative Research: The Inner Life of University Departments*, Pergamon/IAU, Paris.

Bertilsson, M., (1992), From University to Comprehensive Higher Education: On the Widening Gap between Lehre and Leben, *Higher Education*, 24, 333-349.

Brighton, J.A., (1998), Universities Changing to Meet the Needs of the 21st Century, in Wei Xin, Ma Wanhua and Ju Ren (Editors), *The University of the 21st Century*, Peking University, Beijing, pp. 45- 50.

Bloom, A., (1987), *Closing of the American Mind*, Simon and Schuster, New York.

Boyer E.L., Altbach, P. and Whitelaw, M.J., (1994), *The Academic Profession: An International Perspective*, The Carnegie Foundation for the Advancement of Teaching, Princeton.

Brook, G. L., (1965), *The Modern University*, Deutsch, London.

Casper, J., (1998), The Advantage of the Research Intensive University, in Wei Xin, Ma Wanhua and Ju Ren (Editors), *The University of the 21st Century*, Peking University, Beijing, pp. 151- 160.

Diallant, G., (1990), *Universality, Diversity, Interdependence, IAU 1950-1990: A Commemorative Essay*, IAU, Paris.

Ferrer, F., (1999), Some Thoughts on Trends in Educational Research, *Prospects*, 111: 409- 422.

Glion Colloquium, (1998), *The Glion Declaration: The University at the Millennium*, Glion Colloquium, Geneva.

Husen, T., (1994), The Idea of the University: Changing roles, Current Crisis and Future Challenges, in Husen, T., (Editor), *The Role of the University: A Global Perspective*, The United Nations University, Tokyo, 7-31.

Jaspers, K., (1965), *The Idea of the University*, Peter Owen Ltd., London.

Jha, D.M., (1991), Higher Education in Ancient India, in Raza, M. (Editor), *Higher Education in India: Retrospect and Prospect*, AIU, New Delhi, 1-5.

Ker, I.T. (Editor), (1976), *The Idea of a University* by *J.H.Newman*, The Clarendon Press, Oxford.

Kerr, C., (1963), *The Uses of the University*, Harvard University Press, Cambridge, Mass.

Kumar, D., (1988), Challenges of Rural Development and the Responsibilities of Universities, in *What can We do for Our Countries?: The Contribution of Universities to National Development*, ACU, London, pp. 457- 465.

Lucus, C., (1998a), Universities and the Challenge of the Learning Society, in Wei Xin, Ma Wanhua and Ju Ren (Editors), *The University of the 21st Century*, Peking University, Beijing, pp.17- 22.

Lucus, C., (1998b), Knowledge is a Matter of Values, It Poses a Moral Question, in Wei Xin, Ma Wanhua and Ju Ren (Editors), *The University of the 21st Century*, Peking University, Beijing, pp. 267- 270.

Livingstone, H., (1974), *The University: An Organisational Analysis*, Blackie and Son, Glasgow.

Lockmiller, D.A., (1969), *Scholars on Parade: Colleges, Universities, Costumes and Degrees*, The Macmillan Company, London.

Mayor, F., (1991), Inaugural Address, *UNESCO-AAU Seminar on the Institutional Development of Higher Education in Africa*, Legon University, Accra.

Neave, G., (2000), The Pace of Change, *Higher Education Policy*, 13(2): 119-123.

Nehru, J.L., (1947), *Convocation Address*, Allahabad University, Allahabad.

Niland, J., (1998), An Important Function for the University to Play is to Develop the Relation Between Nations, in Wei Xin, Ma Wanhua and Ju Ren (Editors), *The University of the 21st Century*, Peking University, Beijing, pp. 273- 276.

Rhodes, F.H.T., (1999), The New University, in Hirsch, W.B. and Weber, L.E. (Editors), *Challenges Facing Higher Education at the Millennium*, Pergamon and IAU Press, Paris.

Rice, A. K., (1970), *The Modern University: A Model Organisation*, Tavistock Publ., London.

Ross, M.G., (1976), *The University: The Anatomy of Academe*, McGraw-Hill, New York.

Rudenstine, N.L., (1998), Challenges for the Universities of the 21st Century, in Wei Xin, Ma Wanhua and Ju Ren (Editors), *The University of the 21st Century*, Peking University, Beijing, pp. 27-34.

Smith, S., (1988), Two Views from the Past, *ABCD*, 86, 2-4.

Taskar, M. and Packham, D., (1993), Industry and Higher Education: A Question of Values, *Studies in Higher Education*, 18: 127-136.

Teicher, U., (1999), Higher Education Policy and the World of Work: Changing Conditions and Challenges, *Higher Education Policy*, 12: 285-312.

UNESCO, (1995), UNESCO Policy Paper for Change and Development in Higher Education, reproduced in *New Frontiers in Education*, 26, 288-234.

UNESCO, (1996), *'Learning: The Treasure Within', Report of the International Commission on Education for the Twenty First Century (Delors Report)*, UNESCO, Paris.

UNESCO, (1998), *Higher Education in the Twenty-first Century: Vision and Action — Final Report*, UNESCO, Paris.

University Grants Commission, (1987), *University System and Extension as the Third Dimension*, UGC, New Delhi.

Young, R.T.T., (1988), To Set Priorities Within a Limited Research Budget, in *What Can We do for Our Countries: The Contribution of Universities to National Development*, ACU, London, pp. 121-127.

2

Higher Education in India Since Independence: The First Fifty Years*

Introduction

In the five decades since independence the Indian higher education system has undergone a remarkable transformation from an elite system, nurtured by colonial roots, to a mass system attempting to meet the demands of a vibrant democracy. The transformation, marked by a thirteen-fold increase in the number of university-level institutions and a twenty five-fold increase in the number of students, has resulted in the emergence of the world's second largest higher education system comprising (in 1996) of 229 university level institutions, about 8000 colleges and five million students. The network of academic institutions, spread over the entire country, covers diverse physiographic, cultural and socio-economic environments and, consequently, there are great variations in facilities, ethos and quality of education. The state of Indian higher education, faced as it is with myriad problems, can by no means be described as satisfactory. Yet there is much to be proud of. An attempt is here made to trace the development of higher education in India since independence, analyse its problems and look at the options, in this area, for the next millennium. Before doing so it would, perhaps, be relevant to briefly review the changing functions of universities-the principle purveyors of higher education.

India's ancient seats of learning at Nalanda, Vikramshila, Vallabhi and Takshashila were essentially centres of religion and philosophy though the last mentioned also taught professional courses (Jha, 1991). They had their own unique traditions and values. The modern Indian universities, however, have their roots in European institutions and models. The first of these modern universities of Europe, at Bologna, Paris and Oxford, were founded as centres for travelling scholars and

* Background Paper for the National Seminar Commemorating '*Fifty Years of Independence*' organised by the Association of Indian Universities, New Delhi, September 29-30, 1997.

teachers and their main objective was to propagate the intellectual currents of the time (Ben-David, 1968). Later in the thirteenth century, the European universities developed into educational centres of the states, oriented to meet the demand for civil servants, especially priests and lawyers (Bertilsson, 1992). The universities of the Middle Age were essentially teaching and training centres.

The importance of research in universities was recognised by Wilhelm von Humboldt, the German thinker on higher education and founder of the Berlin University. The concept of research universities was initiated with its establishment in 1810; and it found fulfilment in the American research-oriented universities like John Hopkins, Stanford and Berkeley (Bertilsson, 1992). In the late nineteenth and twentieth centuries the need for trained manpower, and an educated labour force, ensured that technology became important in the universities.

The concept of elite universities, for the privileged, was slowly replaced by the concept of egalitarian universities, responsible to society and committed to its needs. By the end of World War II most universities were strongly committed to the welfare of their societies and soon 'extension' became a recognised function of a university — at least in theory. Thus today, a traditional university is charged with the responsibility of undertaking teaching, research and extension activities. The vigorous growth of socially committed universities reflects a confidence in higher education as a major instrument of social and economic progress (Daillant, 1990).

Recent political and economic events, especially the development of free-market economy, highlight the need for 'globalisation of universities' (Alladin,1992). The dynamic nature of higher education imposes upon the universities an obligation to examine their conventional, present and emerging roles, and accordingly modify their functions. Otherwise there is the danger of their being rendered irrelevant.

Policies relating to Higher Education in India

In pre-Independence India

The present system of higher education in India has its roots in Mountstuart Elphinstone's 'minutes' of 1823, in which he pressed for the establishment of schools for teaching English and the European Sciences; his deposition before the Lord's Committee in 1830 in which he reiterated his views; the establishment of such schools at Bombay and Poona, and the founding, in 1834 at Bombay, of the Elphinstone College which was to be instrumental in training "*a class of persons qualified by their intelligence and morality for high employment in the civil administration of India*". Subsequently, Macaulay, in his much-mentioned 'minutes' of 1835, argued that the money which was being provided, under the Act of 1813, for the study of Arabic and Sanskrit literature should be transferred for "*efforts to make natives of the country thoroughly good English scholars*". Macaulay's minutes were approved in a resolution of the Governor General and his Council which stated that the object of the British government ought to be "*the promotion of European Literature and Science amongst the natives of India*". The idea of establishing universities in India, on the model of the London University (i.e. a university of the affiliating type), was first given in Sir Charles Wood's despatch of 1854, which has been called the 'Magna Carta of English Education in India'. It described the aim of (Indian) education as the diffusion of Arts, Science, Philosophy and Literature of Europe, and the study of Indian languages. These recommendations were enlarged to also include Law, Medicine and Engineering, and were followed by the establishment, in 1857, of universities at Calcutta, Bombay and Madras (Govt. of India, 1950). During the next 25 years there was an increase in the number of colleges from 27 to 75. This led to the demand for more universities. The University of Allahabad was established in 1887. By 1923 the number of universities had reached 12. In order to facilitate coordination in the activities of these universities the Inter-University Board (converted, in 1973, to the Association of Indian Universities) was established in 1925.

There was a steady growth in the subsequent years and by 1943 a need was felt for a comprehensive plan for educational development. A report of the Central Advisory Board of Education on Post War Educational Development in India, the Sargent Report of 1944, was the first attempt to formulate a national system of education in India. It pointed out the failure in making university education relevant to community needs and suggested means for improvement (Mohanty, 1993). One of the recommendations was the formation of a University Grants Committee. This was constituted in 1945 with the limited purpose of dealing with the three central universities of Aligarh, Banaras and Delhi. It was empowered in 1947 to deal with all universities but remained a recommendatory body without any funds at its disposal.

In post-Independence India

Even at the time of independence it was known that all was not well with the Indian university system, and successive commissions and committees appointed to examine the situation have highlighted the shortcomings and suggested remedies. The University Education Commission (better known as the Radhakrishnan Commission), appointed in 1948, in its report (Government of India, 1950) stressed amongst other things that Indian education must be rooted in its cultural heritage. It gave guidelines for the structuring of higher education and recommended that the University Grants Committee should be reorganised and should have the powers to allocate grants within total limits set by the Government. An interim University Grants Commission was set up in 1953 and given autonomous, statutory status by an Act of Parliament in 1956.

The state of higher education was re-examined by the Education Commission of 1964-66 (the Kothari Commission) which, in its report (Government of India, 1966), emphasised the need for a built-in flexibility in the system of education, and the necessity for education to be science based and in coherence with Indian culture and values. It visualised education as an instrument for the nation's progress, security and welfare. It advocated far reaching reforms. To quote: *"Indian education needs a drastic reconstruction, almost a revolution. We need to .... introduce work experience as an integral element of general education to improve quality of teachers at all levels...; ... to strengthen centres of advanced studies and strive to attain in some of our universities at least, higher international standards; to lay special emphasis on the combination of teaching and research; and to pay particular attention to education and research in agriculture and allied sciences".*

The Kothari Commission Report emphasised that there had to be:

- a radical improvement in the quality and standard of higher education and research;
- an expansion of higher education to meet manpower requirements of the nation and the rising social ambitions and expectations of the people; and
- an improvement of university organisation and administration.

The Kothari Commission recommended special inputs for major universities to ensure quality of research, development of other universities and affiliated colleges, improvement in teaching and evaluation by reorganisation of courses and examinations, expansion of facilities, selective admissions, opportunities for part-time education and special attention to women's education.

Based upon the Kothari Commission Report, the National Policy of Education, 1968 was adopted. Nearly twenty years later, in 1985, the Government of India document 'Challenge of Education' recognised that "*the general condition of universities and colleges is a matter of great concern to the nation*". It was accepted that the general formulations in the 1968 Policy had not been translated into detailed strategies of implementation.

'The National Policy on Education' (NPE), 1986, aims at not only developing manpower for serving the economy but also inculcating crucial values. The policy envisages education to be:

- a process of empowerment through the development of knowledge, skills and values (Education for Development), and
- an instrument of social change that provides means for upward economic and social mobility, through enhancement of qualifications (Education for Equality).

In the area of higher education the NPE places emphasis on the consolidation and expansion of facilities in existing institutions. The strategies for development of higher education, as outlined in the Ramamurti Committee Report of 1990 'Towards an Enlightened and Humane Society', include the development of autonomous colleges; redesigning of courses and programmes; establishment of State Councils of Higher Education to develop co-ordinating mechanisms; transformation of teaching methods; enhanced support for research; creation of a National Council of Higher Education to co-ordinate general, agricultural, medical, technical and other professional fields of education; use of the open university system as a means of democratising education; delinking degrees from jobs except in the case of occupation-specific courses; and consolidation and development of rural universities for them to be instruments of transformation of rural areas. The Programme of Action, 1992, details the steps to be taken for implementing these ideas.

Our planners and administrators are apparently convinced about the key role that higher education has to play in national development. India's National Policy on Education, as revised in 1992, states (Government of India, 1992, p. 24): *"Higher Education provides people with an opportunity to reflect on the critical social, economic, cultural, moral and spiritual issues facing humanity. It contributes to national development through dissemination of specialised knowledge and skills. It is, therefore, a crucial factor for survival".*

The Growth of Higher Education

As stated earlier, in the fifty years since India gained independence its higher education system has shown remarkable growth. It may be noted that since independence:

- The number of university-level institutions has increased from 18 to 229; and of colleges from 591 to about 8000.
- The percentage of liberal arts colleges has increased from 77.66% in 1947 to 82.91% in 1996; and the percentage of colleges in professional disciplines has correspondingly decreased from 22.34% in 1947 to 17.09% in 1996.
- The number of students has increased from a little less than 0.2 million to about 5 million. The annual growth rate which averaged as much as 27.7% during the first decade after independence fell to 5.9% in the second decade. It increased slightly to 7% in the third decade and then again fell to 6% in the fourth decade. It has slowed down to 3.5% in the last nine years.
- The number of students in professional education has increased from about 46 thousand in 1947 to nearly 550 thousand in 1996. Though there is a substantial increase in absolute terms the percentage of students in professional education has actually decreased from 19.94% in 1947 to 9.93% in 1996.
- Approximately 88% of the students in Indian higher education are in undergraduate programmes in the liberal arts. Enrolment in the faculty of Arts (including Social Sciences) has now stabilised at about 40% after having reached a peak of nearly 45% in 1975-76. The enrolment in Science faculty has come down from about 30% in 1960-61 to only 19.6% in 1992-93. Enrolment in the Commerce faculty is showing a steady increase and is now about 23%. Enrolments in Engineering and Technology, and in Medical faculties, are about 4.9% and 3.4% respectively. The number in Agriculture and Veterinary Science is low, about 1.5%.

The rapid growth of higher education, and the raised expectations regarding its role in nation-building, have highlighted many issues including those of access and equity. The progress made with respect to these aspects needs to be reviewed.

Access

As stated above, after independence there has been a steady and substantial increase in the number of students enrolling for higher education. However, the numbers can be misleading. While 5 million may appear to be a large number in absolute terms it represents only 6% of India's young people in the relevant age group of 18-23 years. This is in stark contrast with the enrolment of 51% in the OECD countries. Moreover, the distribution of students is very heterogeneous. While the colleges in urban centres are inundated with applications for admission, and have strengths exceeding two or three thousand, those in rural areas are sub-viable with less than 500 students; in some cases even less than 100 students.

Students belonging to the low and medium income groups have been finding it difficult to gain entry into private professional colleges because of high fees. Access has been facilitated, to some extent, for merited students by recent rulings of the Supreme Court. It is now mandatory to admit 50% of the students against 'free seats' (that require nominal fees) on the basis of merit. Thus, the thrust of the educational policy is on 'growth with equity', though there may be shortfalls in actual implementation.

There is clearly a need to ensure that a much larger proportion of young people, and especially those from the weaker sections of society, are provided with an opportunity to enrol in higher education programmes and get the benefits of higher education. How this is to be achieved is a matter of concern. Because of financial constraints a notable increase in the number of colleges is not feasible, and from past experience not desirable from the point of view of maintaining quality. Distance education appears to be the most practical way of ensuring the spread of education. It is in keeping with the fact that throughout the world higher education is undergoing a paradigm shift from an instruction-centred college/university model to a learner-centred, integrated network model that is based on student initiative and access to learning resources.

Equity

In a large democratic nation like India, where social and economic disparities are a matter of deep concern, access to higher education must necessarily be linked to equity. There is a need to provide special opportunities to the traditionally under-privileged sections of society. These include women, the scheduled castes and scheduled tribes, other backward classes, the handicapped, and the people of socially backward areas. Several steps have been taken to ensure greater access to the under-privileged groups. Reservations are provided in the educational institutions and for some categories admission qualifications are relaxed. Financial assistance is being provided in the form of scholarships and freeships. These steps have helped in reducing disparities to some extent. The enrolment ratio between male and female students for general education has come down from 8.3:1 in 1947 to 1.7:1 in 1996. For professional education it has come down from 9.9:1 in 1957 to 3.1:1 in 1996. There has been a marked increase in the number of SC/ST students in absolute terms. However, in the case of general education the ratio of enrolment between the general category students and scheduled caste/scheduled tribe students increased from 6.3:1 in 1957 to 7.2:1 in 1996. In the case of professional education the ratio of enrolment has decreased from 11.6:1 in 1957 to 8.7:1 in 1996.

The Affiliation System and Autonomous Colleges

Many of the ills of Indian higher education can be attributed to the system of affiliation. Most conventional Indian universities are teaching-cum-affiliating; and some of the larger universities have more than 300 colleges affiliated to them. The colleges have a common syllabi and the students appear for a common examination usually conducted at the end of the year. For many universities the conduct of examinations has become the most important administrative function.

The affiliating system was devised to regulate and standardise the quality of education. But with the tremendous increase in the number of institutions the system has become counter-productive. Because of it some sub-standard colleges serenely ride piggy-back on the reputation of the mother institution. The affiliating system is a drag on the better institutions that would otherwise regularly revise and update their curricula and introduce innovative programmes. In order to allow the growth of colleges that had the desire to move ahead the concept of autonomous colleges was introduced about a decade back. It allows the college to have autonomy as regards academic matters. However, not many institutions have sought the autonomous status, the present number of autonomous institutions being about 110. Managements, teachers and students all look upon this innovation with suspicion. There is clearly a need for dialogue amongst all concerned so that a conducive environment can be created. Many educationists feel that the programme of granting autonomy to the colleges needs to be vigorously pursued, even to the extent of making every college autonomous and responsible for itself.

The Quality of Indian Higher Education

There is general agreement that the state of Indian higher education is far from satisfactory. The overall impression amongst laypersons is that standards are deteriorating and that the knowledge and skills imparted by our academic institutions are to a great extent irrelevant to the needs of society. The failure of the system to deliver the goods has been attributed to a number of maladies including its colonial roots, the failure to control unplanned expansion, perennial shortage of funds, inflexible academic structures with an antiquated examination system, resistance to change from all its constituents, activism on campuses, highly politicised and bureaucratised systems of management, pressures from politicians and special interest groups, the distancing of the universities from society, and a general lack of concern (Kaul, 1988; Altbach, 1993; Chitnis, 1993). The truth, however, is that there is great variability in the standard of education provided by Indian academic institutions. Centres of undoubted quality, like the Indian Institutes of Technology, and some well-known universities in the metropolitan areas coexist with colleges that are best classified as sub-viable. The overall situation has been described as that being of the existence of islands of excellence in a sea of mediocrity.

The dominance of mediocrity has become a matter of serious concern. Over the years the University Grants Commission, which has been assigned the responsibility of ensuring qualitative development of education, has undertaken various measures for improving quality. These include:

- Laying down minimum standards of instruction for grant of first degree through formal education, and through the distance mode.
- Introducing a College Science Improvement Programme (COSIP) and a College Humanities and Social Science Improvement Programme (COHSSIP) under which financial assistance is granted to predominantly undergraduate institutions for development of teaching capabilities through curricula development; and for procurement of equipment, teaching materials, and books and journals.
- Introducing a programme of the Committee for Strengthening of Infrastructure in Science and Technology (COSIST) under which assistance is given to selected departments, in universities, for acquiring sophisticated and expensive equipment necessary for internationally competitive research.
- Starting of a Special Assistance Programme (SAP) under which selected departments, in universities, are provided support at three levels, namely, as Department of Research Support (DRS), Department of Special Assistance (DSA) and Centre of Advanced Study (CAS).

- Encouraging research by making provision for grants for major and minor projects, and by instituting research associateships, career awards, visiting associateships and fellowships for senior teachers.
- Setting up Curriculum Development Centres for developing model curricula at both undergraduate and postgraduate levels.
- Establishing Academic Staff Colleges for staff development through orientation courses (for new teachers) and refresher courses (for serving teachers).
- Granting of autonomy to selected colleges (Autonomous Colleges) in order to facilitate their undertaking innovations in areas like restructuring of courses, curricula development, teaching-learning process, and evaluation process.
- Providing financial assistance for the development of computer facilities and computer education, and for establishment of Computer Centres.
- Establishing of University Science Instrument Centres (USIC) for training of experimental scientists, and for generating interest amongst students in recent advances in science and technology; and
- Setting up of autonomous Inter-University Centres for facilitating advanced research.

The effect of these measures to improve quality is, however, only marginal. This is because the quantum of assistance is not large and, more importantly, available to only a limited number of colleges and universities. Only about 140 of the 176 traditional universities/ institutions, and about 4500 of the 8000 odd colleges, receive grants from the University Grants Commission. The others are left out as they do not fulfil the minimum requirements. The left-outs are the 'sub-viable' institutions whose need is the greatest.

If the overall standard of education is to improve, much greater attention needs to be paid to our undergraduate programmes in the liberal arts in which 88% of our students are engaged. Bachelor degrees in Arts, Commerce or Science do not count for much in the employment market. In order to make these programmes more meaningful, an ambitious programme of vocationalisation of courses, by including an applied component, has been launched by the University Grants Commission. By the end of 1996-97 about 700 colleges in 30 universities were proposed to be covered. The underlying idea is to produce graduates who meet the requirements of potential employers or acquire the competence to start out on their own. However, it is to be seen whether the introduction of applied aspects in a limited way can achieve the desired objectives. Past experiences have not been encouraging.

The different commissions and committees that have reviewed Indian education have stressed the need to maintain quality in education and research. The Ramamurti Committee, for example, has emphasised: *"The quality of higher and technical education in the country is to be improved in real terms not only to make them more relevant to our society as it is, and as it is envisaged, but also to cater to the needs of competitive industry, indigenisation of technology, including research and development therein, and their application"*. The 'Programme of Action', emanating from the National Policy on Education, 1986, called for the development of assessment and accreditation mechanisms for maintenance of standards. Accordingly the All India Council for Technical Education has set up the National Board of Accreditation and the University Grants Commission, the National Assessment and Accreditation Council. Accreditation by these is voluntary, but looking at the slow progress, it is time that the funding agencies clearly specify that in the future all special funding by them will be dependent on the grant of accreditation by these agencies.

Distance Education

In India, at the Tertiary level, distance education was initiated in 1962 in the form of correspondence courses started by the University of Delhi, The first open university was established in Andhra Pradesh, in 1982, and the Indira Gandhi National Open University was established in 1985. The distance education system has grown substantially since then and today there are eight open universities and 59 Correspondence Course Institutes (CCIs) attached to different universities. The CCIs initially provided largely correspondence programmes with occasional contact programmes. However, with the establishment of open universities, the methodologies of instruction and assessment have substantially changed. The open universities are following rigorous instructional designs in the development of materials and imparting of instructions. The universities provide regular counselling service through networks of study centres and make use of the electronic media. The Indira Gandhi National Open University, which has the dual responsibility of providing open distance education and co-ordinating the distance education system (including the state open universities), has devised a large media networking and teleconferencing system to electronically link all distance teaching institutions in the country. OPENET (Open Education Network) is poised to facilitate voice, image and data transmission through two-way audio and video-conferencing. What is now required is an integration of open education provided by open universities with the distance education programmes of CCIs through networked collaboration between them.

It is visualised that in the near future each state in the country will have an open university and that about 50% of the total future intake in higher education in the country will be catered through the open system. The latter can take care of the needs of all those who desire a liberal arts education. There is optimism that open universities can also offer effective programmes in management and technology. The open universities have taken note of the fact that the prevailing model of higher education, requiring selective learning over a specified period of time, is being slowly replaced by the model of lifelong learning for all. Their programmes include those on industrial and related training, extension education and continuing education in professional areas. The open universities, in network with CCIs, plan to cater to the educational and training needs of about 2 million people. It is evident that open and distance education will have to play a major role in meeting the demand for higher education in India.

Financing of Higher Education

After Independence higher education in India has been largely financed by the government with the social institutions progressively withdrawing. The government's share has steadily increased from 49% in 1950-51 to about 90% today. The government spends about 3.7% of DNP on education of which the share of higher education is about 0.8%. Amongst the different sectors of education the share of higher education was the highest at 25% during the Fourth Five Year Plan (1969-74), remained stable at 22% during the Fifth and Sixth Five Years Plans, but declined to only 8% in the Eighth Five Year Plan (1992-97). There is the promise that allotment for education would be increased to 6% by the end of the Ninth Five Year Plan (1997-2002). However, the share of higher education is not likely to increase. Governments, both at the centre and in the states, are showing an increasing reluctance to support higher education. A recent discussion paper (Government of India, 1997) entitled 'Government Subsidies in India' identifies the spending on higher education as a "non-merit" subsidy. The reason for this categorisation is apparently the belief that the benefits of higher education (unlike those of primary education) do not extend beyond the immediate recipient. This categorisation of higher education funding as "non-merit" subsidy is unfortunate for it does not recognise the very positive role of higher education in socio-economic development. The indications are that in the near future government support to higher education will be progressively decreased. The message to the universities clearly is that they should generate resources in increasing amounts and control their spending. In spite of this efforts must continuously be made to convince the government that it has high stakes in higher education and that it is its duty to provide adequate finances to the universities.

The main sources of funding for most universities are the block- or salary grants received from the government, development grants received from the University Grants Commission, All India Council for Technical Education and like agencies, and research support received mainly from government departments. A small percentage of income is from tuition and other fees recoverable from students, revenue arising from the conduct of examinations, establishments such as the university press and computer centre, and consultancy and alumni support. Though government expectations may be high the possibility of substantially increasing revenue from these miscellaneous sources is not bright. Tuition fees in higher education are very low and there is certainly a need for rationalisation. However, an increase to a reasonable amount, say about 20-30% of actual cost, is possible only if there is political will and government support. Examinations can be a major source of revenue. While some universities show large savings under the budget-head of examinations, others incur large deficits on this account. Some universities have large incomes from correspondence courses and fees realised from international students. The much-touted university-industry interaction has failed to take off in most universities and it would be unrealistic to hope for much revenue from consultancy, except in the case of a few leading universities in industrial areas. Alumni support is something every university can look forward to provided it can motivate past-students through a proper presentation of its achievements and programmes.

Control of expenditure should be as important as generation of funds. A first step in this direction could be the evaluation of unit costs. A methodology of determining unit costs of different types has been evolved by the Association of Indian Universities (Powar, 1996) and an exercise, covering four universities, undertaken by the Research Division of AIU (Powar *et al.*, 1995) shows that the unit costs for similar programmes in these universities is highly variable. The exercise has helped identify 'where the money is going'. It is expected that similar exercises conducted by the universities will help in rationalising expenditure.

The imbalance between the demand for, and the supply of, higher education facilities has encouraged many private trusts and bodies to establish colleges in the professional areas of studies, mainly, medicine, engineering and technology, and management. Additionally, a large number of tutorial classes have cropped up all over the country and apparently attract a large number of students. This 'privatisation' of education is a matter of concern for many. While some of the colleges established under private initiative have a professional approach and are striving to impart high quality education, a depressingly large number lack proper facilities and are in effect business enterprises, established with the primary objective of securing financial profit and/or political power. Strict academic and administrative control of these colleges is essential.

However, if the government is unable to make larger allocations for higher education, private initiatives become necessary and society in general, and industry in particular, will have to play a larger role in higher education. Industry should come forward to finance and design institutions that meet its specific requirements. It is hoped that an early decision will be taken on the Private Universities Bill that is presently before parliament.

The International Perspective

The process of globalisation has changed the character of higher education in many countries. An internationalisation of education is reflected in changes in the academic curricula, which are now more outward-looking, and by the increase in research and teaching partnerships between universities. It has also resulted in 'the export of education'. Indian universities should note these developments.

Traditionally Indian academics have been maintaining close links with their colleagues abroad and collaborating in research at the individual level. There is a need to formalise such links at the institutional level, and extend the partnerships to cover teaching also. In recent years some universities have signed Memorandums of Understanding with foreign counterparts in keeping with the spirit of the UNITWIN programme. Collaboration with foreign universities can include joint research, exchange of teachers and students, and even award of joint degrees. In order to facilitate the incoming of foreign students our curricula, at least at the Master's level, need to be given an international perspective.

There is a case for admitting international students to Indian universities in greater number. Their presence will help broaden the horizons of Indian students by exposing them to new cultures and perspectives. From the long-term viewpoint the international students turn out to be effective ambassadors of our culture, ideals and thoughts. From the more practical viewpoint, if charged differential fees, they can provide the much needed financial resources. The universities, in turn, have the responsibility of providing the international students proper facilities and making their stay comfortable. While the number of international students going to the western countries has increased almost exponentially, the number coming to India has been stagnant. The situation needs to be remedied.

A disturbing development of the nineties has been the influx of foreign universities that prefer to enter into partnership with professional organisations and little-known institutes that do not form a part of the Indian higher education system. The programmes offered by the foreign universities are mainly in the professional areas, especially management. The activities of such universities need to be discouraged. The Association of Indian Universities on its part has not recognised the degrees offered by the foreign universities through programmes in India.

Conclusion

Looking back, during the last fifty years the Indian higher education system has undergone many important changes, the most significant being its unprecedented growth and its consequent transformation from an elite system to a mass system. The fact that higher education is available to the masses, including the underprivileged and weaker sections of society, is an achievement. It is also creditable that we have been able to create some undoubted centres of excellence. However, the system has not been able to change its organisational structure and form. Nor has it been possible to maintain uniform standards of education or ensure that education imparted is relevant to our present needs. Under the circumstance it is necessary that we make systemic changes that will enable the implementation of academic reforms.

The different commissions and committees that have examined the Indian higher education system after independence have identified the maladies that affect it and have also suggested remedies. However, we have failed to follow up on the recommendations. The maladies identified by the Kothari Commission over three decades ago still exist. The latest example of our indifferent approach is the half-hearted manner in which the '*Programme of Action, 1992*' is being implemented. As

Valiathan (1993) points out *"knowing what to do and not caring to do it has cast a shadow on (our) national endeavours"*.

Altbach (1993) perceives the Indian educational system to be a great monolith, with a core of inadequacy, possibly incapable of change, and margined by a rim that has shown significant change and has developed. The better-known institutions, comprising the rim, are perhaps capable of taking care of themselves. We will have to concentrate our attention on improving the infrastructure and facilities in the less-privileged institutions. The colleges deserve greater attention. If there is to be academic revival it will be necessary to grant greater degree of autonomy to the universities and colleges, implement examination reforms, reduce administrative obesity and improve administrative efficiency. There has to be greater commitment on the part of all stake-holders. The open universities have an important role to play in the future and they must be prepared to shoulder greater responsibilities. Above all resources must be found for the colleges and universities. Whether these resources are to come from the government or industry or other sections of society is a matter that has to be decided quickly.

References

Alladin, R., (1992) International Cooperation in Higher Education: The Globalisation of the Universities, *Higher Education in Europe*, 17 (4): 4-13.

Altbach, P.G., (1993), The Dilemma of Change in Indian Higher Education, *Higher Education*, 26: 3-20.

Ben-David, J., (1968), Universities, in Sill, D. (Editor), *Encyclopaedia of Social Sciences*, 16: 191-199.

Bertilsson, M., (1992), From University to Comprehensive Higher Education: On the Widening Gap between Lehre and Leben, *Higher Education*, 24, 333-349.

Chitnis, S. (1993), Gearing a Colonial System of Education to take Independent India Towards Development, *Higher Education*, 26, 21-41.

Daillant, G. (1990), *Universality, Diversity, Interdependence, IAU 1950-1990: A Commemorative Essay*, IAU, Paris.

Government of India (1950), *University Education Commission, 1948-49 Report*, Part I, GOI, New Delhi.

Government of India (1966), *Report of the Education Commission (1964-66) : Education and National Development*, GOI, New Delhi.

Government of India (1985), *Challenge of Education : A Policy Perspective*, GOI, New Delhi.

Government of India (1986), *National Policy on Education - 1986*, GOI, New Delhi.

Government of India, (1989), *Towards an Enlightened and Humane Society*, Report of the Committee for Review of the National Policy on Education, 1986, GOI, New Delhi.

Government of India (1992), *Programme of Action*, 1992, *National Policy on Education, 1986, Revised 1992*, (Reprinted by UGC), New Delhi.

Government of India, (1997), *Government Subsidies in India:* Discussion Paper, Department of Economic Affairs, Ministry of Finance, GOI, New Delhi.

Jha, D M. (1991), Higher Education in Ancient India, in Raza, M. (Ed.), *Higher Education in India : Retrospect and Prospect,* AIU, New Delhi.

Kaul, J.N. (1988), *Governance of Universities: Autonomy of the University Community*, Abhinav, New Delhi.

Mohanty, J. (1993), *Dynamics of Higher Education in India*, Deep and Deep Publications, New Delhi.

Powar, K.B. (1996), *Unit Costs in Higher Education*, AIU Occasional Paper, 96/1, AIU, New Delhi.

Powar, K.B., Panda, S.K. and Sharma, T.C. (1995), *Unit Costs of Education in Indian Universities*, AIU, New Delhi.

Valiathan, M.S. (1993), Presidential Address, *68th AIU Annual Meeting*, AIU, New Delhi.

3

Reforms and Innovations in Higher Education in India: The Relevance and Role of Research*

Introduction

In many countries of the world, and especially in South Asia, reforms in higher education systems have been initiated primarily to overcome inadequacies that became apparent to the different stakeholders of higher education. Changes have been made to take care of immediate requirements, and largely in accordance with the perception of administrators. The reforms, and the studies on them, have therefore been reactive rather than proactive. Practically no research, based on scientific inquiry, has preceded decision-making. The ground realities relating to financial requirements, manpower availability and human shortcomings have usually not been given adequate consideration with the result that the educational reforms that have been introduced in recent years have not yielded the desired results. This is especially true of India. Keeping in view the importance of higher education in promoting sustainable economic development there is a strong case for undertaking adequate research before introducing innovations and reforms in higher education.

Educational Research

The Organisation for Economic Cooperation and Development (OECD) has defined educational research as the "*systematic, original investigation or inquiry.... concerning the social, cultural, economic and political contexts within which educational systems operate and learning takes place; the purpose of education; the processes of teaching, learning and personal development...; the work of educators; the resources and organisational arrangements to support educational work; the policies and strategies to achieve educational objectives; and*

* Paper presented at the International Symposium on '*The Role of Research in Higher Education: Innovation and Reform*' at the Institution of Higher Education, Peking University, Beijing, China, May 1-4, 2000.

the social, cultural, political and economic outcomes of education". (Organisation for Economic Cooperation and Development, 1995, p. 37). In terms of this definition almost all studies relating to education fall within the domain of educational research.

The Swiss Society for Research in Education (SSRE) has a functional approach to research and identifies five functions — analytical and explanatory, synoptic, evaluation, forward-looking and advisory (Socieite Swisse de Recherche en Education, 1988). The last two are important from the viewpoint of innovation and reform. The forward-looking function formulates, on the basis of given political objectives, concepts and models for future development of education. The advisory function advises on planning and development of education.

Following Vielle (1981) educational research may be classified as:

- *Status Research* seeking to study the existing educational system with the view of examining its efficacy, diagnosing its problems and suggesting remedial modifications;
- *Prospective Research* undertaken to design, predict and suggest new models for educational systems; and
- *Creative Research* undertaken for creating, developing or establishing new or alternate educational systems.

As in the case of other major disciplines a number of questions have been raised regarding educational research. The conflicting viewpoints are reflected in the ongoing discussions on such issues as basic research versus applied research, quantitative research versus qualitative research, interdisciplinary research versus multidisciplinary research, contract research versus voluntary research and creative research versus research for circulation (Ferrer, 1999). And one has also to consider the relationship between research and teaching/learning which has often been disregarded (Clark, 1991; Brew and Boud, 1995).

Research relating to problems of higher education is complex and should take into consideration a number of factors, including:

- the social, cultural, economic and political environment of a country;
- the organisation and structure of the higher education system; especially the current administrative, academic and pedagogical practices;
- the goals and objectives of higher education as identified in the country's national policy on education;
- the prevalent financial milieu including the availability of resources and the sources of funding; and

- international relationships, and particularly the extent of inter-dependence and networking with foreign systems.

In the case of India the complexities are accentuated by the fact that it has a multi-cultural society with diverse religions, languages, and socio-economic strata. It is a measure of the country's resilience that it has been able to evolve a homogenous higher education system in spite of much diversity.

India's Higher Education System

In the fifty-odd years since India achieved independence, its higher education system has undergone a remarkable transition from an elite system, having deep colonial roots, to an egalitarian system striving to meet the aspirations of a vibrant democracy (see Powar, 1997). The number of university-level institutions has gone up from 18 in 1947 to 252 at the beginning of the third millennium. At the same time the number of colleges have increased from 591 to over 10,000 and of students from 0.2 million to about 7 million. Today, with over 300,000 teachers the Indian higher education system is the second largest in the world. About 88% of the students are in undergraduate programmes in the liberal arts (Arts, Social Sciences, Science and Commerce). Enrolments in the faculties of Engineering and Technology, and in Medicine are about 5% and 3.5% respectively and in Agriculture and Allied fields about 1.5%. Women constitute about 35% of the student population.

The growth of the Indian higher education system is a result of the nation's policy, adopted immediately after independence, to promote education amongst the masses. The National Policy on Education, 1986 (Government of India, 1986) visualises education to be:

- a process of empowerment, which is to be promoted through the development of knowledge, skills and values (Education for Development), and
- an instrument of social change that provides means for upward economic and social mobility through enhancement of qualifications (Education for Equality).

Hence in the Indian higher education scenario provision of access and promotion of equity are important considerations. It has become necessary to balance these against the demand for quality. Admittedly, in the whole process the latter has suffered.

The state of Indian higher education has been examined by a number of education commissions and committees that have identified the major problems and suggested remedial actions (Government of India, 1950, 1966, 1985, 1986, 1989 and 1992). However, progress towards alleviation of the problems has been limited because of lack of resources and inadequate human resource development.

These reports, especially the reports of the Radhakrishnan Commission (1950) and the Kothari Commission (1966), can be categorised as 'educational research' for they incorporate an incisive analysis of a large volume of data and make valuable suggestions regarding reforms. They have given a substantially improved insight into the Indian higher education system.

The major shortcomings that have been identified in the Indian higher education system are:

- Inadequate access to higher education institutions with the worst sufferers being persons from the weaker sections of society, and those living in the countryside;
- Variable quality of higher education in different institutions with institutions providing education that is internationally recognised co-exist with others that can be described as sub-viable;
- The system of affiliation of colleges, followed by most universities, which centralises decisions and discourages accountability;
- Inflexibility in academic structure that inhibits innovation and promotes mediocrity; and
- Inadequate (and diminishing) financial support for higher education from the government and from society.

It is proposed to discuss, in later sections, educational reforms and innovations in Indian higher education keeping in view these constraints.

Educational Research Centres in India

Information related to studies on higher education in India, published till 1989, is available in a comprehensive annotated bibliography published by the Association of Indian Universities (Raza and Malhotra, 1991). It includes 2485 entries arranged under 50 themes, each sub-classified into four categories, viz., books, articles, committee/commission reports and research studies. As detailed in Table 1 there are 259 entries under the last category. The present report, therefore, covers the period 1990 and onwards.

In India educational research is carried out in university departments undertaking postgraduate teaching; national institutes including the National Institute of Educational Planning and Administration, New

Delhi (NIEPA) and the National Council for Educational Research and Training, New Delhi (NCERT); and in organisations such as the National Council for Teacher Education, New Delhi (NCTE) and the Association of Indian Universities, New Delhi (AIU). Much of the work is, however, on primary and secondary education with emphasis being on teaching methodology and the teaching-learning process. The work on higher education conducted at the major centres is summarised below.

The Universities

In India there are 106 universities providing post-graduate instruction in Education. Educational research is carried out in practically all of them, though the number of faculty members actually conducting research is limited. This is, however, not unusual as the situation is also obtained in many developed countries. Ramsden ((1994), for instance, points out that in many institutions the distribution of research publications is heavily and negatively skewed – most papers are produced by a small number of academics with many faculty members producing little or nothing.

An idea about the research carried out in Indian universities can be obtained from Table 3.2 which summarises information relating to topics of research of Ph.D. dissertations accepted for award of Ph.D. degree by Indian universities during the last decade of the second millennium. The dissertations are grouped into seven categories respectively dealing with:

i) Growth and development,

ii) Access, equity and environment,

iii) Teaching and learning processes,

iv) Academic restructuring and innovations,

v) Policy making, planning and management,

vi) Economics of education, and

vii) Educational psychology.

The allocation of the dissertations to different categories is rather subjective. It is based on a scrutiny of the title only. Some dissertations may also cover more than one aspect. However, Table 3.2 provides an idea about the trend of research and the preference regarding choice of subjects by research students in Indian universities.

Table 3.2 shows that 599 Ph.D.s have been awarded by Indian universities during the last decade of the last millennium on research pertaining to higher education. The number could be higher as some awards may not have been reported to the Association of Indian Universities. The number of awarding universities is 106, with the major output coming from Andhra University, Waltair (33), Osmania University, Hyderabad (26), Panjab University, Chandigarh (22), Kurukshetra University, Kurukshetra (21), Banaras Hindu University, Varanasi (19), Nagpur University, Nagpur (18), Devi Ahilya Vishwavidyalaya, Indore (15), Bangalore University, Bangalore (14), University of Kerala, Thiruvananthapuram (13), Maharaja Sayajirao University of Baroda, Vadodara (13), Maharshi Dayanand University, Rohtak (13), Himachal Pradesh University, Shimla (12), Jamia Millia Islamia, New Delhi (12), University of Calicut, Calicut (11), University of Delhi, Delhi (11), Gorakhpur University, Gorakhpur (11), Karnatak University, Dharwad (11) and Rohilkhand University, Bareilly (11). It is also evident from Table 3.2 that there is a general preference to take up for investigation topics on educational psychology (23.20%) and teaching and learning processes (22.87%) with those on growth and development (15.02%), access and equity (12.52%), policy making and planning and management (12.19%) also attracting students. Students are apparently not drawn to the themes of academic restructuring and innovation (9.02%) and the economics of education (5.18%). The distribution in terms of numbers and percentages is illustrated in Fig. 3.1.

Table 3.1: Number of Research Studies carried out under different Themes till 1989

Theme	No.	Theme	No.
1. General	52	15. Political Aspects	05
2. Administration	09	16. Reform	02
3. Affiliated Colleges	07	17. Research	03
4. Agricultural Universities	02	18. Rural Education	01
5. Autonomous Colleges	01	19. Scheduled Castes and Tribes	15
6. Dropouts	02	20. Semester System	04
7. Economic Aspects	15	21. Students	24
8. Educational Psychology	39	22. Students Unrest	13
9. Educational Sociology	24	23. Teacher Evaluation	03
10. Employment	03	24. Teachers : Role and Responsibility	06
11. Enrolment	01	25. Teaching	09
12. Finance	12	26. Women	03
13. Law	01		
14. Management	01		

(Source: Raza and Malhotra, 1991)

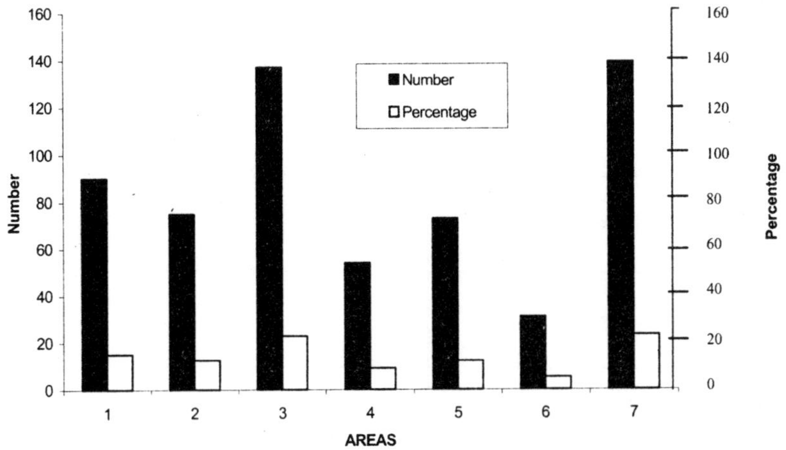

1. Growth and Development
2. Access, Equity and Impact of Environment
3. Teaching and Learning
4. Academic Restructuring and Innovations
5. Policy Making, Planning and Management
6. Economics of Education
7. Educational Psychology

Fig. 3.1: Area-wise distribution of Ph.D dissertations on Higher Education awarded by Indian Universities during 1990-2000

National Institute of Educational Planning and Administration (NIEPA)

The NIEPA is entrusted with the responsibility of undertaking studies related to the planning and administration of education. Its work covers two levels — school and non-formal education, and higher education. The researches attempt to synthesise the theoretical aspects of education with empirical information and thereby provide a base for policy and programme formulation. During the nineties the institute has examined problems relating to access and equity (Nuna, 1993; Aggarwal and Sibou, 1994), economics of education (Sharma, 1992; Shri Prakash and Choudhary, 1998; Ruddar Datt, 1994), innovations relating to college management (College Development Council, Indiresan, 1991) and quality improvement (Autonomous Colleges, Sudha Rao, 1999; Sudha Rao et al., 1999). Information on other studies are available in an annotated bibliography of research studies undertaken at NIEPA compiled by Malhotra (1996).

Table 3.2: Area-wise distribution of Ph.D. dissertations on Higher Education awarded by Indian Universities during 1990-2000

Sl No	Theme	1990	1991	1992	1993	1994	1995	1996	1997	1998	1999	2000	Total
1	Growth and Development	11	12	14	10	9	-	6	6	4	10	8	90 (15.02)
2	Access, Equity and Impact of Environment	11	3	15	12	7	4	4	4	4	2	9	75 (12.52)
3	Teaching and Learning Processes	11	18	21	19	17	4	6	10	10	8	13	137 (22.87)
4	Academic Restructuring and Innovations	3	5	9	11	2	-	3	7	3	7	4	54 (9.02)
5	Policy Making, Planning and Management	4	5	7	12	13	1	3	7	4	12	5	73 (12.19)
6	Economics of Education	3	2	4	3	3	3	1	2	-	7	3	31 (5.18)
7	Educational Psychology	17	11	16	15	20	5	10	9	17	7	12	·139 (23.20)
	Total	60	56	86	82	71	17	33	45	42	53	54	599

Note: Figures in Parentheses indicate percentage

National Council for Educational Research and Training (NCERT)

The NCERT conducts studies essentially in the areas of primary and secondary education. It has also published a resource book on teacher education in India which includes a chapter on 'Research and Innovation in Teacher Education' (Singh and Bhat, 1994), and published a bibliography on 'Educational Research and Innovations' covering the period 1988-92 (Dave and Murthy, 1993). The Fifth Survey of Educational Research for the period 1988-92 includes a review of the trend of research in the field of education (Sharma, 1997).

National Council for Teacher Education (NCTE)

The NCTE has published reports on the status of teacher education in the states of Haryana, Himachal Pradesh, Karnataka, Meghalaya, Mizoram and Uttar Pradesh. (National Council for Teacher Education, 1998a,b, 1999a,b,c,d.) It has also published a handbook on educational research which provides guidelines for the identification, formulation and conduct of educational research (National Council for Teacher Education, 1999e).

Association of Indian Universities (AIU)

The Research Division of the AIU collects information on various aspects of higher education and also conducts research on areas of current interest in higher education. In the nineties it has undertaken research on (i) the economics of education especially unit cost of education (AIU, 1995; Powar, 1996a), (ii) quality in higher education (quest for quality — Powar and Panda, 1995; accreditation — Powar, 1996b; and quality in distance higher education — Powar and Bhalla, 1999a), and (iii) examination reforms, including question banking (Bhalla, 1999). The AIU has published question banks on 28 subjects. It also brings out the 'Universities Handbook' every alternate year (Association of Indian Universities, 1998) and handbooks on engineering education, medical education, management education, computer education, distance education, and education in library and information science every year.

Educational Reforms and Innovations

Educational reforms, and especially those that call for a large-scale revamping of the educational system, are often the result of a shift in social and political ideologies (Vielle, 1981). These have been witnessed in China and Cuba and the erstwhile Socialist countries. Educational reform may also be undertaken when there is a realisation that the system in place is no longer capable of delivering goods because of a changed socio-economic milieu and a consequent change in the objectives of higher education. This is true of post-British India. And educational reforms may result from a desire for improvement and a quest for quality. In the last case the changes relate to teaching, learning and evaluation methodologies, and more often than not are designed at macro-level for implementation at micro-level. One cannot say that the changes are always promoted by, or a result of, educational research. On the other hand educational research may reflect the desire to know what are the impact of changes already undertaken because of social, political or economic considerations.

Innovation is the introduction of new ideas, methods or devises, generally with the objective of bringing about improvement. As discussed by Vielle (1981) educational research may be innovative with regard to:

- Knowledge about education (patterns, theories, ideologies)
- Processes of decision making (those relating to monitoring, control and management of educational systems)
- Educational systems (structure, organisation, management, practices, procedures and methods)
- Behaviour of stakeholders (policy-makers, administrators, sponsors, teachers and students).

In India the biggest obstacle to innovation and reform has been the inability of academics and academic administrators to break the shackles of its colonial inheritance. Raza and Malhotra (1991) have summed up the situation thus: *"Some of the crucial problems being faced by Indian higher education today are a function of the persistence of the chronic malady injected in the system by the colonial power and the inability of the ruling elite of independent India to uproot the poisonous weeds from academic pastures"*. The India academe haunted by *"historical fears and deep-rooted prejudices"*, and afraid of change, have not been able to transform an essentially dysfunctional system into a live and vibrant one that can act as a support system for the social and economic revolution postulated in the country's national policy.

External perceptions are important for they provide a clearer picture, uncluttered with details and free of personal preferences and bias. It is for this reason that the views of Altbach (1993) on the state of Indian higher education are significant. He perceives the Indian higher education system to be a great monolith, with a core of inadequacy, possibly incapable of change, and margined (by a rim) that has shown significant change and has developed. Institutions constituting the rim have been receptive to innovative ideas and have adapted themselves to global requirements and enjoy good reputation. It is the core of the educational system that requires revitalisation through major reforms and innovative changes.

In the following pages an attempt is made to highlight key issues and enumerate publications, of the last decade of the twentieth century, that provide an insight into the problems related to them. The references are by no means comprehensive but are hopefully representative of all the areas and themes being investigated by Indian educationists.

Growth, Development and Policy

As mentioned earlier, in the fifty-odd years since India achieved Independence its higher education system has undergone considerable expansion. The growth in terms of number of institutions, teachers and students, and in terms of financial inputs, has been described by Powar (1997). He has drawn attention to the need to achieve a balance between the need to satisfy the demand for equity and the necessity of maintaining the quality of education, especially in the non-urban centres. Dasgupta (1997), reflecting government concern, has identified the major challenges of higher education as those posed by inequity, disregard for values and financial constraints. Earlier Desai (1995), defining the approach of the University Grants Commission, had stressed the role of education in development, and in promoting social change. She emphasised the need for making academic programmes relevant to the basic requirements of society, and assuring its quality. Tilak (1999) has drawn attention to the fact that in India higher education is undergoing transformation from a public-financed, welfare system to a system financed by both the government and private sectors often with a market-based commercial approach. The aspect of privatisation of higher education has been examined by a number of workers including Ruddar Datt (1993), Sharma (1996) and Pani (1998). The feeling is that keeping in view the conditions prevailing in India privatisation of education should not be encouraged as it leads to commercialisation. However, there is a case for privatisation, especially because of the fact that government is unable to support higher education to the required extent. Privatisation should be allowed after taking adequate safeguards. These include provision for the merited, but needy, student, and appropriate control on the fees charged.

It is an accepted fact that all that was visualised in the National Policy on Education, 1986, and the subsequent Programmes of Action could not be achieved. There has been only limited success in some areas and total failure in a few others. The reasons for the failure have been examined by Pinto (1996). He believes that this was due to the fact that the policy was politically motivated and assigned to education functions that were beyond its capacity. The policy is essentially a policy of the central government which was drawn up without consulting the state governments or those who were to implement it. Nor was there adequate financial support. One may add that there was also a lack of will. If a policy is to succeed it has to have support at both the macro and micro-levels and this was lacking. Looking to the future Takwale (1998) has pointed out the need to develop a knowledge network and forge partnership with foreign providers. There is evidently a need for building a strong data-base, for networking, and for research leading to projections on future requirements in different disciplines.

Access and Equity

The National Policy on Education, 1986, explicitly states that the doors of academic institutions should be open to all and also provides for special provisions for the weaker sections of society. Access and equity are, therefore, matters of great concern and many research workers, and especially those belonging to the weaker sections of society, have undertaken investigations on these themes.

The student population of about seven million appears to be high in absolute terms. However, this represents only 6-7% of the young people in the age group of 17-23 years. This is abysmally low in comparison to the over 50% obtained in the OECD countries, and the 20% considered essential for sustained economic development. The position regarding access to higher education has been examined by Majumdar and Vaidyanathan (1994) and Acharya (1996). There is clearly a need to ensure that a much larger percentage of young people avail of higher education. Increasing access substantially would require the creation of new educational facilities at considerable cost. However, in view of financial constraints the opening of a large number of new academic institutions in the formal stream is not possible. Distance education has, therefore, emerged as a viable and effective option (Madan, 1995). Today, with 10 open universities and 61 conventional universities, with centres of distance education/correspondence courses, distance education is catering to about 20% of India's student population. Comprehensive status reports on distance education in India have been published by Yadav and Panda (1996) and Powar and Bhalla (1999b).

The research conducted on distance education till the mid-nineties have been reviewed by Panda (1995). Studies conducted by Pillai (1993) and Ruddar Datt (1994) show that distance education is cost effective. Pillai's study revealed that: (i) the starting of the Indira Gandhi National Open University (IGNOU) widened access as 90% of the students who registered were from non-traditional groups, (ii) the flexibility, both in terms of timeframe and course content, was welcomed by the students, and (iii) the cost of the academic programmmes is relatively low while the value addition is high. The effectiveness of distance education is clear from the fact that today about 20% of the student population is catered to by the open universities and distance education centres in conventional universities. A subsequent study on IGNOU conducted by Pandey (1997) substantiates the increasing popularity of distance education as an alternative to education through the formal stream. However, the IGNOU has largely attracted the urban population (77%) and the number of students from the scheduled castes and scheduled tribes is less than 5%. This is probably due to the fact that the medium of instruction at IGNOU is largely English.

An important national commitment is that of extending the benefits of higher education to the under-privileged classes and groups. These include the scheduled castes, the scheduled tribes, other backward classes, women and the physically handicapped. Consequently many scholars have undertaken studies related to the status of these classes and the mechanism by which their position in society can be improved. As an example we may consider the case of the scheduled castes and scheduled tribes (dalits). They have been provided 15% seats in higher education and are also financially supported. Yet the enrolment today is only about 10% and they have a very high drop-out rate of nearly 80% (Khajapeer, 1996; Pinto, 1998; Aggarwal, 1998; and Choudhury, 1998). Pinto attributes this to social, cultural and economic disparities, and the elitist culture and curriculum of universities. He pleads for a special 'dalit' culture and for courses with content that is relevant to the backward classes. This move for separate universities and colleges and separate courses is opposed by others, like Barik (1998), who believe that assimilation into the mainstream through the provision of better facilities is the correct way. Aggarwal points out that the mere provision of better infrastructure is not enough. There is the need for a movement to mobilise 'dalits' into higher education.

There has been much inquiry and discussion on the role of women in higher education (see Powar and Shafi, 1999). As previously stated the number of women students in higher education in India is about 35%. A study by Padmini (1999) on the Shivaji University, Kolhapur, which is located in a rural setting, reveals that the percentage of women students at the undergraduate level during 1997-98 was 37.9% in Arts (including Social Sciences), 40.8% in Science, 42.5% in Commerce, 32.2% in Education, 34.4% in Medicine and 12.7% in Engineering. At the post-graduate level it was 33% in Arts (including Social Sciences), 46.2% in Science, 25.5% in Commerce, 35.5% in Education, 50% in Medicine and 19.9% in Engineering. The number of women teachers in universities is comparable to that obtained in western countries. A survey covering 64 universities carried out by AIU reveals that 27% of Lecturers, 18% of Readers and 17% of Professors in Indian universities are women (Bhalla and Rai-Negi, 1999).

Academic Restructuring and Innovations

The majority of the conventional Indian universities are of the teaching-cum-affiliating type. There is a central campus on which is conducted post-graduate teaching and research. To the university are affiliated a large number of colleges (often exceeding 200) which are primarily undergraduate institutions, but sometimes undertake post-graduate teaching as well. All colleges have common programmes and syllabi determined by the university and the students appear for a common examination, usually conducted at the end of the academic year. The affiliating system was devised to regulate and standardise the quality of education, but with the tremendous increase in the number of colleges the system has proved to be counter-productive. Because of it some sub-standard colleges serenely ride piggy-back on the reputation of the mother institution. At the same time the system is a drag on the better institutions that would otherwise regularly revise and update their courses, and introduce innovative programmes. Efforts to discard the affiliating system have not succeeded. In order to maintain the quality of education several reforms and innovations have been tried out. These are briefly reviewed below.

***Autonomous Colleges*:** Realising the difficulties faced by good institutions in revising syllabi, evolving methods of teaching and learning and introducing innovative programmes, the concept of autonomous colleges was adopted in the National Policy on Education, 1986. It was visualised that by the end of Seventh Five Year Plan (1990) there would be about 500 such autonomous colleges. But as of today there are only some 120-odd colleges. The functioning of the autonomous colleges has been studied at NIEPA (Sudha Rao, 1999, Sudha Rao et al., 1999). The study yields a positive picture. Most of the colleges have been successful in remobilising community support, have undertaken meaningful extension and some research activities, restructured their courses, introduced examination reforms (including semester system, internal assessment, continuous evaluation), ensured accountability of teachers, and implemented UGC guidelines regarding administration and management. However, Thangamuthu (1993) has drawn attention to the lop-sided spatial distribution of the colleges (practically all of them are in the southern states of India) and to the fact that they are privately managed. The government colleges (or the governments) are evidently lukewarm to this innovation. It has to be studied why most colleges are unwilling to apply for autonomous status. One reason that is often cited is the unwillingness of teachers to shoulder extra responsibility. Thangamuthu is of the view that the teacher unions feel that the autonomous colleges would become elitist institutions and thus help in perpetuating inequity. Another fear is that autonomy gives undue strength (power) to the managements. Whatever the reason the reluctance of colleges to take up autonomous status must be researched into, for otherwise an excellent innovation could become ineffective. The problem of personnel management in autonomous colleges has been reviewed by Krishnan and Raj (1995).

***Academic Staff Colleges*:** As a measure of staff development the University Grants Commission established, more than a decade ago, 48 Academic Staff Colleges in different universities of India. These offer orientation programmes for fresh teachers and subject-specific refresher courses for serving teachers for the updating of their knowledge. These colleges have been functioning with varying degrees of success depending upon the local ethos and the disciplines handled. A difficulty that has often been faced by the colleges is the shortage of competent faculty (Rastogi, 1999). The UGC is reviewing the functioning of the different Academic Staff Colleges. Verma (1998) and Rastogi (1998) have spelt out criteria for such an evaluation. Benakanal and Sahoo (1994) and Rao (1996) have undertaken a detailed survey of an Academic Staff College in which they have ascertained the views of the Director, resource persons and participants (lecturers) on the objectives, duration, content, nature of activities and use of educational technology. Harichandan and Ramabrahmam (1999) have reviewed the impact of orientation courses offered by an Academic Staff College.

***Vocationalisation of Education*:** In order to increase the employability of university graduates, and/or the absorptive capacity of the job market, the UGC decided to vocationalise the first degree programme in the faculties of arts, social science, science and commerce. This was to be done by making a provision for offering a course, that imparted knowledge and skill required for gainful employment, especially self-employment, in place of one course in the regular degree programme. The scheme was implemented in some 35 selected colleges all over the country, initially for a period of three years. It has been received with some skepticism in view of past experiences. It is felt that the skills that would be imparted in one course would not be sufficient for the purpose that is mooted. Gnanam (1995) has suggested that it would be a better option to provide a short training programme of three-to-six months, duration after the completion of general education. Azad (1995) has drawn attention to the practical difficulties, including availing the services of competent persons for teaching, prevailing upon industry to offer facilities for practical training and providing financial support on a continued basis after the three-year initial period is over. He has also expressed fear that vocationalisation at the degree level would fail for the same reasons that vocationalisation at higher secondary level failed. Das Gupta (1998) has drawn attention to the need of offering agro-based vocational courses for colleges in rural areas. He has made a case for rural-based vocational courses to be offered in collaboration with the Indian Council for Agricultural Research.

***Academic Restructuring*:** Universities in India, in general, have rigid academic structures. The programmes are time-specific, and at undergraduate level offer limited choice regarding combination of subjects, and little or no option regarding choice of courses within a subject. In recent years there have been demands for a more flexible structure. Many academics have asked for a cafeteria-type approach that would allow students to select courses from a wide range of options. A very small number of universities have responded by adopting a Choice-Based Credit System. There have also been demands for restructuring with the view of making the academic programmes more relevant to societal needs. The scheme of vocationalisation of education discussed above is an outcome of this demand. Alternate approaches have also been suggested, amongst others, by Azad (1995), Das (1996) and Narain (1996).

The Abid Hussein Committee Report of the University of Delhi (University of Delhi, 1997), on employment-oriented courses, has made recommendations regarding the nature of the job-oriented courses to be offered at the university. It has also recommended the starting of job-oriented Bachelor's programmes in subjects like accountancy, food technology, computer applications, graphic arts, and fashion technology. The teachers of Delhi University have proposed a revised structure for the B.Sc. programme that incorporates foundation courses in all science subjects and supports a multi-disciplinary approach (Centre for Science Education and Communication, 1997). In keeping with the concept of foundation courses a revised structure for the B.A. programme has been suggested by Das (1996). A proposal for an integrated 4-year B.Sc. programme has been made by the Srivastava Committee of UGC (University Grants Commission, 1995). Earlier a working group of the Planning Commission had suggested the introduction of a 5-year integrated M.Sc. programme (Indian Academy of Sciences, 1994). Modak (1996) has put forward a proposal for a 5-year integrated programme for Life Science. These and other such proposals need to be examined seriously.

***Curriculum Development*:** In India there are strong boundaries between the content units of a curriculum and only a limited option is available to teachers as regards selection, organisation and pacing of knowledge acquisition (Vijya and Chand, 1998). This is related to the fact that there is a single curriculum in a subject for all colleges affiliated to a university and this curriculum is prepared by a 'board' comprising of a few teachers. A teacher does not necessarily have a say in what he teaches and there is, therefore, little scope for innovation or experimentation. The need for uniformity in standards makes it necessary for all universities to have a relatively homogeneous curriculum that incorporates all fundamentals as also the latest developments in a subject. With the view to maintaining quality the University Grants Commission set up in 1986 Curriculum Development Centres for different subjects, to prepare curricula with the active participation of teachers from different universities and outside experts. It was expected that the universities would adopt the model curricula with minor modifications dictated by local needs. However, a survey carried out in 1994 indicated that very few universities had seriously considered them (Malhan and Bhalla, 1977).

In spite of this negative feedback it is to be appreciated that many academics have shown interest in developing curricula in different disciplines. In an important contribution Mathur (1995) has discussed the necessity of restructuring teaching curricula in engineering education to meet national needs. Mandke (1993) has stressed the need for engineering inputs in non-engineering curricula. Passi and Pal (1996) have put forward suggestions regarding a curriculum for orientation programmes in higher education. Sharma (1998) has examined curriculum development in distance education. Verghese *et al.* (1993), Pathak and Singh (1998) and Kumar and Prakash (1993) have respectively contributed to curriculum on hospital management, population studies and energy studies through distance mode.

Examination Reforms: Under the affiliating system most Indian universities have an annual examination with at least some external examiners. Efforts have been made since the late seventies to replace this system by the semester system with internal assessment and continuous evaluation. Many universities introduced the semester system but quite a few have reverted to the older system. The reasons for this need to be analysed in depth.

As a part of the examination reforms effort question banking was introduced in India largely through the efforts of AIU (Bhalla, 1994). It has prepared 28 question banks in different subjects. Bhalla (1999) has discussed the principles and practice of development of question banks. Other, more specific contributions on examination reforms are those by Khare *et al.* (1993) on tutor marked assignments, Shreemathi (1996) on multiple choice examination, Kachroo (1999) on evaluation of distance education programmes in liberal arts, and Kannan et al. (1998) on assessment of science laboratory courses.

Teaching and Learning Processes

A great amount (and variety) of research has been done at micro-level on innovations and improvements in the teaching and learning processes (also see Chand, 1998) but only illustrative examples are presented here. Some of the research published relates to effectiveness of teaching (Dixit, 1994), innovations in teaching of specific subjects (Verma, 1994; Reddy and Ramar, 1995), cooperative teaching (Sundaram, 1997), questioning technique (Rajendran, 1998), development of self-instructional materials (Bagchi, 1996), use of educational technology (Chandra and Pandya, 1996; Khemchandani, 1998) and educational psychology (Biswas, 1999).

A major concern has been the effectiveness of teaching and learning as it ultimately controls the quality of both education and the product. In order to evaluate these a few performance indicators have been evolved to meet the requirements of the Indian scenario (Shafi, 1990; Powar, 1996; Kishore, 1998). Criteria and methods for the evaluation of teaching, research and institutions have been described by Powar (1996). Powar and Sabale (1995) have used statistical parameters to evaluate the effectiveness of teaching in engineering colleges.

Financing Education

In the fifty-odd years following Indian Independence the Indian higher education system has shown massive growth. This has been possible largely because of the support provided by the governments – both Central and State (Powar, 1997, 1998). Even today in the case of most universities over 90% of the expenditure is met from public funds. The government is now placing greater emphasis on primary education and school education. The consequence is that funds are no longer flowing into higher education and in the future financial stringency is likely to increase. In a discussion paper issued in 1997 by the Department of Economic Affairs, Ministry of Finance expenditure on higher education was classified as a 'non-merit' subsidy implying that its benefits were restricted to the individual. This has been strongly contested in analytical papers by Desai (1998), Powar (1998) and others (see Special Issue of *University News*, Vol.36, No. 24 on *Higher Education – A Non-Merit Good?: A Symposium*). At the same time it is accepted that in India higher education is extremely cheap. The situation has been analysed at various levels (Dandekar, 1991; Balchander, 1991; Panchmukhi, 1996; Tilak, 1997) and proposals have been made to rationalise tuition fees (University Grants Commission, 1993, 1997; Powar, 1995, 1996a). Likewise the cost of professional education has also been studied (Manipal Academy of Higher Education, 1996; Christo, 1996), as also the mechanisms of funding (Sharma et al., 1992; Government of India, 1997; Ahmad, 1998; Azad, 1999). As detailed earlier studies have also been conducted on the cost of distance education. There is considerable scope for research on this aspect also.

Internationalisation of Higher Education

In the context of globalisation there is a need to study the process of internationalisation of education in India. Very little has been done in this area which, however, has great potential for research. Lavakare *et al.* (1995) have published a study on the export of Indian education in general, and Chahal (1999) on the marketing of business education in particular. Powar *et al.* (1997) have comprehensively discussed the position of international students in Indian universities. Natrajan (1998) has discussed the internationalisation of Engineering studies.

On retrospection one is led to the conclusion that macro-level innovations in higher education, introduced during the last two decades, have failed to yield the expected results. The concept of autonomous colleges is viewed with suspicion by a large part of the teaching community and has not found favour in many states. Academic Staff

Colleges have only been partially successful, and vocationalisation of education at the undergraduate level has not achieved demonstrable success. Attempts at restructuring academic programmes have failed and it has not been possible to impart flexibility to the academic structure in most universities. The recommendations of the Curriculum Development Centres have been more or less completely disregarded. Most universities have not been able to implement examination reforms, and at least a few that tried out the semester system with internal assessment and continuous evaluation, have reverted to the old system. The innovations, thought out by senior and well-meaning academics, have failed to improve quality across the board though there are some success stories. This can be possibly attributed to the country's psyche. As Valiathan (1993) succinctly puts it: "*knowing what to do and not doing it has cast a shadow on (our) national endeavours*". A possible alternate reason could be that the innovations were formulated by persons of superior intellect and commitment without adequately taking into consideration the infrastructure, financial resources and human resources available at the levels of implementation. Under the conditions of scarce resource, success is possible only if there is all-round commitment and sustained effort.

Conclusion

In the coming years higher education is destined to play an important role in the progress of nations because socio-economic development will, to a considerable extent, depend upon the capacity of humans to convert information into knowledge. It is, therefore, essential that in the incoming 'knowledge age' higher education systems be dynamic. They should have the capacity to adapt themselves to the constantly changing needs of a knowledge-based society.

Reforms and innovations have to be based upon a proper understanding of the factual position and a clear perception of future requirements. Research, which is essentially the collection, analysis and interpretation of information, should logically have an important part to play in decision-making relating to reforms. It should also provide the inspiration for innovation. The results of research, however, need to be clearly and forcefully presented in order to minimise the effect of political and administrative considerations that, in most societies, influence decision-making. Further, research must continue even after reforms are implemented, for, constructive evaluation is required in order to effect mid-course corrections or modifications. In order to be effective the research must be undertaken promptly and conducted expeditiously.

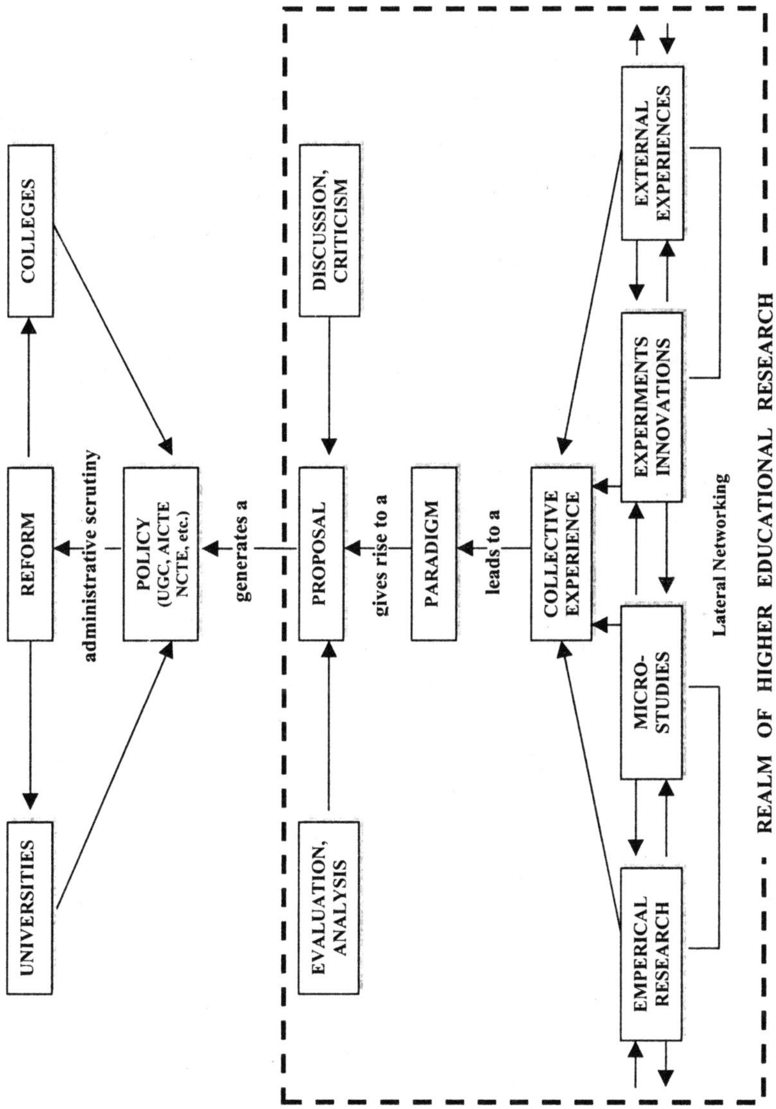

Fig. 2: A Conceptual Framework for Reforms in Indian Higher Education based on Educational

If we accept Altbach's (1993) perception, that the Indian higher education system is a great monolith with a core of inadequacy, possibly incapable of change, and margined by a rim that is receptive, and has developed, then it would be wise to concentrate on the 'core', and let the 'rim' develop on its own momentum. After all it represents excellence, achieved through conceptualisation, hard work and innovation. In a country characterised by great diversity and vast inequalities, uniform implementation of reforms and acceptance of innovation are not to be expected, nor sought. It would, therefore, be prudent, as Chand (1998) asserts, to lay emphasis on small efforts and encourage innovation and change at the micro-level. Propagation of results through 'good practice' accounts should lead to lateral networking and progression. Our experience shows that ideas generated and developed at higher echelons, and prescribed as panacea for deeply entrenched ills, do not necessarily find acceptance at the levels where they are to be implemented. Innovation evolved in the classrooms and laboratories should be the subjects for research, which in turn should be the basis of reforms.

A conceptual framework that attempts to depict the possible relationship between educational research on one hand, and policy formulation and reform on the other, is presented in Fig. 2. The foundation blocks include empirical research carried out in the spirit of academic inquiry, micro-studies on specific aspects of higher education, experiments and innovations carried out in the classrooms and in the field, and external experiences from foreign countries. Lateral networking and interaction should result in a pool of collective experience, leading to the development of a paradigm, which in turn could give rise to a proposal. The proposal on analysis, evaluation, discussion and criticism, could lead to the generation of a policy, which on administrative scrutiny, may result in a reform.

References

Acharya, S., (1996), Access and Returns to Education: Analysis for Maharashtra, *Journal of Educational Planning and Administration,* 10(4): 383- 396.

Altbach, P.G., (1993), The Dilemma of Change in Indian Higher Education, *Higher Education,* 26: 3-20.

Aggarwal, Y., (1998), Some Aspects of Social and Economic Inequities amongst SCs in India, *Journal of Higher Education*, 21(3): 415-432.

Aggarwal, Y. and Sibou, S., (1994), *Educating Scheduled Caste: A Study of Inter-District and Intra-Caste Differentials*, NIEPA, New Delhi.

Ahmad, N., (1998), Financing Central Universities: An Overview, *Journal of Educational Planning and Administration,* 12(1): 67- 75.

Association of Indian Universities, (1995), *Unit Cost of Education in Indian Universities*, AIU, New Delhi

Association of Indian Universities, (1998), *Universities Handbook*, 27th Edition, AIU, New Delhi

Azad, J.L., (1995), Restructuring of University-level Courses: Need for a Cautious Approach, *Journal of Higher Education*, 18(2): 233- 242.

Azad, J.L., (1999), Criteria-Based Funding of Higher Education, *Journal of Educational Planning and Administration*, 13(4): 443-449.

Bagchi, J.P., (1996), Developing Self-instructional Materials for Science Programmes: A Pragmatic Approach, *Indian Journal of Open Learning*, 5(2): 47-52.

Bajpai, J.P., (1996), Developing Self-instructional Materials for Science Programmes: A Pragmatic Approach, *Indian Journal of Open Learning, 5(2):* 47- 52.

Balchander, K.K., (1991), Funding of State Universities in India: Some Critical Issues, *Journal of Educational Planning and Administration*, 5(3): 285- 299.

Barik, R.K., (1998), Education for Dalits: No Separate Colleges and Universities for Dalits, *Journal of Higher Education*, 21(3): 433- 436.

Benakanal, V.A. and Sahoo, P.K., (1994), Faculty Development and Academic Staff Colleges, University News, 32(51): 8- 14.

Bhalla, V., (1994), Status of Question Banking in Indian Universities, *Journal of Higher Education*, 17(3): 451- 454.

Bhalla, V., (1999), *Development of Question Banks; Principles and Practice*, Contributions to Examination Reforms 99/1, AIU, New Delhi.

Bhalla, V. and Rai-Negi, U., (1999), Representation of Women in Teaching Positions in the Indian Universities, *University News*, 37(18): 20.

Biswas, P.K., (1999), Freshers at IGNOU: A Study of their Awareness, Interest and Motivation, *Indian Journal of Open Learning*, 8(3): 273- 282.

Brew, A. and Boud, D., (1995), Research and Learning in Higher Education, in Smith, B. and Brown, S., (Editors), *Research, Teaching and Learning in Higher Education*, Kogan Page, London, p. 30-39.

Centre for Science Education and Communication, (1997), *Science Education and Career Opportunities,: An Exercise in Looking Ahead*, CSEC, University of Delhi, Delhi.

Chahal, H., (1999), GLOBUS: A marketing Model for Globalising Business Education, *Journal of Educational Planning and Administration*, 13(2): 135-166.

Chandra, A. and Pandya, R., (1996), An Experiment to Test Effectiveness of Video Films in imparting Legal Education, *Journal of Higher Education*, 19(4): 571- 574.

Choudhary, K., (1998), Dalits in Higher Education: Cooption or Domination, *Journal of Higher Education*, 21(3): 437- 452.

Christo, C.G., (1996), *The Privatisation and Pricing of Professional Education with Special Reference to Medical Education*, Centre for Policy Research, New Delhi.

Clark, B.R., (1991), The Fragmentation of Research, Teaching and Learning, in Throw, A. and Thorsten, N. (Editors), *University and Society,* Jessica Kingsley Publ., London, p. 101- 111.

Dandekar, V.M., (1991), Reform of Higher Education, *Economic and Political Weekly,* 26(4): 2631- 2637.

Das, V., (1996), Towards the Restructuring of Undergraduate Education, *Journal of Higher Education*, 19(2): 275- 280.

Dasgupta, P,R., (1997), Challenges Facing Indian Education, *Journal of Higher Education*, 20(4): 519- 522.

Das Gupta, D.K., (1998), Rural-based Vocational Courses, *Journal of Higher Education,* 21(1): 59- 75.

Desai, A., (1995), Policies of Higher Education in India, *Journal of Higher Education*, 18(4): 667- 686.

Dave, P.N. and Murthy, C.G.V., (1993), *Educational Research and Innovation (1988-92): A Bibliography*, NCERT, New Delhi.

Dixit, A., (1994), Transmission Losses in Teaching-Learning Process, *Journal of Higher Education*, 17(3): 445- 450

Desai, A., (1998), Government Subsidies for Higher Education, *University News*, 36(24): 2-7

Ferrer, F., (1999), Some Thoughts on Trends in Educational Research, *Prospects,* 111: 409 –422.

Government of India, (1950), *University Education Commission, 1948-49: Report*, (Radhakrishnan Commission Report), GOI, New Delhi.

Government of India, (1966), *Report of the Education Commission (1964-66): Education and National Development,* (Kothari Commission Report), GOI, New Delhi.

Government of India, (1985), *Challenge of Education: A Policy Perspective,* GOI, New Delhi.

Government of India, (1986), *National Policy on Education, 1986*, GOI, New Delhi.

Government of India, (1989), *Towards an Enlightened and Humane Society,* (Ramamurthi Committee Report), GOI, New Delhi.

Government of India, (1992), *Programme of Action, 1992*, GOI, New Delhi, Reprinted by UGC, New Delhi.

Government of India, (1997), *Review Report on Revised Pattern of Funding Scheme for IITs, IIMs and IISc.*, (Ayyar Committee Report), GOI, New Delhi.

Gnanam, A., (1995), Vocationalisation of What? The Student or Education, *Journal of Higher Education*, 18(2): 217- 222.

Harichandan, M. and Ramabrahmam, I., (1999), Towards Quality Assurance in Higher Education: Impact of Orientation Courses, *Journal of Educational Planning and Administration,* 13(1): 81- 89.

Indian Academy of Sciences, (1994), *University Education in India*, Academy Papers 1, IASc, Bangalore.

Indiresan, J, (1991), *College Development Councils: Prescription versus Performances*, Research Study, NIEPA, New Delhi.

Kachroo, Kanchan Bala, (1999), Distance Education Programmes at College and University Levels in Jummu Region: An Evaluation Study, *Indian Journal of Open Learning*, 8(3): 293- 305.

Kannan, S., Raghavan, V.V. and Goel, V., (1998), Need for Quality in Assessment — Part I: Concept of Assessment of Science Laboratory Courses in Open Learning System, *Journal of Open Learning*, 7(2): 191- 197.

Khajapeer, M., (1996), Democratisation of Higher Education in India with Special Reference to the Weaker Sections, Minorities and Women, *Journal of Educational Planning and Administration,* 10(2): 143- 152.

Khare, P., Byrne, C.J. and Jacob, A., (1993), Different Formats of TMAs: Observation Account, Case-study and Application (Skill), *Indian Journal of Open Learning*, 2(2): 13-20.

Khemchandani, B. S., (1998), A Study of the Use of Technological Device by Academic Counsellors at IGNOU Study Centres of Ahmedabad District, *Journal of Higher Education*, 21(2): 273- 277.

Kishore, S., (1998), Student Support and Quality Indicators in Distance Learning, *Indian Journal of Distance Learning*, 7(2): 205-212.

Kumar, K. and Prakash, J., (1993), Science Curriculum for Distance Learners: A Case Study for Teaching Energy Studies, *Indian Journal of Open Learning*, 2(2): 32- 36.

Lavakare, P.J., Gulhathi, S.K. and Sukhija, S.S., (1995), Exporting Indian Higher Education: Opportunities and Challenges, *Journal of Higher Education*, 18(1): 105-119.

Krishnan, K. and Raj, A.E., (1995), Personnel Management in Autonomous Colleges, *Journal of Educational Planning and Administration,* 9(2): 189- 192.

Madan, V.D., (1995), Access to Higher Education through Distance Mode, *Journal of Educational Planning and Research,* 9(1): 93-100.

Majumdar, M. and Vaidyanathan, A., (1994), Access to Education in India: Retrospect and Prospect, *Journal of Educational Planning and Administration*, 8(4): 353-404.

Malhan, P. and Bhalla, V., (1997), Report on Acceptance and Implementation of Model Curricula Developed by the Curriculum Development Centres in Geosciences, *Journal of Higher Education*, 20(4): 633- 638.

Malhotra, N., (1996), *NIEPA Research Studies: Annotated Bibliography*, NIEPA, New Delhi.

Mandke, P., (1993), Engineering Inputs in Non-Engineering Curricula, *Journal of Higher Education*, 16(3): 389- 399.

Mathur, N.C., (1995), The Role of Teaching Curricula in Meeting National Needs: A Case Study of IITs — Final Report, *Journal of Higher Education*, 18(1): 121-180.

Manipal Academy of Higher Education, (1996), *Computation of Cost of Education* (Bopanna Committee Report), MAHE, Manipal.

Modak, S.P., (1996), Science Education in Indian Universities: Proposal for a 5-Year Integrated Course in Life Science, *Current Science*, 71(2): 960- 967.

Narain, N., (1996), Restructuring of Undergraduate Education, *Journal of Higher Education*, 19(2): 275- 280.

National Council for Teacher Education, (1998a), *Teacher Education in Haryana*, NCTE, New Delhi.

National Council for Teacher Education, (1998b), *Teacher Education in Himachal Pradesh*, NCTE, New Delhi.

National Council for Teacher Education, (1999a), *Teacher Education in Karnataka*, NCTE, New Delhi.

National Council for Teacher Education, (1999b), *Teacher Education in Meghalaya*, NCTE, New Delhi.

National Council for Teacher Education, (1999c), *Teacher Education in Mizoram*, NCTE, New Delhi.

National Council for Teacher Education, (1999d), *Teacher Education in Uttar Pradesh*, NCTE, New Delhi.

National Council for Teacher Education, (1999e), *A Handbook on Educational Research*, NCTE, New Delhi.

Natrajan, R., (1998), Internationalization of Engineering Studies, *Journal of Higher Education*, 21(1): 9- 16.

Nuna, S.C. (Editor), (1993), *Regional Disparities in Educational Development*, South Asian, New Delhi.

Organisation for Economic Cooperation and Development, (1995), *Educational Research and Development – Trends, Issues, Challenges*, OECD, Paris.

Panchmukhi, P.R., (1996), University Finances in India, *Journal of Economic Planning and Administration*, 10(1): 15- 24.

Panda, S.K., (1995), Review of Research on Indian Distance Education, *Journal of Higher Education*, 18(4): 469- 484.

Pandey, S., (1997), Popularity and Effectiveness of Open Educatiion System: A Case Study of IGNOU, *Journal of Higher Education*, 20(1): 71- 60.

Padmini, M.S., (1999), Women in Higher Education Scenario of Shivaji University, in Powar, K.B. and Shafi, Z. S. (Editors), *Women Participation in Higher Education*, AIU, New Delhi, pp. 35- 53.

Pani, B.S., (1998), Privatisation — Some Issues, *Journal of Higher Education*, 21(3): 453- 462.

Passi, B.K. and Pal, R., (1996), Curriculum for Orientation Programs in Higher Education, *Journal of Higher Education*, 19(1): 53- 66.

Pathak, K.B. and Singh, S.K., (1998), Distance Education Programme in Population Studies, *Journal of Higher Education*, 21(2): 241- 249.

Pillai, C.R., (1993), Accommodating Social Demand for Higher Education: Cost Effectiveness of IGNOU, *Journal of Higher Education*, 16(3): 453-486.

Pinto, A., (1996), Whither Education Policy, 1986? *Journal of Higher Education*, 19:219-230.

Pinto, A., (1998), Dalit in Higher Education: Need to Establish a Counter-Culture, *Journal of Higher Education*, 21(3): 403- 414.

Powar, K.B., (1996a), *Unit Costs in Higher Education*, AIU Occasional Paper, 96/1, AIU, New Delhi.

Powar, K.B., (1996b), *Accreditation in Higher Education: An Indian Perspective*, Viva Books, New Delhi.

Powar, K.B., (1997). *Higher Education in India Since Independence: Retrospect and Future Options*, AIU Occasional Paper 97/1, AIU, New Delhi.

Powar, K.B., (1998), Government Support for Higher Education, *University News*, 36(24): 8- 9.

Powar, K.B. and Bhalla, V., (Editors), (1999a), *Quality Assurance in Distance Higher Education*, AIU, New Delhi.

Powar, K.B. and Bhalla, V., (1999b), Distance Education in India, in Powar, K.B. and Bhalla, V. (Editors), *Quality Assurance in Distance Higher Education*, AIU, New Delhi, pp. 33- 70.

Powar, K.B. and Panda, S.K., (Editors), (1995), *Higher Education in India: In Search of Quality*, AIU, New Delhi.

Powar, K.B., Pandey, S., Panda, S.K. and Bhalla, V., (1997), *International Students in Indian Universities*, AIU, New Delhi.

Powar, K.B. and Sabale, B.S, (1995), Using Performance Indicators for Performance Appraisal of Engineering Colleges, *Journal of Higher Education*, 18(4): 607- 618.

Powar, K.B. and Shafi, Z. S., (Editors), (1999), *Women Participation in Higher Education*, AIU, New Delhi

Rajendran, G., (1998), A Study of Questioning Technique Adopted by Lecturers in JNR Mahavidyalaya, Port Blair, *Journal of Higher Education*, 21(2): 275- 295.

Ramsden, D.W., (1994), Describing and Explaining Research Productivity, *Higher Education*, 28: 207-226.

Rao, B.G., (1996), Academic Staff Colleges and the Development of Higher Education, *Journal of Educational Planning and Administration*, 10(2): 179- 183.

Rastogi, S., (1998), Academic Development in Higher Education: An Overview, *University News*, 36(44): 14- 17.

Rastogi, S., (1999), Academic Staff Development in Higher Education: Training for Efficiency in Teaching, Research and Management, *Journal of Higher Education*, 22(1): 147- 153.

Raza, M. and Malhotra, N., (1991), *Higher Education in India: A Comprehensive Bibliography*, AIU New Delhi, pp. 477.

Reddy, G.L. and Ramar, R., (1995), Effectiveness of Multimedia-based Modular Approach in Teaching Mathematics to Low Achievers, *Journal of Higher Education*, 18(2): 283- 288.

Ruddar Datt, (1993), Aspects of Privatisation of Education, *Journal of Higher Education*, 16(2): 211- 237.

Ruddar Datt, (1994), *Cost of Distance Education in India: A Study of Cost of Distance Education Institutes with Different Size, Classes*, South Asian, New Delhi.

Shafi, Z. S., (1990). Performance Indicators in Education System: A Study of its Uses and Implications, *Journal of Educational Planning and Administration*, 4: 43- 56.

Sharma, G.D., (1992), *Funding Mechanisms of Thrust Areas of Higher Education in India*, IIEP Research Report No 82, IIEP, Paris, New Delhi.

Sharma, G.D., (1997), Higher Education, in *Fifth Survey of Educational Research (Trend Reports*), NCERT, New Delhi, p. 326- 338.

Sharma, M., (1996), Privatisation of Higher Education in India: Some Lessons from USA, *Journal of Higher Education*, 19(3): 375- 399.

Sharma, R.C., (1992), Curriculum for Distance Education, *Journal of Higher Education*, 21(2): 235- 239.

Shreemathi, Y., (1996), Multiple Choice Papers: Is Guessing Better than Omission? — An Illustration, *Journal of Higher Education*, 19(3): 405- 411.

Shri Prakash and Chowdhury, S., (1994), *Expenditure on Education: Theory, Models and Growth*, NIEPA, New Delhi.

Singh, L,C. and Bhat, V., (1990), Research and Innovation in Teacher Education, in Singh, L.C. (Editor) *Teacher Education in India: A Resource Book*, NCERT, New Delhi, pp. 130- 156.

Somaiah, M., (1993), *Financial Management of Indian Universities: A Case Study*, IIM, Bangalore.

Societe Suisse de Recherche en Education, (1988), *Developmental Plan for Educational Research in Switzerland*, CSRE, Aaran.

Sudha Rao, K., (1999), *Management of Autonomy in Autonomous Colleges*, NIEPA-Vikas Publishing House, New Delhi.

Sudha Rao, K., Mathew, G., and Samanray, S.K., (1999), *Autonomous and Non-Autonomous Colleges: Selected Case Studies*, NIEPA-Vikas Publishing House, New Delhi.

Takwale, R.G., (1996), IGNOU's Challenge of Quality, Quantity and Equity, *University News*, 24(22): 7- 15.

Takwale, R.G., (1998), Partnership with Foreign Providers for Extending Higher Education, *Journal of Higher Education*, 21(2): 157- 163.

Thangamuthu, C., (1993), Autonomy for Colleges: The Vision and the Reality, *Journal of Higher Education*, 16(2): 273- 282.

Tilak, J.B.G., (1995), Union Budget: Education, a Loser, *Mainstream*, 33(26): 15- 20.

Tilak, J.B.G., (1997), The Dilemma of Reforms in Financing Higher Education, *Higher Education Policy*, 10(1): 7- 21.

Tilak, J.B.G., (1999), Higher Education Reform in India, *Journal of Higher Education*, 32(1): 59- 76.

University of Delhi, (1997), Launching of Employment Oriented Courses: Dr Abid Hussein Committee Report, *Journal of Higher Education*, 20(1): 107- 151.

University Grants Commission, (1993), *UGC Funding of Institutions of Higher Education, 1992- 93,* (Punnayya Committee Report), UGC, New Delhi.

University Grants Commission, (1995), *Report of Srivastava Committee on 'National Science University: Concept and Structure*, UGC, New Delhi.

University Grants Commission, (1997), *Report on the Recommendations of the Punnayya Committee relating to Unit Cost of Higher Education,* (Pylee Committee Report), UGC, New Delhi.

Valiathan, M.S., (1993), *Presidential Address, 69th Annual Meeting, Association of Indian Universities*, AIU, New Delhi.

Varghese, S., Pullinod, B.M. and Sengu Havan, V.C., (1993), An Innovative Distance Education Programme for Hospital Managers, *Indian Journal of Open Education*, 2(1): 1-5.

Verma, S.K., (1994), Teaching of English at the Tertiary Level: Focus on Functions, *Journal of Higher Education*, 17(1): 101-106.

Verma, Y., (1998), Evaluation of Academic Colleges: Certain Criteria and Issues, *University News*, 36(18): 9-10.

Vielle, J.P., (1981), The Impact of Research on Educational Change, *Prospects,* 11(3): 313- 325.

Vijya, P.G. and Chand, S., (1998), Lateral Learning: Networking Small Reforms for Revitalisation, *Journal of Higher Education*, 21(3): 325- 332.

Yadav, M.S. and Panda, S.K., (1996), Distance Higher Education in India; A Historical Overview, *Journal of Higher Education*, 19(3): 437- 487.

4

Higher Education in the Twenty-first Century*

Introduction

The last decade of the twentieth century witnessed dramatic changes that were ushered in largely because of the breakdown of political barriers and the unprecedented developments in communication technology. The higher education scenario has been significantly altered. The importance of higher education in national development, and in the development of an individual, has been universally recognised. Governments are now acutely conscious of the need to ensure access and equity. The character of higher education itself has changed with a significant paradigm shift from tutor-centred to learner-centred learning and an acceptance of the concept of lifelong education for all. Higher education systems, the world over, are being subject to ever-increasing financial constraints with governments steadily withdrawing support. A private higher education sector has emerged and market forces have started operating. Quality has become an over-riding concern. There has been an internationalisation of education in more than one sense. It is evident that higher education in the twenty-first century will be significantly different from what it was in the twentieth and, therefore, there is urgent need to plan for the coming years.

The Need for Higher Education

There is a general appreciation of the fact that higher education provides the competencies that are required in different spheres of human activity, ranging from administration to agriculture, business, industry, health and communication, and extending to the arts and culture. The World Bank document *Higher Education: The Lessons of Experience* (World Bank, 1994) allocates a low priority to higher education in its scheme of funding, yet admits: *Higher education is of paramount*

* Background paper for the AIU National Seminar on '*The Role of Universities in the 21st Century*', Gauhati University, Guwahati, December 6, 2000.

importance for economic and social development. Institutions for higher education have the main responsibility for equipping individuals with the advanced knowledge and skills required for positions of responsibility in government, business and the professions". It adds, *"Higher education investments are important for economic growth. They increase (the) individual's productivity and incomes, as indicated by rate-of-return analysis, and they also produce significant external benefits not captured by such analysis".* UNESCO (1995) in its policy paper on *'Change and Development of Higher Education'* emphasises that *"State and society must perceive higher education, not as a burden on federal budgets but as a long-term domestic investment, in order to increase economic competitiveness, cultural development and social cohesion".* Finally, the foreword to the report of the *World Conference on Higher Education,* held in Paris in 1998, maintains: *"It is no longer necessary to demonstrate the importance of education for sustainable, endogenous development, for democracy and peace, for a strengthening of the defence of peace as a human value, and for respect and protection of all human rights and fundamental freedoms. The far-reaching changes now taking place in the world, and the entry of human values into a society based on knowledge and information, reveal how overwhelmingly important education and higher education are".* (UNESCO, 1998)

Significantly, it is the developed nations that attach the greatest importance to education - including higher education. Dhanarajan (1998) quotes two examples to illustrate this. In the United Kingdom, the country that gave birth to Thatcherism, the present Prime Minister Tony Blair stated in a lecture delivered to Ruskin College: "... *the three priorities for (his) government (should his party come to power) would be education, education and education".* Likewise, Bill Clinton in his second inaugural address called for *'a new land (in which) education will be every citizen's most prized possession...And the doors of higher education would be open to all".* Evidently, the importance of higher education is recognised by all – except, perhaps, by those responsible for the distribution of funds.

Inference 1: Those in authority in India must accept the fact that higher education is essential for national development and that in the first decade of the new millennium it should receive the highest priority.

Access

During the second half of the twentieth century higher education acquired an egalitarian character with the process of 'massification' being especially intense in the developing countries, India included.

Worldwide, there has been a near seven-fold expansion in the number of students from about 13 million in 1960 to about 85 million at the turn of the century. In India the expansion has been much more spectacular. In the fifty-odd years since independence, the number of universities has grown from 18 to 256, of colleges from 591 to about 10,000, and students from 0.2 million to about 7 million. In absolute terms the number 7 million is large, and the 35-fold growth since independence is very impressive. Yet, the stark reality is that only about 6-7% of India's population in the relevant age group of 17 to 23 is getting the benefit of higher education. This is insignificant compared to the figure of over 50% obtained for the countries belonging to the Organisation of Economic Cooperation and Development (OECD). The importance of higher education is brought into focus by the World Bank document, of 1994, which states: *"The development of higher education is correlated with economic development: enrollment ratios in higher education average 51 per cent in countries that belong to the Organisation of Economic Cooperation and Development (OECD), compared with 21 per cent in middle-income countries and 6 per cent in low-income countries.* In this context attention may be drawn to Article 26(1) of the Universal Declaration on Human Rights, adopted by the UN General Assembly in 1948, which enjoins that: *"Everyone has the right to education. ...Technical and general education shall be made generally available and higher education shall be equally accessible to all on the basis of merit."* (UNESCO-NIHR, 1986).

In the Indian situation it is necessary to ensure that a much larger number of young people, and especially those belonging to the under-privileged classes or living in the rural area, get the benefit of higher education. Otherwise there is the real danger of an increased socio-economic stratification with the gap between the 'haves' and 'have-nots' increasing. In order to promote equity it may be necessary to substitute the word 'merit' by 'minimum merit' while dealing with applications from the extremely under-privileged. The immediate requirement is to raise the percentage of young people in higher education to at least 20 per cent. Looking at the financial constraints there can be only limited promotion of access though the establishment of new educational institutions in the formal stream of higher education. Distance education, however, promises great possibilities.

Inference 2: Every effort has to be made to increase access. It is necessary to raise the gross enrollment ratio to at least 20 per cent by the end of the first decade.

The Role of Information and Communication Technologies

The twenty-first century promises to be a 'knowledge era' in which a highly competitive 'knowledge society' will make unprecedented demands on universities and other institutions in the area of higher education. These demands can be met only through imaginative and effective utilisation of information and communication technologies. A tremendous increase in the information available in libraries and data-bases will bring to the forefront the critical question as to what a student really needs to know. The education process will, therefore, have to aim at training people in the science (or art) of processing information and transforming it into knowledge that promotes effective decision-making and its implementation. Educational methodologies are bound to change in accordance with the now accepted concept of student-centred learning. On-line learning, making use of the personal computer and information highways, promises to make the virtual classroom an effective reality. One can anticipate a boom in packaged educational products with the educational experience being dramatically enhanced by multi-media, computer simulation, virtual reality and other searching tools. Global universities will emerge bringing together students and faculty from different countries via computer networks, satellite television and other advances (Corrish, 1996). Communication technology will also play an important role in increasing accessibility, in promoting the professional development of teachers and administrative personnel, in streamlining educational administration and management, and advancing quality research.

Inference 3: In the early part of the twenty-first century education, and in particular the teaching-learning process, will be dramatically changed because of developments in information and communication technologies.

Distance and Flexible Education

Distance education, regarded not long ago as the 'poor cousin' of conventional university education, has emerged in recent years as a viable alternative to the formal variety. The flexibility that it offers in terms of choice of programmes and courses, and the period over which these may be pursued, makes it attractive to those already in employment. It allows access to higher education to those who live in areas that do not have adequate educational facilities, or do not have adequate financial support to undertake full-time education, or have not been able to secure admission to courses of their choice in the formal higher education institutions.

Distance education offers a solution to the problem of access, and already about 18 per cent of India's student population is in the non-formal distance education stream. It is visualised that in the coming years a much larger number of students will be in a position to take advantage of this option. There are already 10 open universities and 61 dual mode universities offering programmes through their correspondence course institutes (Powar and Bhalla, 1999). It is hoped that within the first decade of the present century open universities will be functioning in every state so that about 50 per cent of the total future intake in the country will be catered to through the distance/open education system (Powar, 1997). The programmes offered through the distance mode are no longer confined to the arts, social science and commerce streams. Advances in communication and educational technologies have rendered it possible to offer management, science, technology, agriculture and even medical programmes through the distance mode. It is significant that the formal institutions (e.g., the Birla Institute of Technology and Science) have already entered the 'virtual class' mode. It is expected that by the end of the first decade of the new century virtual classes will be common.

Distance and flexible education is particularly important from the point of furtherance of the concepts of continuing education and lifelong learning for all. It offers immense possibilities to industry and business where updating of knowledge and retraining in terms of skills is essential. This is especially significant in view of the development in recent years of technologies with low half-life periods, and the reduction in the time-lag between a major scientific discovery and its application, to only a few years.

Inference 4: Distance education has great potential and will play a major role in providing access to higher education and furthering the concept of lifelong learning.

Financing Higher Education

For the major part of the twentieth century education, including higher education, was financed almost entirely by the State. Till the late eighties, in most countries across the world, governments met nearly 90 per cent of the expenditure on higher education. The state's share was 88 per cent in Australia in 1988; 89.5 per cent in France in 1984; 90 per cent in Norway in 1987, and about 90 per cent in India in 1990; and even in the United States it was about 70 per cent (Tilak, 1997). However, since then there has been a rethinking about the role of the government in the financing of higher education, partly because of its (higher education's) considerable expansion and partly because of demands on the government from other sectors of society. It is paradoxical that as long as higher education was elitist governments were able to meet almost the full cost of higher education. But with its 'massification' governments now find it difficult to meet even the essential requirements (Ziderman and Albrecht, 1995). Thus, most governments are tending to withdraw from higher education, citing the need to first guarantee funds for primary education. This in spite of the fact that higher education institutions:

- produce and train human resources (engineers, doctors, lawyers, accountants, business managers and all kinds of support personnel) required by every productive system;
- conduct scientific and technological research that forms the basis for industrial development and which is essential for a country's progress and survival; and
- examine various areas of human activity, that generate information and knowledge essential for promoting a better social and economic order.

The position regarding the financing of higher education is summarised in the oral report of the World Conference on Higher Education as follows: *"The financing of higher education remains a major problem at the dawn of the twenty-first century. ... In view of the development of higher education, the state cannot hope to be the sole or even the main source of financing for the sector as a whole. ... But, it in no way detracts from the state's responsibility for ensuring that higher education is adequately financed.... It is advisable to create at the decision making level an atmosphere conducive to greater diversification of funding sources for higher education. The solutions are many and varied. In any event an effort should be made to foster an entrepreneurial spirit in institutions which are striving to raise funds not only by traditional research and training activities but also by commercial or production operations. ... New ways of diversifying resources, resulting from a variety of pressures and opportunities, are continuously emerging. ... All these possibilities of diversification are fraught with dangers that must be avoided. The most serious of all is that of undermining equality of access to higher education. ... Involvement of the state and the retention of a public service are still the best guarantee of equal opportunities and the democratisation of higher education".*

All that has been stated above applies to India. However, we find that the governments, at both the centre and the states, are attempting to abdicate their responsibility towards higher education without waiting for institutions to develop the required 'entrepreneurial spirit' and fund-generating capacity. Profit-oriented organisations have stepped in. Professional education has been privatised to a considerable extent and privatisation is leading to commercialisation. Indications are that this trend will gather strength in the first decade of the new millennium. It is necessary to encourage society's participation in higher education yet at the same time ensure that only genuine players enter the field. The existing institutions should be encouraged, trained and facilitated to generate resources and fees need to be rationalised. Decisions have to be taken without allowing political compulsions to dominate. There is perhaps a need to systematically develop the private higher education sector especially for quality professional education. A healthy competition between the state and private institutions is likely to promote the cause of quality. In extreme circumstances, at a time when the policy of disinvestment of public sector undertakings has been accepted, privatisation of poorly-functioning government academic institutions could be a possibility.

Inference 5: In the early part of the twenty-first century state support for higher education will steadily decrease making it necessary for academic institutions to generate revenue through their own efforts. New and innovative means for generating funds and diversifying resources will have to be found. The development of the private higher education sector is perhaps inevitable and necessary. However, government should not be allowed to abdicate its responsibility towards higher education.

Relevance

Today there is general apprehension that the education being imparted through our higher education institutions is not relevant to the needs of society. An extreme view is that the 'average' graduate, at least the one in the liberal arts, is not fit for employment. There appears to be a mismatch between what is taught in our academic institutions and what is required by industry, business, administration, the professions and society-at-large. As the World Declaration on Higher Education states: *"Relevance in higher education should be assessed in terms of the fit between what society expects of institutions and what they do"*. Discussions at the World Conference on Higher Education held at Paris in 1998 brought out the fact that relevance is a dynamic concept varying with context and target groups. It emerged from the deliberations that *'relevance can only be the outcome of dialogue and consultation among the different partners concerned, including the students themselves"* (UNESCO, 1998). In the Indian scenario relevance has assumed importance because of the high rate of unemployment amongst the educated youth. The non-relevance of the academic programmes offered by our academic institutions, especially in the non-professional areas, is further manifested in the emergence of a large number of training institutes that attract many students who are willing to pay relatively high fees for professional training that can secure employment. These institutes place emphasis on the development of skills required by business and industry. Thus, there are two parallel systems of education in India. The formal system represented by the universities and colleges that offer programmes that may be outdated and non-relevant but provide the academic base without emphasising the practical aspects. And the non-formal system represented by institutes of various size, constituting the so-called 'training industry', that impart skills that become irrelevant soon because of the short half-life of modern technology, requiring a re-visit to the institution.

In the first decade of the twenty-first century the universities will perforce have to address the question of relevance. This will have to be done through the updating of curricula following dialogue with different constituents of society, development of proper infrastructure, and closer coordination with the 'users'. In the case of professional education the concept of 'practice school' needs to be more widely adopted. One can also visualise a convergence of the formal and the non-formal systems. Academic programmes can be offered jointly by institutions belonging to the two systems; the formal system providing the strong fundamental base that is so essential for the learning process, in an era of rapid development and change, and the non-formal system providing the required skills.

Inference 6: The academic programmes offered by the universities in the twenty-first century have to be relevant to the needs of society in terms of a fit between what society expects of institutions and what they offer. There is a need for collaboration between the formal and non-formal systems.

Relationship with Society

The expectations of society from its higher education system are reflected in the perceived relationship of academic institutions with its constituents, and especially with the 'world of work'. There is a growing realisation that there has to be a symbiotic relationship between the 'world of knowledge' and the 'world of work'. Industry and business appreciate the fact that with expansion of higher education the information-base has grown almost exponentially and the resultant new-knowledge is a key factor in productivity. Likewise academics accept that practical experience is a necessary component of the learning process and this can be available only through cooperation of the 'world of work'. As Casper (1998) points out, Silicon Valley is today a metaphor, the world over, for productive relationship between a university and its surrounding region. The example needs to be emulated. It is expected that in the twenty-first century there will be close cooperation between the universities and industry, the last word being used in the broadest sense. As Fredrico Mayor, Director General, UNESCO put it: *"I should like the university to cultivate closer relations with the worlds of business, commerce, industry, agriculture, journalism and administration. Research links need to be forged with all these sectors; greater effort should be made to seek out consultancy and service work."* (Mayor, 1991) One can, therefore, visualise the universities, in the coming years, building partnerships with various sectors of society, across interfaces that are porous and allow a free exchange of thoughts and ideas. And, more importantly, the partnerships need to be a relationship of equals, not necessarily controlled by market forces (UNESCO, 1998).

Inference 7: In the coming years one can expect greater interaction between the universities and different sectors of society; the relationship between them being one of equals and not necessarily controlled by market forces.

Quality Assurance

During the last fifteen years considerable attention has been directed towards quality in higher education largely because of the realisation that higher education is essential for national development and economic prosperity. As stated in Article 11 of the World Declaration on Higher Education, *"Quality in higher education is a multidimensional concept which should embrace all its functions, and activities: teaching and academic programmes, research and scholarship, staffing, students, buildings, facilities, equipment, services to the community and the economic environment. Internal self-evaluation and external review, conducted openly by independent specialists, if possible with international expertise, are vital for enhancing quality".* Quality assurance in higher education has, in fact, become a global issue with many countries calling for international global standards. This aspect is particularly relevant to India where the quality of institutions is variable, ranging from the excellent to poor, and with a long tail of mediocrity. In view of the increased student mobility, and the need to provide international experience to both faculty and students, quality assurance should be a priority concern. All institutions must reach a certain minimum standard, and even the best must strive for continuous improvement. Therefore, in the initial years of the twenty-first century all academic institutions will have to develop internal mechanisms for monitoring activities, identify lacunae and shortcomings, and undertake effective measures to improve quality. There is a need for all academic institutions to undergo evaluation by an external agency for overall performance. In India the agencies established for this purpose are the National Assessment and Accreditation Council (NAAC) under the University Grants Commission (UGC) and the National Board of Accreditation (NBA) under the All India Council for Technical Education (AICTE). However, looking at the number of institutions and programmes to be evaluated it would be practical to identify other agencies, like the Association of Indian Universities (AIU), for the purpose of evaluation. The development of reliable, applicable and acceptable performance indicators is a pre-requisite. This exercise has to be immediately followed by appropriate benchmarking, which is generally understood to be the process of identifying standards or standard institutions that represent high quality, and against which other organisations or institutions can be compared and measured. Student mobility, faculty exchange, research collaboration, joint programmes, all require uniform (and high) standards and, hence, quality assurance needs to be accorded the highest priority by all educational institutions.

Inference 8: In the coming years it will be necessary for all academic institutions to maintain minimum standards in all aspects of higher education and adopt quality assurance mechanisms to ensure that their teaching and research programmes are of globally acceptable quality.

Internationalisation of Higher Education

The process of globalisation has affected all spheres of human activity and higher education is no exception. As the foreword to '*Higher Education in the Twenty-first Century: Vision and Action*' states: "*We must be fully alive to the fact that higher education can no longer be conceived solely in terms of national situations and criteria. Research and training that are worthy of the name cannot henceforth be conducted in purely local terms*" (UNESCO, 1998). This reflects the fact that during the last decade of the twentieth century there has been a noteworthy internationalisation of higher education. The main incentive has, unfortunately, been financial gain. This internationalisation has been achieved through:

- advertising, by the developed countries, of their 'educational wares' in order to attract international students;
- offering, through franchise, programmes leading to diplomas and degrees in the professional areas, to 'buyers' in other countries (mostly developing);
- offering 'virtual programmes' in specialised areas via the internet;
- promoting student mobility by adopting credit-transfer mechanisms and emphasising the importance of international experience in higher education; and
- updating and adding an international component to existing academic curricula, and developing special programmes for international students.

Internationalisation of education is to be promoted not only because it yields financial benefits but also because of the academic, political and social advantages that accrue from the presence of international students on campuses. To quote Altbach (1989): "*Foreign students and scholars are one of the most important elements of the international knowledge system... They are the carriers of knowledge across borders... They are the embodiment of the cosmopolitan culture... (and they) are one of the most visible and important parts of the worldwide exchange of ideas*".

It is evident that in the twenty-first century higher education will be increasingly internationalised. Student mobility will substantially increase as twinning programmes develop between universities, the less developed countries try to improve their status, the requirement of being able to function effectively in a global environment is stressed by potential employers, and the desire to have cross-cultural relations increases. Indian universities need to make planned efforts to internationalise their education, if only for the financial benefits. The low value of the Indian Rupee ensures substantial income through the charging of differential (economic) fees from international students (including the Non-Resident Indian). However, it must be emphasised that internationalisation of education will require definitive changes including the strengthening of infrastructure, creation of additional seats, streamlining of admission procedures, revision of curricula to include an international component, establishment of linkages with institutions in other countries, providing facilities for English language courses, and simplification of visa procedures etc. (Powar *et al.*, 1997). Vigorous promotional efforts will also be necessary. It is to be seen if the Indian universities wake up to the promise internationalisation offers or let the opportunity slip by.

Inference 9: Internationalisation of higher education is a fact of life that cannot be neglected. It can both enrich the teaching-learning process and provide financial stability to institutions. It is for the Indian universities to take advantage of the opportunities that exist.

The Basic Functions of Universities: Teaching and Research

Traditionally, teaching and research have been the basic functions of the higher education system. The universities, and the individuals manning them, have been making every effort to adequately discharge both responsibilities, and often the added responsibility of social service also. However, the time has come when a serious retrospection is required in this matter. The two functions – teaching and research — require vastly different abilities that are normally not present in the same individual. Cardinal Newman (Ker, 1976) was quite categorical in stating that teaching and research were distinct functions: the first belonged to the universities, the second to the (research) academies. In his 'discourse' he said: "*To discover and to teach are two distinct functions; they are also distinct gifts, and not commonly found united in the same individual. He too who spends his time in dispensing his existing time to all is unlikely to have either leisure or energy to acquire new* ......". "*The greatest thinkers have been too interested in their subject to admit of interruption .... . And have more or less shunned the lecture room and the public school*". A recent study of the academic profession in 14 countries (Boyer *et al.*, 1994) favours the above contention. It shows that contrary to popular belief most academics prefer to either teach or do research. Interestingly, in the United States and Russia nearly two-thirds of the faculty prefer, or are inclined towards, teaching.

Universities, and more importantly the individuals that constitute them, have apparently been expected to perform both functions because they are mutually beneficial. Perhaps, this 'mutually beneficial' aspect has been over-stressed. Looking at the difference in the interest and aptitude of individuals, the fact that performance of high quality will be required in the 'knowledge-age', and the fact that modern research can be very expense, it would be prudent to allow the universities of the twenty-first century to decide for themselves whether they should concentrate on teaching, or on research, or undertake both teaching and research in equal measure. This could possibly lead to the universities being separated into two groups – the principally-teaching universities and the research-intensive universities.

Modern-day research, especially in science, technology and medicine, can be expensive and can be effectively promoted only by the better-endowed institutions. Further, basic (or fundamental) research requires sophisticated infrastructure, strong financial backing for running expenses, and high creative abilities. These normally would not be available in many universities, which may, therefore, not favour it. Applied (or developmental) research, which requires relatively less expensive infrastructure and gives immediate benefits to society, is more within the means of the less-endowed universities. It would be pragmatic for them to evolve a strategy to promote an 'applied research ethos'. Applied research should logically culminate in participatory research, in which the common man is also involved, and in which there is a convergence of traditional knowledge with modern research.

Inference 10: Looking at the need to ensure quality, and the financial constraints under which many universities are operating, it would be practical to allow universities of the twenty-first century to choose whether they would like to concentrate on teaching (the principally-teaching university), or undertake both teaching and research in equal measure (the research-intensive university). For the average university it may perhaps be more beneficial to promote applied research involving, if possible, different sectors of society, than to undertake fundamental research.

Universities of the Twenty-first Century

In the developed countries there has been an ongoing debate on the future of universities. There are not a few who predict the demise of the universities, as we know them today, in the near future. However, noting that the universities have a history of over 900 years, and that they have successfully adapted themselves to changed situations in the past, one is tempted to think that they will survive, and even thrive, in the new century, albeit in a modified form. It is clear that the universities of the twenty-first century will have to function under the all-pervading influence of the communication technology revolution which has under-written world economy, globalised knowledge, accelerated innovation and facilitated the individual's access to information and skills (Lucus, 1998a). The universities will have to teach the students how to cope with the vast amount of information that keeps pouring in; to discriminate between what is useful and what needs to be confined to the trash bin; to analyse information competently and thereby convert it into knowledge. The universities will have to globalise in terms of both curricula and quality. Functioning under the intense scrutiny of a society that will have high expectations the universities will have to deliver programmes that are both relevant and of high quality. This will require commitment, collaboration and coordination within the institution. It will not be possible to deliver the goods working in isolation. Hence alliances, partnerships and networks would be prime requisites as called for under Article 17 of the World Declaration of Higher Education. The alliances and partnerships will have to be not only with other academic institutions but also with government agencies, non-government community organisations and the corporate world. Finally, at a time when higher education is being viewed in terms of global economy (Lucus, 1998b) or international relationships (Niland, 1998), the universities have the task of restoring values as the key factor in education. In India, this aspect has been a matter of concern for some time now. A few universities have taken an initiative by establishing units for promotion of value education but the efforts need to be intensified.

Lucus (1998b), summarising the views presented by a galaxy of Presidents and Vice Chancellors at a Conference on 'Universities of the 21st Century' held at the Peking University, concluded that in the near future there would essentially be two types of universities – the research-intensive universities and the principally-teaching universities. The research-intensive universities will continue to be of relatively small size and, in keeping with their characteristic, have a highly selective type of entry, with quality teaching and a faculty active in research. The teaching universities will cater to the demands of mass higher education and will seek different forms of delivery, and therefore a different relationship between teacher and taught. In this category, at one end would be the virtual universities, delivering education through the internet, and at the other end multi-campus universities with a consortia of (affiliated) colleges. In the Indian context we may identify within the category of teaching universities a distinct sub-category – the professional universities, whose primary functions will be imparting quality professional education and providing consultancy services to industry.

What does one seek in a university of the new millennium? As Rhodes (1999) visualises it, the 'New American University' will be one possessing institutional autonomy and academic freedom but with strong, impartial public governance; increasingly privately supported but publicly accountable and socially committed; campus-rooted but internationally oriented; academically independent but constructively partnered; knowledge-based but student-centred; research driven but learning focussed; technologically sophisticated but community dependent; quality obsessed but procedurally efficient; and professionally attuned but humanely informed. In the Indian context one may also add that the university will be open to all who desire to enroll but will have a close teacher-student relationship; it will be development oriented but will also lay stress on values. A Utopian ideal but one to cherish!

Inference 11: It appears that in the near future the universities will be basically of two types – the research-intensive university and the principally-teaching university. Working under the all-pervading influence of the communication technology revolution they will have to provide quality education that is internationally competitive. It will be necessary for them to work in partnerships, and networking would be a prime requisite.

The Future

To conclude: Higher education in the twenty-first century promises to be not only demanding but also refreshingly different. Imparted under the all-pervading influence of the communication technology revolution it will be student-centred, committed to the concept of lifelong learning, responsive to the needs of society, increasingly privately financed, and influenced by market forces. It will be international in character placing emphasis on quality, with partnerships and networks being important. In the early part of the twenty-first century life will be influenced not only by the 'knowledge society' but also by the 'stakeholder society' and the 'market society'. The universities, while creating and disseminating knowledge, will have to cater to the interests of its various stakeholders (students, parents, faculty, government, society-at-large), and to market demands.

A submission: The 'inferences' given at the end of each section are, in fact, generalisations that, on scrutiny, can have various proviso appended to them. They are statements, hopefully provocative, that can serve as starting points for stimulating discussions, and should be viewed as such.

References

Altbach, P.G., (1989), The New Internationalisation: Foreign Students and Scholars, *Higher Education*, 14(2): 125- 136.

Boyer, E.L., Altbach, P. and Whitelaw, M.J., (1994), *The Academic Profession: An International Perspective*, The Carnegie Foundation for the Advancement of Teaching, Princeton.

Casper, J., (1998), The Advantage of the Research Intensive University, in Wei Xin, Ma Wanhau and Ju Ren (Editors), *The University of the 21st Century*, Peking University, Beijing, pp. 151-160.

Corrish, E., (1996), The Cyber Future, *The Futurist*, Jan-Feb. 1996, pp. 1-15.

Dhanarajan, G., (1998), Reflections on Collaborative and Networked Learning, *Keynote Address*, International Conference on *Collaborative and Networked Learning*, Indira Gandhi National Open University, New Delhi.

Ker, I.T. (Editor), (1976), *The Idea of a University* by J.H. Newman, The Clarendon Press, Oxford.

Lucus, C., (1998a), Universities and the Challenge of the Learning Society, in Wei Xin, Ma Wanhua and Ju Ren (Editors), *The University of the 21st Century*, Peking University, Beijing, pp. 17- 22.

Lucus, C., (1998b), Knowledge is a Matter of Values, It Poses a Moral Question, in Wei Xin, Ma Wanhua and Ju Ren (Editors), *The University of the 21st Century*, Peking University, Beijing.

Mayor, F., (1991), *Inaugural Address*, UNESCO-AAU Seminar on *Institutional Development of Higher Education in Africa*, Legon University, Accra.

Niland, J., (1998), An Important Function for the University to Pay is to Develop the Relation between Nations, in Wei Xin, Ma Wanhua and Ju Ren (Editors), *The University of the 21st Century*, Peking University, Beijing.

Powar, K.B., (1997), *Higher Education in India Since Independence: Retrospect and Future Options*, AIU Occasional Paper 97/1, AIU, New Delhi.

Powar, K.B. and Bhalla, V., (1999), Distance Education in India, in Powar, K.B. and Bhalla, V. (Editors), *Quality Assurance in Distance Higher Education,* AIU, New Delhi, pp. 33- 55.

Powar, K.B., Pandey, S., Panda, S.K. and Bhalla, V., (1997), *International Students in Indian Universities*, AIU, New Delhi.

Rhodes, F.H.T., (1999), The New University, in Hirsch, W.B. and Weber, L.E. (Editors), *Challenges Facing Higher Education at the Millennium,* Pergamon and IAU Press, Paris.

Tilak, J.B.G., (1997), The Dilemma of Reforms in Financing Higher Education, *Higher Education Policy*, 10(1): 7- 21.

UNESCO, (1995), Policy Paper for Change and Development in Higher Education, Reproduced in *New Frontiers in Education*, 26(3): 288- 334.

UNESCO, (1998), *Higher Education in the Twenty-first Century: Vision and Action*, UNESCO, Paris.

UNESCO-NIHR, (1986), *The International Bill of Human Rights: Normative and Institutional Developments, 1948-85,* UNESCO-Netherlands Institute of Human Rights, Utrecht.

World Bank, (1994), *Higher Education: The Lessons of Experience*, The World Bank, Washington, D.C.

Ziderman, A. and Albrecht, D., (1995), *Financing Universities in Developing Countries*, The Palmer Press, London.

5

Indian Higher Education in the Knowledge Era: The Challenges Within

Introduction

The beginning of the new millennium finds higher education systems, the world over, in a state of flux. This is because a new generation, nurtured by the communication- and information technology revolutions, and a revitalised society which is slowly becoming attuned to life in a new 'knowledge era', are making unprecedented demands. In the first decade of the twenty-first century, academic administrators will have to continue to grapple with 'perennial problems' carried over from the last century, like those of access and equity, relevance and quality, and financial constraints; and face new issues, like those of 'on-line' learning and internationalisation of education. These 'perennial issues' are, in many ways, related to the rapid, largely unplanned, expansion of the system that took place in the post-independence period. The problems are complex and interrelated, and the experiences of the past five decades indicate that they are not likely to be overcome by the further expansion of formal higher education facilities. New and innovative methods have to be tried out. Distance education possibly provides a viable option. In this article these major problems are briefly reviewed and the possibilities offered for their alleviation, by technological developments, are examined. It is suggested that a possible solution is the convergence of the three main systems of higher education – the formal system, the distance education system and the non-formal system. Perhaps, the new developments may help in the resolution of old problems.

The Role of Higher Education

Higher education has always been considered as being essential for human development. When universities were 'elitist' young men and women entered their portals for broadening of perspective and the development of personality. After the universities became 'egalitarian' they were seen as vehicles for economic and social progression. It is against this background that the 'Universal Declaration of Human Rights', adopted by the United Nations General Assembly in 1948, emphasised in its Article 26.1, "*Everyone has the right to education.... Technical and general education shall be made generally available and that higher education shall be equally accessible to all on the basis of merit*" (UNESCO-NIHR,1986). Endorsing this basic principle the *Convention against Discrimination in Education* (1960), through its Article 4, called upon the governments of the States, party to the declaration, to "*make higher education equally accessible to all on the basis of individual capacity*". It is clear that all aspirants should be assured that they have a reasonable chance of being able to get the benefits of higher education at the most appropriate period in their lives (UNESCO, 1960). In keeping with this objective UNESCO's 'Learning Without Frontiers' programme seeks to overcome every kind of obstacle and barrier to learning throughout life (Mayor, 1998).

Today, there is a general appreciation of the fact that higher education provides the competencies that are required in different spheres of human activity, ranging from administration to agriculture, business, industry, health and communication, and extending to the arts and culture. The World Bank document "*Higher Education: The Lessons of Experience* (World Bank, 1994), though allotting a low priority to higher education in its scheme of funding, admits: *Higher Education is of paramount importance for economic and social development. Institutions for higher education have the main responsibility for equipping individuals with the advanced knowledge and skills required for positions of responsibility in government, business and the professions*". It adds: "*Higher education investments are important for economic growth. They increase (the) individual's productivity and incomes as indicated by rate-of-return analysis, and they also produce significant external benefits not captured by such analysis*". It also states: "*Estimated social rates of return of 10 per cent or more in many developing countries also indicate that investments in higher education contributed to increase in labour productivity and to higher long term economic growth, which are essential for poverty alleviation*".

The significance of higher education is also stressed by UNESCO, which in a policy paper (UNESCO, 1995) emphasises: "*State and society must perceive higher education, not as a burden on federal budgets but as a long-term domestic investment, in order to increase economic competitiveness, cultural development and social cohesion".* Finally, as the foreword to the report of the *World Conference on Higher Education (UNESCO,* 1998) maintains: *"It is no longer necessary to demonstrate the importance of education for sustainable, endogenous development, for democracy and peace, for the strengthening of the defense of peace as a human value, and for respect and protection of all human rights and fundamental freedoms. The far-reaching changes now taking place in the world, and the entry of human values into a society based on knowledge and information, reveal how overwhelmingly important education and higher education are"* (UNESCO, 1998).

The recognition that higher education is essential for development should make it easier for academic institutions to generate (financial) support for their activities. The universities need to highlight the fact that they:

- produce and train human resources (engineers, doctors, lawyers, accountants, business managers, and all kinds of support personnel) required by every productive system;
- conduct scientific and technological research that forms the basis for industrial development, and which is essential for a country's survival and development; and
- examine every area of human activity and in the process generate information and knowledge that is essential for promoting a better social and economic order.

Access and Equity

During the second half of the twentieth century higher education acquired an egalitarian character with the process of 'massification' being especially intense in the developing countries, and particularly in India. Worldwide, there has been a near seven-fold expansion in the number of students, from 13 million in 1960 to 82 million in 1985 (UNESCO, 1998), and 85 million at the turn of the century. In India the expansion has been even more spectacular. In the fifty-odd years since independence, the number of universities have grown from 18 to 258 (end of 2000), of colleges from 591 to over 11,000 and of students from 0.2 million to 7.4 million. According to the data for 1998 given in the Universities Handbook, 28th Edition, (Association of Indian Universities, 2000) the students attending the higher level institutions affiliated to universities number about 7.4 million. The figures represent an approximate 37-fold growth in the student population since independence. The student-strength of about 7.4 million, though high in absolute terms, represents only 7.5 per cent of India's population in the relevant age group of 18 to 22 years (Rajput, 2000).

The World Bank document of 1994 (*op. cit.*) states: *"The development of higher education is correlated with economic development: enrollment ratios in higher education average 51 per cent in the countries that belong to the Organisation of Economic Cooperation and Development (OECD), compared with 21 per cent in middle-income countries and 6 per cent in low-income countries".* The low overall enrollment percentage of 7.5 indicates that there is a need to further promote higher education in India and we cannot afford to relax in our efforts in this direction. Rajput's study (*op. cit.*) further shows that programme-wise the enrollment percentages are as follows: B.A./B.Sc./B.Com. 9.51 per cent; B.Ed. 7.70 per cent; B.E./B.Sc (Engg.)/B.Arch. 0.40 per cent; M.B.B.S. 0.15 per cent; and M.A./M.Sc./ M.Com. 1.56 per cent. This suggests the need to lay stress on vocational education and programmes leading to professional degrees. The immediate goal should be to raise the enrollment ratio to at least 20, a figure comparable to that obtained in middle-income countries.

In a democratic society access to higher education must necessarily be linked to equity. In keeping with this policy the National Policy on Education, 1986 (Government of India, 1986) emphasises the need to remove disparities and to equalise educational opportunities, especially for those sections of society that have been denied equality in the past. The categories identified for special consideration by the Government of India are women, the scheduled castes, scheduled tribes and other backward classes, the educationally backward sections and the educationally backward areas. Reservations are provided in educational institutions, and admission-criteria relaxed for students from most of these categories. In addition, financial assistance is provided to them by governments in the form of freeships and grants. Reservations are also operative in respect of recruitment to teaching and non-teaching positions in Indian universities. In an effort to remove gender disparities women's studies are being encouraged in Indian universities and efforts are being made to introduce teaching and research on gender issues. The access to private professional colleges, where the fees charged are beyond the reach of most students from low and middle income groups, has also now been facilitated by judgements of the apex court. It is now mandatory to admit 50 per cent of students against 'free seats' (that require nominal fees), on the basis of merit. Thus, in India the thrust of the educational policy is on 'growth with equity', though there may be shortfalls in actual implementation (Powar, 1996).

The efforts made during the last five decades have reduced disparities but the overall picture is not satisfactory. Specifically:

- The percentage of female students has steadily increased since independence. In the case of general higher education it has risen from 10.77% in 1947 to 39.71% in 1998. In the case of professional and special education the increase has been from 9.11% in 1947 to 28.85% in 1998. However, the growth, appears to be largely within the upper and middle classes of the open (non-reserved) segment of the population. Amongst the scheduled castes and scheduled tribes female students constitute 23.30% in the general higher education and 25.72% in professional and special education.
- In accordance with the demographic pattern the percentage of students belonging to the scheduled caste and scheduled tribe categories should be about 23%, and keeping in view the need to encourage their access 15% reservation is provided for them in academic institutions. Yet, these categories have remained very much under-represented in higher education throughout the last five decades. In fact, the percentage of students of the reserved category in general higher education has fallen from 13.76% in 1957 to 10.68% in 1998. In the case of professional and special higher education there has been a marginal increase from 7.93% in 1957 to 11.29% in 1998.

There has been much inquiry and discussion on the role of women in higher education (see Powar and Shafi, 1999). As previously stated the number of women in higher education in India is a little more than 39%. It is encouraging that the situation is steadily increasing even in the non-urban area. For example a study by Padmini (1999) on the Shivaji University, Kolhapur, Maharashtra, which is located in a rural setting, reveals that the percentage of women students at the undergraduate level during 1997-98, was 37.9% in Arts (including Social Sciences), 40.8% in Science, 42.5% in Commerce, 32.2% in Education, 34.4% in Medicine and 12.7% in Engineering. At the post-graduate level it was 33.0% in Arts (including Social Sciences, 46.2% in Science, 25.5% in Commerce), 35.5% in Education, 50.0% in Medicine and 19.9% in Engineering. The number of women teachers in universities is comparable to that obtained in western countries. A survey, covering 64 universities, carried out by AIU revealed that in the mid-nineties 27% of Lecturers, 18% of Readers and 17% of Professors in Indian universities were women (Bhalla and Rai-Negi, 1999).

A number of scholars have undertaken studies related to the status of the under-privileged classes and the manner in which it could be improved. As an example the case of the scheduled castes and scheduled tribes may be considered. Reservations have been provided for them and they are also financially supported. Yet the enrolment today is unsatisfactory, and they have a very high drop-out rate of nearly 80% (Khajapeer, 1996; Pinto, 1998; Aggarwal, 1998; and Choudhary, 1998). Pinto (*op. cit.*) attributes this to social, cultural and economic disparities, and the elitist culture and curriculum of universities. He has pleaded for a separate 'dalit' culture and for courses with content relevant to the backward classes. This move for separate universities and colleges, and for separate courses, has been opposed by Barik (1998) who asserts that assimilation into the mainstream through the provision of better facilities is the correct way. Aggarwal (*op. cit.*) points out that mere provision of better infrastructure is not enough. There is a need for a movement to mobilise 'dalits' into higher education.

It is necessary to ensure that a much larger number of young people, and especially those belonging to the under-privileged classes, or those living in rural areas, get the benefit of higher education. Otherwise there is the danger of an increased socio-economic stratification with the gap between the 'haves' and 'have-nots' increasing. In order to promote equity it may be necessary to substitute the word 'merit' by 'minimum merit' while dealing with applications from the extremely under-privileged. The immediate requirement, as mentioned above, is to raise the enrollment ratio to at least 20 per cent. Looking at the financial constraints, operating on the higher education system, access can be promoted to only a limited extent, through the establishment of new educational institutions in the formal stream of higher education. Distance education, however, offers hopes and its possible role is discussed later.

Relevance and Quality

Today, in India, there is a general apprehension that the education being imparted through its higher education institutions is not relevant to the needs of society. An extreme view, often expressed, is that the 'average' graduate, at least in the liberal arts, is not fit for employment. There appears to be a mismatch between what is taught in our academic institutions and the requirements of industry, business, administration, the professions and 'society-at-large'. As the, World Declaration on Higher Education, states: "*Relevance in higher education should be assessed in terms of the fit between what society expects of institutions and what they do*". Discussions at the World Conference on Higher Education, at Paris, brought out the fact that relevance is a dynamic concept varying with context and target groups. It emerged at the discussions that "*relevance can only be the outcome of dialogue and consultation among the different partners concerned, including the students themselves*" (UNESCO, 1998). The non-relevance of many of the programmes offered by most Indian universities is brought into focus by the high rate of unemployment amongst graduates and the emergence (and success) of training institutes, of varying types, that have sprung up to offer courses concentrating on the development of skills required by business and industry. The question of relevance will have to be addressed in its entirety. To impart real relevance to higher education it will be necessary to have close coordination between the supplier and the user, develop infrastructure, have networking amongst institutions at national and international levels, undertake academic re-structuring, emphasise curricula development and work (as discussed later) towards a convergence of the formal system of education (represented by the conventional and professional universities), the distance education system (represented by the open universities), and the non-formal system (represented by the training industry).

Closely related to relevance is the aspect of quality. Society has generally viewed quality in higher education in terms of 'fitness for purpose' or 'value for money' and sometimes as 'a transformative' (Green and Harvey, 1993). It must, however, be assigned a broader meaning not necessarily laying stress on the result. To quote Article 14 of the 'World Declaration on Higher Education': "*Quality in higher education is a multi-dimensional concept which should embrace all its functions and activities: teaching and academic programmes research and scholarship, staffing, students, building, facilities, equipment, services to the community and the economic environment*". Quality assurance in higher education has become a global issue with many countries calling for international global standards. This is particularly relevant to India where the quality of institutions, and therefore of the education imparted, is extremely variable from the excellent to poor. There is, what may be called, a long tail of mediocrity. Efforts have to be made to see that all institutions reach a certain minimum standard, and even the best need to strive for continuous improvement. All academic institutions need to develop internal mechanisms for monitoring activities, identifying lacunae and shortcomings, and undertaking appropriate measures to improve quality. The immediate requirement is for the development of reliable, easily applicable and acceptable performance indicators and the establishment of benchmarks.

Realising the need to monitor quality two accreditation agencies have been established in India. These are the National Assessment and Accreditation Council (NAAC) under the University Grants Commission (UGC) and the National Board of Accreditation (NBA) under the All India Council for Technical Education (AICTE). While the former is undertaking institutional evaluation the latter is doing programme evaluation for professional courses. The tasks before the two agencies are monumental. To illustrate: NAAC, established in 1994, has to undertake, at least in theory, the assessment of about 260 universities and over 9000 colleges in 5-year cycles. Till the end of 2000 it had completed assessment of 22 universities and 123 colleges. NBA has completed evaluation of 500 programmes of about 80 institutions against the approximately 600 institutions of engineering and technology, and 350 institutions of management, affiliated to Indian universities. Clearly there is a need to identify more assessment agencies. The various statutory councils could be asked to set up assessment and accreditation agencies for their own institutions; and established agencies like the Association of Indian Universities (AIU), which presently undertakes evaluation for purposes of granting equivalence, could also be given a status equivalent to NAAC.

Monitoring alone will not be of much use from the viewpoint of raising standards. Much greater attention needs to be paid to other crucial aspects like the development of infrastructure, teacher recruitment and staff training. The UGC has been concerned about the two latter aspects and, over a decade back, started a National Eligibility Test for recruitment of teachers and research scholars, and also established Academic Staff Colleges for the orientation and enhancement of knowledge of teachers. However, the functioning of the latter needs to be reviewed. The lack of infrastructure in our academic institutions is a matter of critical concern. In an age of internationalisation, when foreign opinions count, one recalls the assessment made nearly a decade back by Maddox (1993a) *"...the long-standing neglect of the universities, recently intensified, is a serious black-spot in the present state of affairs".* His evaluation of the situation (Maddox, 1993b) is: *"In the circumstances, it is hardly surprising that shabbiness is the hallmark of the regular Indian university. Classrooms are much as they were when first built, perhaps in the early decades of this century. When university libraries are agonizing over the need steadily to reduce their purchases of books and journals, who can wonder that paintwork is allowed to flake, or that classrooms and offices accumulate dirt faster than it is cleaned away?. The shortage of equipment drives people to despair. Departmental budgets for repair and maintenance are negligible. ... It is no wonder... that academics say they are ashamed at being unable to do their duty by their students".* The need for proper infrastructure is evident. Surprisingly, only feeble attempts have been made to improve it in spite of the fact that the 'Programme of Action, in 1992' (Government of India, 1992) has recognised the need to provide a minimum level of infrastructure for maintenance of quality and standards. Finances must be found because it is imperative to have all-round improvement in quality. We cannot have national development with only a few 'showpieces of excellence' (whose products largely contribute to brain-drain).

Financing of Higher Education

Academic institutions are today subject to strong financial constraints. This is related to the fact that governments, the world over, are tending to withdraw from higher education citing the need to first meet commitments to priority areas like those of primary education and health care. A contributory factor has been the great expansion in higher education during the last fifty years. It is paradoxical that when education was elitist, governments were able to meet almost the full cost of education. However, with the 'massification' of education, governments find it difficult to meet even the essential requirements (Ziderman and Albrecht, 1995). In the case of India the decline in government support commenced in the early eighties. Thus the share of higher education in GNP which was nearly 1% in 1980-81 declined the 0.5% in the early nineties and to less than 0.4% in the late nineties. Likewise, as a proportion of total plan expenditure on education, the share of higher education decreased from 25% in the Fourth Five-Year Plan (1969-74), to 22% in the Fifth and Sixth Five-Year Plans (1974-79 and 1980-85), 16% in the Seventh Five-Year Plan (1985-90), 12% in the following 'holiday', and to 8% in the Eighth Five-Year Plan (1992-97). However, there has been a small increase in the Ninth Five-Year Plan.

The message from the government to the universities and colleges is clear. The latter cannot depend wholly on state resources and will have to generate resources on their own. The possible sources are tuition- and other fees, consultancy, corporate support and alumni contributions. All will have to be explored carefully. The revenue from fees cannot be large unless provision is made for reserving seats for international students (including Non-Resident Indians) and they are charged differential fees. The private sector is destined to play an increasingly important role in higher education. In some states of India it has entered this field in a big way, and to an extent higher professional education has been commercialised. Perhaps, professional education will be able to survive (and even prosper) without government support. But the outlook for liberal arts education (Arts, Social Sciences, Commerce and Science) seems to be bleak. A possible remedy would be to allow private trusts to start professional institutions only if they support, fully or to a major extent, a liberal arts institution in the same area. There is perhaps a need to systematically develop the private higher education sector, especially for professional education, after taking care that only genuine players are allowed to enter the field. A healthy competition between the state and private institutions is likely to promote the cause of quality.

Distance Education

In recent years distance education, long regarded to be the 'poor cousin' of the conventional form of education, has gained acceptance and has emerged as a possible alternative to the formal variety. The flexibility it offers, in terms of choice of programmes and the period over which these can be pursued, makes it attractive to those who are employed and cannot attend regular classes. It also offers an alternative to others who are unable to secure admission to academic institutions in the formal stream. Distance education has been projected as an answer to the problems of access and equity.

In India higher education is imparted through the distance mode by two types of institutions – the correspondence course institutes (CCIs) attached to the conventional universities, and the open universities (OUs). The first were promoted largely to meet the rapidly increasing demand for higher education in the years immediately following independence; the second to provide a flexible and open form of education in which the quality of education could be ensured through an optimum use of technology. Today, both forms of distance education are firmly established. At the turn of the millennium there were 810,000 students in the 64 CCIs. The total cumulative enrollment in the ten open universities was over 1,700,000, with the registered strength being 618,000. Thus about 19.3% of registered students in Indian higher education belong to the distance education stream. The number can increase greatly through proper promotion. The programmes offered through the distance stream are no longer confined to the Arts, Social Science and Commerce streams. Advances in communication technology has now made it possible to offer management, science, engineering, agriculture and even medical programmes through the distance mode. It is significant that formal institutions (e.g. the Birla Institute of Technology and Science, Pilani) have already entered the 'virtual class' mode. It is expected that by the end of the first decade of the new century virtual classes will be common.

The founding fathers of the Indira Gandhi National Open University (IGNOU) visualised distance education as being the most promising medium through which higher education could be made available to the disadvantaged groups, and to those living in rural area. However fifteen years down the line it is clear that things have not worked out as anticipated. The student profile of IGNOU for 1999 is revealing. There were 75.53% males against 26.47% females, 22.40% students were from rural areas against 77.60% from the urban areas, and 95.30% students were from the general category against only 4.60% (3.14% scheduled castes and 1.46% scheduled tribes) from the reserved category (Vijayshri and Garg, 2000). These and other facts, given in the earlier section on access and equity, point to the urgent need for re-appraisal of the strategies adopted. Looking back one perceives that the programmes offered by IGNOU, in the first decade of its existence, were those adapted from the formal stream (Bachelors in the Liberal Arts), and professional courses in the newly developing areas (e.g. computers). This was, possibly, dictated by the interests of the faculty (largely recruited from the formal system of education) and the immediate necessity of meeting the requirements of the employed, and others seeking professional skills that facilitated employment. The stated objectives of meeting the needs of those living in the rural areas and providing opportunities for higher education to the disadvantaged sectors were given secondary importance. The necessity of generating funds and making distance education self-supporting may have also been a contributing factor in decision making. The state open universities followed the example of IGNOU while developing their programmes. It is only the Yashwantrao Chavan Maharashtra Open University (YCMOU) that has made conscious efforts to develop diploma and certificate programmes for those residing in rural areas, and for people belonging to the lower income group (see information in Distance Education Council, 2001). Negi (1999) has suggested that in order to encourage increased access of persons from the disadvantaged groups the university should:

- Increase the number of study centres in rural/tribal areas;
- Design programmes that would suit the needs of learners from the disadvantaged groups, and preferably offer programmes in the regional languages; and
- Undertake promotional programmes to create greater awareness about the distance learning programmes and offerings.

Recently, IGNOU has devised some measures for improving the access of these groups. It has now adopted a two-pronged strategy of offering both conventional degrees and continuing/awareness programmes. The aim is to develop a programme-profile comprising knowledge-based as well as competency-based technical/vocational and skill-development courses (Vijayshri and Garg, 2000). Hopefully, this would encourage a greater percentage of people from the disadvantaged groups to join the open universities.

Online Learning

The role of information and communication technologies in changing the character of education has long been recognised. These have been instrumental in introducing new educational methodologies that have allowed the development of the concept of student-centred learning. Computer Aided Learning (CAL) was introduced in India more than a decade back. Packaged educational products are freely available, and the learning process has been dramatically enhanced by multi-media, computer simulation, audio-video conferencing and virtual reality. Today, online learning (or E-learning), which is anchored in computer networks (Internet), is making its presence felt. It is being made use of by both the distance education and formal education systems. Most formal academic institutions in the developed countries have started including a few online courses in their degree programmes. In these countries higher education has shown a perceptible shift from the conventional form of classroom teaching to online learning on the Internet. High-tech entrepreneurs and also traditional universities are taking advantage of E-learning to eliminate temporal and spatial barriers from higher education. A variety of courses are being offered on the web. Originally thought of as a means of providing continuing education to older people the Internet is today a means of imparting professional education to all (including the young) in areas as different as management, engineering and medicine, as also undergraduate education in the liberal arts. The potential of online education (*cf.* Frank, 2000) is evident from the following:

- The Global Network Agency has listed, as on June 2000, 516 Bachelor-level programmes on the Internet.
- A recent article in the *Los Angeles Times* states one out of three U.S. colleges has at least one degree online.
- According to projections of the International Data Corporation 84% of U.S. colleges will be offering E-learning programmes by 2002.
- Warwick Universitiy, UK proposes to make it compulsory for all students from 2003 to have laptop computers with Internet connections.

- Massachusetts Institute of Technology (MIT) has announced that it will put all its courses on the Internet for free. This includes 200 courses across MIT's entire curricula covering architecture and planning, engineering, humanities, arts, social sciences, management and science. For this MIT will be spending $100 million in 10 years.
- A number of western universities are offering programmes in different areas, and especially in management 'across borders'. Most of them have secured accreditation from a national or international agency.

Against this background India, as global leaders in information technology, have no other option but to follow suit. The question is, will 'Social India' and 'Economic India' be able to keep up with 'Technological India'? And will 'Academic India' allow 'Business India' to run away with the opportunities offered? Already, some online portals have started functioning. The Indian universities must make a start, if necessary in collaboration with communication technology business houses. Incidentally, it is reported that the Anna University, Chennai and the Karnataka State Open University, Mysore have taken the first step by signing agreements with 'virtual education' agencies. The Ministry of Information Technology recognising the importance of E-learning has, as one of its focus, the promotion of web-based education. It has identified a number of projects through its scientific and academic institutes. C-DAC has, for example, taken up E-learning as a focus area and is pursuing the development of E-learning technologies.

Internationalisation of Higher Education

An important fallout of the globalisation process has been the internationalisation of higher education (see Powar, 2001). This has taken different forms including:

- Increased mobility of students and faculty at the international level;
- Greater collaboration between institutions, research groups and individuals, and the formation of networks of institutions for teaching-learning purposes;
- Entry of universities from the developed countries into the developing and under-developed worlds, and the marketing of degrees through franchise; and
- Increase in 'education across borders' via distance education, including online learning.

As far as India is concerned the effects have been both beneficial and deleterious. The beneficial effect is the realisation that greater emphasis needs to be placed on quality of education in view of the fact that the developed (and some developing) countries are now insisting on international standards and benchmarking. There has, therefore, been a conscientious effort to update curricula and introduce international components in syllabi, at least at the Masters level. The deleterious effect is that the country has been invaded by universities from the developed world (including some institutions of doubtful standards) who have been marketing their educational wares through franchise; or have been recruiting students for study abroad. The ill-effects of internationalisation of higher education, from the Asian viewpoint, have been highlighted by Altbach (1999). He has pointed out that the current wave of internationalisation has a late 20th century flavour being motivated by profits. Universities from the developed countries have been active in offering 'off-shore degrees', working with institutions that are not educational, and are using the internet to deliver degrees with few controls concerning quality.

Be what may, in the present 'knowledge era' internationalisation of higher education is an accepted fact of life. It needs to be encouraged for it promotes values and culture, generates goodwill, enhances the quality of education, encourages competitiveness and helps generate resources. However, it is essential that care is taken that it does not lead to gross commercialisation. The best option would be to develop institutional links between universities in India and abroad in which the partners contribute (and benefit) in equal measure. Franchising of programmes by the foreign universities to non-academic institutions and business concerns should be disallowed. Education can have financial overtures but it must essentially remain a profession with values.

Convergence of Educational Systems

In the Indian higher education scenario there are today three distinct educational systems in operation. These are:

- *The Formal System* represented by the universities, other institutions deemed to be universities, and colleges affiliated to the conventional universities. The programmes offered by the formal system provide a strong academic base to the student, as they place emphasis on facts and the fundamental concepts of a subject. They are, however, generally weak in practical aspects, and tend to be stereotyped and inflexible.
- *The Distance Education System* that operates through the open universities and the correspondence course institutes in the dual-mode universities, and offers programmes that usually replicate those of the formal system in content.

- *The Non-formal System* or the 'Training Industry' comprising commercial institutions that provide skill-based training in vocational areas that are needed by industry and business. While the programmes neglect the fundamental aspects of the subject they ensure that the student excels in hands-on operations.

Perhaps, none of these three systems can fully meet, by themselves, the requirements of a knowledge-based society in which job requirements are constantly changing because of technological developments and increasingly shortened periods of obsolescence of equipment. However, one must appreciate the fact that the programmes offered by the three systems could be exclusive, mutually complementary or supplementary. A convergence of these different systems, through networking and partnership, could meet the requirements of different sectors of society, and at the same time provide education that would equip the individual to meet changing demands. A convergence of the formal and distance education systems should not be difficult, and can be made possible through the adoption of such measures as that of credit-transfer and joint degrees. A pre-requisite would be the establishment of a national qualifications framework. Since professional training offers added-value to a degree one must examine the possibilities of developing a mechanism that would facilitate effective collaboration between the conventional and open universities, on the one hand, and the training institutions of the non-formal stream on the other. Such a convergence is necessary if we are to achieve the objective of providing the coming generations with knowledge and skills required for human development.

Conclusion

The first decade of the new century is crucial for Indian higher education, for it is during this period that major decisions, that will influence the functioning of higher education in the following decades, will have to be taken and acted upon. Governments will have to decide on the extent of support they will provide to higher education keeping in view their commitment to the disadvantaged sectors of society. The moot question is will we follow the example of a number of developed countries and allow education to be commercialised by giving a free rein to private business enterprise? Universities will urgently have to re-orient and re-structure themselves and their activities, as otherwise there is the fear of their becoming redundant. The academics will have to adapt to the changed paradigms of education and learn to function in the new context of the information and communication technology revolutions. And the Indian administrators will have to undertake academic planning on the basis of authentic data. Before the decade is out we will have to find real answers to some real questions. A few of these (Anandakrishnan, 2001) are: What is the level of anticipated demand for higher education for 2010 and 2020? What are the expected disciplinary balances and how can these be moderated? What is the level of resource commitment from public funds, and how much will society contribute? How do we undertake academic restructuring, and introduce flexibility and innovation into the system, to meet the requirements of quality? What is the scope for a consortia and coalition approach, and how do we go about networking our institutions? How do we ensure the convergence of different systems and their effective coordination? How do we achieve greater transparency in operations? The outlook is hazy and all that one can say at present is that higher education in the early decades of the twenty-first century promises to be not only demanding but also refreshingly different (Powar, 2000).

References

Aggarwal, Y., (1998), Some Aspects of Social and Economic Inequities among SCs in India, *Journal of Higher Education* 21(3): 415-432.

Altbach, P.G., (1999), The Perils of Internationalising Higher Education: A Perspective, *International Higher Education,* 15:4-5.

Anandakrishnan, M., (2001), Planning for Academic Development: A Perspective, *Fifth AIU Roundtable of Vice Chancellors on 'University Management',* AIU, New Delhi.

Association of Indian Universities, (2000), *Universities Handbook*, AIU, New Delhi.

Barik, R.K., (1998), Education for Dalits: No Separate Colleges and Universities for Dalits, *Journal of Higher Education.* 21(3): 433-436.

Bhalla, V. and Rai-Negi, U., (1999), Representation of Women in Teaching Position in the Indian Universities, *University News,* 37(18): 20.

Choudhary, K., (1998), Dalits in Higher Education: Cooption or Domination, *Journal of Higher Education,* 21(3): 437- 452.

Distance Education Council, (2001), *Open Universities in India, 2001: Brief Information,* IGNOU, New Delhi.

Frank. T, (2000), Universities Compete for a Presence Online, *University Affairs,* October, 2000, pp. 10-15.

Government of India, (1986), *National Policy on Education, 1986,* GOI, New Delhi.

Government of India, (1992), *Programme of Action, 1992, on National Policy on Education 1986,* GOI, New Delhi.

Green, D. and Harvey, L., (1993), Quality Assurance in Western Europe: Trends, Practices and Issues, in Santa, T.W., Anderson, C.L., Berendt, B., (Editors), *Proceedings, Fifth International Conference on Assessing Quality in Higher Education,* Indiana University-Purdue University, Indianapolis.

Khajapeer, M., (1996), Democratisation of Higher Education in India with Special Reference to the Weaker Sections, Minorities and Women, *Journal of Educational Planning and Administration,* 10(2): 143-152.

Maddox, J, (1993a), Science in India: India's Great Ambition to Succeed, *Nature,* 366: 611- 614.

Maddox, J., (1993b), Science in India: Higher Education with Lower Budgets, *Nature,* 366:617.

Mayor, F., (1998), The Universal University, *Higher Education Policy*, 11(4): 249-255.

Negi, D.B., (1999), Impact of IGNOU on Disadvantaged Groups: A Critical Assessment, *Proceedings, AAOU Conference, Beijing.*

Padmini, M.S., (1999), Women in Higher Education: Scenario of Shivaji University, in Powar, K.B. and Shafi Z.S., (Editors), *Women Participation in Higher Education,* AIU. New Delhi, pp. 35-53.

Pinto, A., (1998), Dalit in Higher Education: Need to Establish a Counter-Culture, *Journal of Higher Education,* 21(3): 403-414.

Powar, K.B., (1996), Assuring Equity and Quality in Mass Higher Education: The Indian Context, *University News*, 34(22): 3-6.

Powar, K.B., (2000), *Higher Education in the Twenty-first Century*, AIU Occasional Paper, 2000/3, AIU, New Delhi.

Powar, K.B., (2001), Promoting the Internationalisation of Indian Higher Education, in Powar, K.B. (Editor), *Internationalisation of Indian Higher Education,* pp. 87-100, AIU, New Delhi.

Powar, K.B. and Shafi, Z.S., (Editors), (1999), *Women Participation in Higher Education,* AIU, New Delhi.

Rajput, J.S., (2000), Harnessing Youth Power, *University News,* 39(5): 8-10.

UNESCO, (1960), *Convention Against Discrimination in Education, Adopted by the General Session of UNESCO at its Eleventh Session, December 14, 1960, Paris,* UNESCO, Paris.

UNESCO, (1995), Policy Paper for Change and Development in Higher Education, Reproduced in *New Frontiers in Education*, 26(3): 288-334.

UNESCO, (1998), *Higher Education in the Twenty-first Century: Vision and Action – Final Report,* UNESCO, Paris.

UNESCO-NIHR, (1986), *The International Bill of Human Rights: Normative and Institutional Developments, 1948-85,* UNESCO-Netherlands Institute of Human Rights, Utrecht.

Vijayshri and Garg, S., (2000), Reaching the Unreached: From Rhetoric to Practice, *Conference Paper, IDEA 2000,* IGNOU, New Delhi.

World Bank, (1994), *Higher Education: The Lessons of Experience,* The World Bank, Washington, D.C.

Ziderman, A. and Albrecht, D., (1995), *Financing Universities in Developing Countries,* The Palmer Press, London.

The Indian Context

- Management of Universities: Focus on India
- Science Education in Indian Universities
- Dilemma of Research in Indian Universities
- Autonomy of Indian Universities
- Accountability in Indian Higher Education
- Environmental Studies in Indian Universities
- The Internationalisation of Indian Higher Education

6

Management of Universities*

Introduction

The successful management of universities and other similar academic institutions requires detailed planning, timely and appropriate decision-making, and skillful coordination of activities. The organisational structure of the institution, the model of governance it follows, and the work-culture are the determinative factors in management. An efficient information management system, good inter-personal relationship and relative financial stability are pre-requisites. In the case of Indian institutions management styles are constricted by the fact that universities are almost entirely dependant on governments for funds. The existence of a number of statutory bodies that tend to control, rather than facilitate, functioning does not help matters. It is not possible to prescribe a uniform pattern of management for the Indian universities, and other university-level institutions, because they are of different types – central-, state- or privately-funded, unitary or affiliating, conventional (multi-faculty often dual-mode) or professional (usually single-discipline), deemed (usually specialised, often single-subject) and open. In this article the different aspects of management of universities are reviewed and some suggestions for effective management are made.

Management and the Manager

Before considering the management of universities *per se* it may be desirable to understand what is implicit in the term 'management' and also to define the role of a manager. Broadly, management is the art of guiding actions and controlling situations in a manner that yields results that best meet the objectives of an organisation or institution. By implication this means that a manager's basic task is to continuously

* Background paper for the *Roundtable of Vice Chancellors on 'University Management'* organised by the Association of Indian Universities at Jamia Hamdard, New Delhi, May 28-31, 2001.

strive to improve the situation and take it as close as possible to the ideal. As Checkland and Scholes (1990) put it: *"The 'Manager' tries to improve situations which are seen to be problematical – or at least as less than perfect – and the job is never done... because as the situation develops new aspects calling for attention emerge, and yesterday's solution may be seen as today's problems".*

It has to be remembered that effective managerial performance depends upon the successful interplay of a number of factors including the personal competence (in terms of skills, knowledge and aptitude) of the chief executive and his senior colleagues; and the existence of a stable institutional framework in the form of policies, rules, guidelines, conventions and information. It can be enhanced by provision of opportunities (say, to experiment or to innovate) and extension of support (in the form of appreciation, reward or promotion) to subordinates (Davies, 1996, Fig. 2).

The leadership provided to the institution is a crucial factor in management. The chief executive needs to have, amongst other things, a clear perception about the goals and objectives of the institution, a yearning for success along with the willingness to accept setbacks with stoicism, a confidence in colleagues and subordinates but not over-dependence on them, equanimity coupled with a sensitivity to the feelings of co-workers, an understanding of strengths and weaknesses of the institution, a full knowledge of the functioning of all divisions and units in the institution, the (inborn) capability of having a holistic overview, the ability to take timely (and sometimes unpleasant) decisions, an appreciation of the need to change and with it the willingness to adopt new and innovative strategies, a commitment towards quality, and finally the ability to listen patiently and communicate effectively. The chief executive has to be not only a leader but also a motivator, coordinator and facilitator.

The successful chief executive is one who can take decisions that satisfy the majority without antagonising the others. This requires a capacity to correctly judge the mood of different stakeholders, and the time to announce a decision. Good judgment is the essence of successful management. The capacity for good judgment relates with Goleman's concept of 'emotional intelligence', which is based (Goleman, 1998; Watson, 2000) on five attributes:

- Self-awareness: An understanding of one's administrative style and behavioural pattern and its impact on others.

- Self-control: The ability to control one's disruptive impulses and moods; and to think before acting.
- Motivation: The ability to pursue goals and work with commitment without thought of personal benefits.
- Empathy: The ability to understand people and their emotions; and treat them accordingly.
- Social skills: Proficiency in managing relationships, finding common ground and building bridges.

Obviously it is difficult to find people with all these attributes inborn in them. However, these can be developed through effort, and a chief executive is expected to do so.

Organisational Models and Working Cultures

The successful governance of an academic institution is dependant, to a considerable extent, on its organisational structure. The most experienced managers may find it difficult to take decisions, and implement them effectively, if the organisational structure is heavily bureaucratised and requires confirmation of decisions by varied committees/bodies or even by a central authority. In this context it may be noted that Paul (1990) has recognised four major operational models that are to be found in different organisations and institutions. These are:

- The Bureaucratic Model that has a well-established hierarchy, from the chief executive down to the lowest support staff, and is governed by laid-down rules and procedures.
- The Collegiate Model that has a collection of specialised professionals who try for consensus in decision-making in an attempt to protect the autonomy of the individual professional.
- The Political Model in which due recognition is given to power groups and to the need to protect their interests in decision-making.
- The Anarchic Model in which the institution is considered to be 'an organised anarchy' where goals are vague and diffuse, technology unclear and participation fluid.

Each of these models results in different working cultures that determine the style and effectiveness of management. Following McNay (1995) and Davies (1996), we recognise four types of working cultures that are a function of the degree of looseness or tightness in the definition of policy (*dp*) and in the implementation of policy (*ip*), i.e. in the control of activity. These are:

- A Corporate Culture where the emphasis is on the leadership provided by the senior management personnel, top-down planning and monitoring through performance indicators (tight dp, tight ip).
- A Enterprise Culture where there is a strong quality framework but considerable freedom for the individual to interact with external agencies, and where results are expected (tight dp, loose ip).
- A Bureaucratic Culture where there is a dominance of administration and committees, with emphasis on rules and precedent, and also a desire for uniformity and stability (loose dp, tight ip).
- A Collegial Culture where there is a respect for the individual's autonomy, freedom of expression, considerable devolution of authority, the dominance of academic committees and a tendency to be loose regarding procedures (loose ip, loose dp).

Specific to the distance education institutions Mugridge (n.d.) recognises:

- An Educational Culture that focuses on fostering freedom of expression, critical thinking, respect for individuality, independence, and emphasis on process.
- An Industrial Culture that is characterised by hierarchies, division of labour, standardised mass production and line management.

What is the typical culture of a university? Opinions, in the past, have varied. Millet (1962) described it as collegial, Stroup (1966) as bureaucratic, and Baldridge (1971) as political (in which the interests of power groups become paramount in decision making). Today most people agree that, by and large, the universities have a culture that is a mix of the bureaucratic and collegial cultures. Thus, while the central administration manned by officials may act in a bureaucratic manner, the academic units (faculties, departments, schools) are decidedly collegial in their approach. Open universities and other flexible learning institutions have an additional production aspect as they mass-produce considerable amounts of learning materials. This adds a touch of Mugridge's industrial culture.

The bureaucratic approach of a chief executive of an academic institution, and of his immediate subordinates in administration, is possibly necessitated by the fact that they are expected to function within the framework of a pre-ordained organisational structure which imposes hierarchy, formal rules, laid-down procedures and an impersonal approach (Weber, 1947), and which fosters a tendency to follow precedent and as far as possible maintain *status quo*. The schools and departments, on the other hand, are constituted largely of academic personnel who like to work at their own pace for attaining scholarly objectives, and are not unduly bothered by procedures, or even rules. Even this assessment of a mixed-model culture may be simplistic. A few decades back Cohen and March (1974) considered the modern university to be an 'organised anarchy' because its goals are vague, technology unclear, issues ill-defined and approaches (of individuals) self-defined and, therefore, multi-directional. Hence, getting the best out of the professionals (teachers, researchers, technical experts) becomes a skill or even an art. Paul (1990) has drawn attention to this inherent conflict between the orientation of the professionals (academics) and the norms of bureaucracy. The silver lining is provided by the fact that most chief executives of universities, as also their senior officers, are former academics, drawn from within the system, who (presumably) understand the minds of the professionals working with them.

The culture of a university is described in terms of being weak or strong, internally focused or externally oriented (Arnold and Capella, 1985; Sporn, 1996). A weak culture is reflected by the presence of loosely linked sub-units having their own style of functioning. A strong culture is characterised by a high degree of conformity in the values, goals and approach of different units (and individuals) within the organisation. Internally focused culture is one in which the individual concentrates on his own work and does not necessarily identify himself with the university as a whole. In contrast an externally oriented culture is one in which there is an awareness and an appreciation of the external environment. Unfortunately, most universities have a weak and internally oriented culture. There may be individuals and centres that represent excellence but this fact is not represented in the image of the university. The social requirement is for a strong, externally oriented culture. It is for the university management to examine the culture (and sub-cultures) prevalent; and if there are different sub-cultures try to unite them. This is easier said then done; and long and sustained efforts need to be put in towards the attainment of this objective. It is necessary for universities to develop a culture that is responsive to social needs. Instilling commonality in values and beliefs, and developing an orientation towards quality and productivity, need to be important goals of management.

Macro-issues

Universities are complex institutions with many distinctive features that set them apart from other social and business organisations. A unique characteristic, from the point of view of management, is that they are manned by sets of people having different professional outlook, and possibly different values. Thus the academics, though deeply committed to their work, often meander through their career doing much as they please. The administrative personnel on the other hand are largely concerned with the work on hand, and are strictly concerned about rules and procedures, to the extent of being sometimes accused of pulling their weight or 'placing obstacles' in the work of academics.

Weick (1976) has referred to academic institutions as weakly-coupled systems. Sporn (1996) has drawn attention to the facts that the goals of universities are ambivalent and their decision-making process ambiguous; that they are 'people-oriented' with the requirement of stakeholders being more important than profit; that their procedures and techniques are non-routine and diverse; that the main professionals (the teachers) have a strong wish for autonomy and freedom; that decision making, mainly by experts, is complex; and that they are vulnerable to their environment – political, social, economic or technological.

In view of the above, management in universities cannot be undertaken according to any set pattern. Many-a-times, a compromise has to be sought between the collegial culture of the academic and the bureaucratic culture of the administrator. To add to the complexity, education is now becoming a business and shades of corporate and enterprise cultures are being seen. There is, today, a spectrum of management patterns in universities. Dopson and McNay (1996) draw attention to the fact that while collegiality is to be found in its undiluted form at Oxford and Cambridge, in the statutory universities of UK the Vice Chancellor is a 'Jarratt Chief Executive' leading to a situation Ryder (1996) describes as 'authoritarian management'. In the United States the management style has been mainly corporate with the President being greatly involved in fund raising. The situation is, perhaps, most tenuous in India with, in many cases, political influence being strong, bureaucracy dominant, and administration following an undefined path.

In recent years there have been continued effort to bring 'professionalism' into university management by seeking to adopt management techniques of industry and business. Academic institutions have experimented with techniques like Management by Objectives (MBO), Total Quality Management (TQM), Continuous Quality Improvement (CQI) and Responsibility Centred Management (RCM). 'Zero-based budgeting' has been tried, 'pay-by-performance' advocated and 'benchmarking' emphasised. Despite claims of successful adoption of these techniques successful application has rarely been demonstrated.

'Success' is usually a case of Birbaum's 'virtual adoption' – proclaiming something is in place without actually doing anything about it (Ewell, 1999). To illustrate this we may take the case of introduction of TQM in academic institutions. Chaston (1994), following a study to ascertain whether universities were in a position to implement TQM, came to the conclusion that there were a number of initial barriers that had to be overcome before its implementation became a feasible option. The reasons behind non-acceptance of the TQM concept by the academic institutions had earlier been identified by Crawford (1991) as the need for cultural change, and also staff development to appropriate levels of education and training. He made the point that there is always an initial apathy to change that can be overcome only after considerable efforts.

The fact of the matter is that ideas and concepts imported from an alien sector rarely succeed. Any innovation related to management of large academic institutions, like the universities, must have its roots in the ethos and working culture of higher education. However, as Ewell (*op. cit.*) points out, there are three reasons why borrowed concepts are tried out. These are:

- Because one must: An example is some Indian universities reluctantly experimenting (most unsuccessfully) with 'zero-based budgeting' in the late 1980s because the government insisted upon it.
- To accomplish something specific: To bring about changes in specific areas that are not an integral part of the teaching-learning or research processes. For example ideas related to out-sourcing of specific non-academic activities like provision of security service.
- To help think about what is being done: Introducing a new concept makes it necessary to examine the existing one. For example trying to introduce the practice of treating students as clients or customers invokes thought about what they really are. Alternatives that emerge include: 'raw material to be transformed', 'co-producer of learning', 'manager of the learning process' (Ewell, *op. cit.*).

To sum up one may conclude: Do not try too hard to implant alien concepts of management especially in the fundamental areas related to teaching and research.

An academic-turned-administrator does not have much difficulty in adapting to the sophisticated aspects of management, like planning-for-development, as he or she is trained to think logically, interpret facts, and find solutions. Such a person is also mostly able to detect bottlenecks and duplications, and, therefore, to streamline administrative procedures. However, what often proves difficult is the coping with the perennial issues. Examples of these are problems related to financial constraints, requirements (and expectations) of students, demands related to career advancement and working conditions of faculty and support staff, and certain administrative matters, as those related to examinations. Sociologists term these as 'wicked issues' for which there are no logical solutions. Watson (2000) argues that for such issues there are three possible approaches:

- The 'Fire-fighting' approach that ordains that no action need be taken till the problem develops into a crisis.
- The 'Interventionists' approach that means taking all these problems seriously even though one is aware that the circumstances do not permit a solution.
- The 'Pragmatists' approach that tends to examine things calmly and methodically, and take decisions after a judicious exercise of judgment.

In India, activism is rampant in many of the universities – especially the conventional universities (the professional universities are fortunately an exception). Decisions of the management are often not accepted in good grace, especially when they are not in the interest of any of the stakeholders. The Vice Chancellor is the object of adverse criticism and subject to searching scrutiny. This provides an additional dimension to the 'wicked issues'. Under the circumstances he or she has no option but to take the pragmatists' approach to all problems. This, however, requires that the Vice Chancellor and his senior colleagues be prepared for all eventualities. There has to be an efficient information system that can provide full information, and the history of all recurring problems. The Vice Chancellor must have a good public relations network, and must have channels of communication with all major activist groups. The Vice Chancellor is subject to so much (usually unfair) criticism, and it is often said that a prime requisite of the office is that the incumbent should be 'thick-skinned'. Actually he needs to be extremely 'thin-skinned', sensitive to all that is taking place and to all that he hears. Only then is it possible for him to anticipate trouble and take precautionary steps.

Models of Universities

The style of management is influenced, if not dictated, by the working culture which, in turn, depends upon a number of factors including the social milieu, the traditions of the university, and its mission, goals and objectives. Accordingly there are 'universities and universities'. A number of 'models' have been recognised for the European and North

American scenes. (*cf.* Husen, 1994) Models that are represented in India (Powar, 2000) include:

- The Humboldtian Research University Model in which there is emphasis on post-graduate teaching and research, and on interaction between the two functions for their mutual benefit. Indian university-level institutions that approach this model are the Indian Institute of Science, Bangalore and the University of Hyderabad, Hyderabad.
- The Oxbridge Model that stresses close formal and informal contacts between students and teachers, through classroom lectures, tutorials, seminars and other forms of personal contacts. In India, these ideals are possibly met at some unitary universities like the Jawaharlal Nehru University, New Delhi.
- The Grandes Ecoles Model imparting elitist, professional education, mainly in science and technology, to the most talented and intellectually-select students. The Indian examples are the Indian Institutes of Technology and the Indian Institutes of Management.
- The Liberal Education Model that places emphasis on all-round development, and the development of independent and critical thinking. A few Indian institutions like the St. Stephen's College, Delhi and the Banasthali Vidyapeeth, Banasthali can be cited as possibly representing this model.
- The Affiliating University Model wherein there is a central campus for post-graduate teaching and research, and a large number of affiliated colleges (largely undergraduate) distributed over the area over which the university has jurisdiction. A little over 120 Indian universities fall within this category and these are often referred to as the 'conventional' universities.
- The Agricultural University Model that concentrates on agricultural studies including forestry, horticulture and veterinary sciences. At present there are 35 agricultural universities in India.
- The Professional University Model that provides for specialised instruction in a single professional area like engineering, medicine and health services, journalism or law. Examples are the universities established for these areas in some of the states of India.
- The 'Deemed University' Model representing academic institutions that have been granted the status of universities in recognition of their long-standing or excellent academic reputation. Examples are the Birla Institute of Technology and Science, Pilani and the Deccan College Post-Graduate and Research Institute, Pune.

- The Open University Model that provides open and flexible education through the distance mode. There are ten open universities including the Indira Gandhi National Open University, New Delhi.

The organisational structure, work culture and mechanism of governance may differ significantly in these different types of universities, and accordingly be reflected in the style of management.

The Authorities, Officers and Sub-systems of Universities

The management of a university is carried out by bodies and committees (generally referred to as the 'authorities'), and by officers appointed on long-term or tenure basis. Successful management requires close and effective coordination between the two. The public-funded universities, and especially the conventional universities, have three important decision-making bodies, namely the Senate or Court, the Executive Council or Syndicate or Board of Management, and the Academic Council.

- The Senate, also designated as the Court, is in most universities the supreme body with a large membership representing the cross-section of society. It is responsible for formulating policies, making statutes, and overseeing the functioning of the university. In the case of the deemed universities and other specialised categories of universities (like the open universities, professional universities and agricultural universities) the senate is usually replaced by a smaller body called the Governing Council or Planning Board which is mainly responsible for policy formulation and planning of developmental activities.
- The Executive Council (also known as Syndicate or Board of Management) is the decision-making and implementing body and wields considerable power, because much administrative and financial authority is vested in it. Being the body that grants final approval to academic decisions, it also has some say in academic matters.
- The Academic Council which is concerned with all academic matters including starting of programmes, framing of curricula, grant of equivalence to degrees, recognition of institutions and award of degrees and diplomas. The recommendations of the Council are, almost invariably, accepted by the other authorities.

The Vice Chancellor (or Director) is the Chief Executive Officer of a University and functions as both its administrative and academic head. He or she is assisted by Pro-Vice Chancellors (or Rectors). Other important functionaries are the Registrar, Finance Officer and Controller of Examinations who look after administrative aspects; and Deans and Directors who supervise academic activities.

A number of Committees, statutory and non-statutory, function in an advisory capacity under these three authorities. For example, the Finance Committee, Staff Affairs Committee and Campus Development Committee advice the Board of Management; and the Academic Council receives inputs from Faculties, Boards of Studies and Departmental/ School Committees. Thus, in the case of the majority of institutions the administration is committee-oriented with the officers being responsible for the implementation of decisions. This often leads to piquant situations, for while the authorities and committees may take difficult-to-implement, and even impracticable, decisions the responsibility of implementing them rests with the officers.

Increased democratisation often leads to difficulties for the management. It is for this reason that bodies like the Senate or Court have been done away with, even in countries like the United Kingdom. The Gnanam Committee constituted by the University Grants Commission to report on university management (University Grants Commission, 1990) has, for this reason, recommended that elections to various university bodies should be kept to the 'bare minimum', and that the Senate/Court should be a deliberative and consultative body, and not a decision-making authority, with only nominated/ex-officio members and a maximum strength of 100 members. It is, perhaps, no coincidence that universities with Boards of Management or Governing Councils having small memberships seem to have lesser problems.

From the management point of view a higher education institution can be said to comprise of five major sub-systems that function under the overall supervision of the Vice Chancellor. These sub-systems are respectively represented by the:

- *Administrative Divisions* including those dealing with general administration, finance, campus maintenance and development, student registration, and evaluation. The chief functionaries are the Registrar, Finance Officer and Controller of Examinations.
- *Academic Units* including faculties, schools and departments responsible for development and implementation of academic (teaching and evaluation) programmes, and for conduct of research. The chief functionaries are the Deans of Faculties, Directors of Schools/Heads of Departments.

- *Academic Support Units* including the Central Library, Computer Centre, Common Facilities Centre for research (Sophisticated Instruments Centre); and in the case of distance education the Regional Centres and Counselling Centres. The important functionaries include the Librarian and the Directors of the different Centres.
- *Student Welfare Units* like the Health Centre, Sports facilities and Cultural Centre. The chief functionary is the Dean of Students' Welfare.
- *Production Units* like the Press, Instrumentation Centre, Audio-Video Aids Centre (as also Material Distribution Centre). The main functionaries are the heads of these units.

Distance education units have well-developed production units but may not require student welfare units. The conventional universities, likewise, may not have production units except for a press.

The different sub-systems may have differing norms of work and working cultures, and hence coordination is important. It is for the management at different levels to ensure that there is efficiency and productivity within individual sub-systems. Further each of the sub-systems must function in harmony with other sub-systems; and also with external (sub) systems with which the university has an interface.

Decentralisation

A university is a large and disparate organisation with varied functions to perform. Centralised decision-making is often counter-productive leading to lack of cohesion, loss of interest and even frustration. Academics, for example, have been known to express resentment over delays in release of grants for research projects they have worked hard to obtain from outside agencies. The answer lies in decentralisation of authority with appropriate responsibility. The management strategy should be to:

- *Delegate* authority and assign responsibility to heads of different departments and units to evolve, under the supervision of the central authorities, procedures of functioning that would ensure productivity and quality of outputs.
- *Coordinate* the activities of different departments and units through frequent meetings and interactions.
- *Monitor* the progress of each department and unit through a system of constant reporting and feedback.

- *Assess* performance periodically, through the use of recognised performance indicators.

It follows that the middle-level management (department and unit heads) must be conversant with the basic administrative and/or managerial functions. These (Sengupta, 1996) include:

- *Planning*, which is determining objectives and policies, and accordingly formulating systemised programmes. Office planning involves determining the various necessities of the office, selecting the best possible method(s) for performing various operations, and deciding when, where and how they are to be performed.
- *Organising*, which is identifying and grouping of work, defining and delegating authority and responsibility, and establishing relationship.
- *Staffing*, which is finding the right person for the right job. It could be through the selection of a person having the requisite qualifications and training, but more often than not it is identifying a person who could be trained and assigned the work.
- *Directing*, which is the inter-personal aspect of management through which subordinates are led to contributing efficiently and effectively to the attainment of objectives. This is best achieved through effective communication and providing motivation.
- *Coordination*, which is keeping the team together, and in good spirit, thus ensuring that work is carried out harmoniously. This is best achieved by a suitable and equable allocation of work (according to capabilities) and even-handed treatment.

Management Information System

Planning, monitoring, evaluation and promotional activities all require a steady inflow of data and other information from various units within an institution, and also from external sources. All the information needs to be integrated, analysed and interpreted. Hence, it is essential that universities have an efficient, computer-based, Management Information System (MIS). Its basic purpose is to provide information to support operational, managerial and decision-making functions. Consequently the MIS has a pyramid structure (Nigavekar, 1994) with the:

- Basal layer consisting of information for transaction processing (information relating to Acts, Statutes, Regulations, Rules and also Precedents);

- Second layer consisting of information required for conducting day-to-day operations and control (basic information and data relating to students, faculty, finances, products);
- Third layer with information required for tactical planning and decision-making (functions and responsibilities of various authorities, different activities); and
- Top layer, or apical part, containing information critical for strategic planning and policy formulation by the highest authorities (viewpoint, and possible impact on stakeholders).

There has to be a complete flow of data from one level to another. Keeping in tune with the requirements of higher education the MIS is designed as a planned federation of the different sub-systems. If properly developed the MIS can be an invaluable aid in institutional management.

A word of caution is necessary. MIS is difficult to use because:

- The major stakeholders of the higher education system, i.e., students, faculty and administrative staff, operate within a dynamic framework and, therefore, may be disturbed by decisions taken on insufficient or old information. It is possible that they may express their dissatisfaction in different ways.
- Decision-making is through the democratic process (by authorities, committees) and, therefore, can be subjective. On the other hand the implementation is by an executive process (through officers) and is circumscribed by legal requirements (rules, regulations). Implementation may also be difficult because of 'ground realities'.
- Information is partly obtained from spatially separated units (colleges) that are not under the direct supervision of central authorities. The possibility of data being incomplete, and even non-authentic, cannot be discounted.

MIS facilitates decision-making and management if the information is complete and provided to the decision-makers in time.

Inter-personal Relationships

In a multi-faceted system like that of higher education, where there is a need for effective coordination between, and within, different sub-systems, there has to be a harmonious relationship between all employees and so inter-personal relationship assumes importance. The initiative in this matter has to be taken by the chief executive and his senior management.

Following Verma (1994) inter-personal relationship in higher education institutions can be examined in terms of the following dimensions:

- *Intra-institutional relationships* involving the central administration, the academic divisions and the support services.
- *Human relationships* involving the members of the decision-making bodies, the academic fraternity, the administrative staff and the members of the community.
- *Academic relationships* involving the basic academic activities namely teaching, research, course development, and student guidance.

In each of the above relationships the personal, or human, approach is likely to yield the best results. The head of the institution and senior management must meet the different stakeholders (students, faculty, administrative and technical staff, members of the community) at regular intervals. The policies and programmes of the institution must emerge as a result of interaction and after considering the inputs provided by the stakeholders.

Verma (1994) emphasises the fact that interactional, bi-directional activities can strengthen inter-personal relationships. The activities include:

- *Involvement:* It is productive to have the stakeholders involved in the decision-making process. The views of the students on the mechanisms of evaluation and the usefulness of a course, that of the faculty on course-development, of technical staff on matters related to maintenance and of the community on the general quality of the programmes offered, are invaluable for decision-making.
- *Dialogue:* Unilateral decisions often create unpleasant situations and lead to tensions and even confrontations. It is best to have a dialogue with representatives of students, teachers or employees before taking decisions that are likely to affect many persons. Even if there is no agreement after discussions the two sides know each other's thought process and position. This helps to remove bottle-necks and misunderstandings. Even if things do not work out the management is aware of the other side's position and can prepare for eventualities.
- *Equality:* There has to be a feeling of equality even in a hierarchical system and an employee must feel that he is being given his due, whatever the nature of work done. The basic norms and rules (say about leave and timing) must be the same for all categories of employees. There cannot be two sets of employees, one bound by

rules and regulations and the other with a right to bend or disregard them.

- *Freedom of Expression:* Every stakeholder must have the freedom to express his view, of course in a disciplined manner, as also the right to be heard. Simply allowing a person to express his or her feelings can relieve a lot of tension.
- *Cooperation:* The cooperation of every member of a unit must be sought. A friendly word, a little encouragement, permission to innovate generates a feeling of involvement.
- *Motivation:* In order to get the best out of an employee it is necessary to motivate him or her. This can be done in a variety of ways including giving him a job of his liking, keeping him informed, soliciting his views, appreciating good ideas, giving adequate incentives and rewards, providing job security and showing concern about his or her welfare. It is, however, sometimes necessary to stress on discipline and instill a modicum of fear.

Financial Aspects

Most plans related to the management of an institution, and to its development, are based on the assumption that enough funds are available for their implementation. If resources are readily available institutions can be managed successfully and plans for expansion of infrastructure, activities and programmes implemented. Unfortunately, this is rarely the case and in reality insuitutions have to function under financial constraints. Hence careful budgeting and monitoring of expenditure is an essential part of management.

A characteristic of higher education institutions is that both income and expenditure can be high. The income is from governmental grants (usually for payment of earmarked expenditure like that for salaries and for developmental purposes) and fees. In case of many institutions that have huge enrollments the latter can be considerable. Expenditure on academic matters (e.g., upkeep of laboratories) and on maintenance may also be large, and in many cases difficult to control. However, if the programmes offered are of a general nature, like the Bachelor's programme in the liberal arts offered through distance mode, and the learning material mass-produced according to the 'Fordist' production strategy (Raggat, 1993), then considerable savings can accrue. This is the position in the dual-mode universities. In such a situation the additional revenue generated may be diverted to other expenditures. It is for the authorities to ensure that this does not happen, and that all savings are retained by the university for the development of infrastructure and new programmes.

As Rumble (1986) points out, when funds are in plenty institutions expand with a proliferation of programmes and activities, the growth, however, being relatively unplanned. When funds are constrained institutions have to make effective and efficient use of resources. This succeeds only to a certain extent and if the situation of reduced resources continues there is an ultimate curtailment of activities. As, in most cases, resources are limited the efficient management of finance is crucial to the functioning of an educational institution. This can be achieved through efficient functioning and careful budgeting. Tightening up of performance is possible only to a certain extent. Financial managers often take recourse to an all-round financial cut of equal proportion (say 10% of budgeted amount). This is an unhealthy practice for it favours the proliferate spender, while penalising the efficient. It also is a case of the financial personnel taking decisions which others (administrative and academic heads) have to implement. Financially constrained institutions usually resort to revenue budgeting (when there are tight but predictable resources) or to 'zero-based budget' when resources are scarce and future uncertain. It is a good practice in such cases to have a 'core budget' that can take care of all essential requirements and an 'additional' or 'peripheral budget' to meet the optimum needs of a programmme. Constant monitoring of expenditure should be able to control the overall situation, and with the availability of many financial software packages this should not prove to be difficult.

Conclusion

Universities are complex, multi-dimensional organisations that have a number of sub-systems and a plurality of working cultures. The style of management that is to be adopted depends on many factors including the organisational structure of the institution and its working culture. Management concepts borrowed from other sectors, like business and industry, are not likely to be effective. The Vice Chancellor and other senior management personnel have a key role to perform. Within this dynamic system there is a continuous inflow of information and management can be made easier with support from a fully functional and efficient Management Information System. Inter-personal relationship is a key factor and has to be fostered. As most institutions work under resource-constraints there has to be carefully planned budgeting and monitoring, along with an efficient functioning of all sub-systems and effective coordination between them.

References

Arnold, R.A. and Capella, L.M., (1985), Corporate Culture and the Marketing Concept: A Diagnostic Instrument for Utilities, *Public Utilities Forthnightly,* 116(8): 32- 38.

Baldridge, J.V., (1971), *Power and Conflict in the University,* John Wiley, New York.

Chaston, I., (1994), Are British Universities in a Position to Consider Implementing Total Quality Management, *Higher Education Quarterly,* 48: 118- 134.

Checkland, P. and Scholes, J., (1990), *Soft System Methodology in Action,* John Wiley and Sons, Chichester.

Cohen, M.D. and March, J.G., (1974), *Leadership and Ambiguity,* McGraw-Hill, New York.

Crawford, F., (1991), Total Quality Management, *CVCP Occasional Paper,* CVCP, London.

Davies, John L., (1996), Higher Education Management, Training and Development Quality Indicators, *New Papers in Higher Education Studies and Research,* UNESCO, Paris.

Dopson, Sue and McNay, I., (1996), Organisational Culture, in Warner, D. and Palfreyman, D (Editors), *Higher Education Management: The Key Elements,* SRHE and Open University Press, Buckingham.

Ewell, P.T., (1999), Imitation as Art: Borrowed Management Techniques in Higher Education, *Change,* 31((6): 11- 15.

Goleman, D., (1998), What makes a Leader?, *Harvard Business Review,* Nov.-Dec., pp. 93-102.

Husen, T., (1994), The Idea of the University: Changing Roles, Current Crisis and Future Challenges, in Husen, T., (Editor), *The Role of the University: A Global Perspective.* The United Nations University, Tokyo, pp. 7-31.

McNay, I., (1995), From Collegial Academy to Corporate Enterprise: The Changing Culture of Universities, in, Schuller, T., (Editor), *The Changing University,* SRHE/Open University Press, Buckingham.

Millet, J., (1962), *The Academic Community,* McGraw-Hill, New York.

Mugridge, Ian, (n.d.), Managing the Institution, *Course Material, M.A./Diploma Course 4, Block D, Unit 13,* UK Open University, Milton Keynes.

Nigavekar, A.S., (1994), Management Information System for University Administration: Concept, Structure and Development, in Powar, K.B. and Panda, S.K., (Editors), *University Administration and Management,* AIU, New Delhi, pp. 49-63.

Paul, Ross H., (1990), *Open Learning and Open Management,* Kogan Page, London.

Powar, K.B., (2000), *The Changing Role and Functions of Universities*, AIU Occasional Paper 2000/2, AIU, New Delhi.

Raggat, P., (1993), Post-Fordism and Distance Education – A Flexible Strategy for Change, *Open Learning,* 8(1): 21-31.

Rumble, G., (1986), The Planning and Management of Distance Education, Croom Helm, London.

Ryder, A., (1996), Reform and UK Higher Education in the Enterprise Era, *Higher Education Quarterly,* 50(1): 54- 70.

Sengupta, S., (1996), Office Administration and Management, in Powar, K.B. and Panda, S.K. (Editors), *Staff Development in Indian Universities,* AIU, New Delhi, pp. 9-20.

Sporn, Barbara, (1996), Managing University Culture: An Analysis of the Relationship between Institutional Culture and Management Approaches, *Higher Education,* 32: 41- 61.

Stroup, H., (1966), *Bureaucracy in Higher Education,* Free Press, New York.

University Grants Commission, (1990), Report of the UGC Committee *'Towards New Educational Management'*, UGC, New Delhi.

Verma, S.K., (1994), Management in University Administration: Interpersonal Management, in Powar, K.B. and Panda, S.K., (Editors), *University Administration and Management,* AIU, New Delhi, pp. 35-40.

Warner, D. and Palfreyman, D., (Editors), (1996), Editors' introduction to Chapter 2, 'Organisational Cultures', of *Higher Education Management: The Key Elements,* SRHE and Open University Press, Buckingham.

Watson, D., (2000), Managing in Higher Education: The 'Wicked' Issues, *Higher Education Quarterly,* 54(1): 5- 21.

Weber, M., (1947), *The Theory of Social and Economic Organisations* (Trans. Hendeison, A.M. and Parson, T.), Oxford University Press, New York.

Weick, K., (1976), Educational Organisations as Loosely Coupled Systems, *Administrative Science Quarterly,* 21: 1- 19.

7

Science Education in Indian Universities*

Historical Aspects

In India, science education dates back to later Vedic times when both pure and applied sciences were taught at Takshashila. The subjects included astronomy, medicinal biology and ayurvedic medicine. Amongst the great teachers of that time was Atreya (Sixth century BC), whose contributions to Ayurveda were unrivalled. Subsequently, Nalanda (Fifth century AD) became well-known as a centre for astronomical and mathematical studies (Jain, 1982). In the medieval period the teaching of science languished though medicine, mathematics, astronomy and geography were taught at Banaras and in the *chatuspathis* (Hindu colleges) of Bengal. The study of natural and physical sciences was altogether unknown (Alam, 1991).

The revival (if one could use the word) of scientific studies and science education took place during colonial times, initially in Bengal, with the establishment of the Asiatic Society (1784) and the founding, in 1817, of the Hindu College (later Presidency College) at Calcutta. Further impetus was given by the establishment, in 1857, of the three universities of Calcutta, Bombay and Madras. During the first half of the twentieth century, the teaching of science subjects became important in Indian universities. However, science received greatest encouragement in the years immediately following independence, largely because of the thinking of Pt. Jawaharlal Nehru, who believed that the economy of the country could be improved only through scientific and technological development. Consequently scientific research, and with it science education, gained importance.

* Keynote Address at the National Seminar on '*Science Education in Universities and Colleges: Retrospect and Prospects*' organised by the Nagpur University, Nagpur, February 12-14, 1999.

Present Status

In India science education at the tertiary level is presently imparted largely through the 150-odd conventional universities and the over 4000 science colleges affiliated to them. Science is also taught in the 37 agricultural universities/institutions, 22 institutions for engineering and technology, and 15 medical universities/institutions (Association of Indian Universities, 1998). During 1997, over one lakh students were studying science at the Masters level and nearly 11 lakh at the Bachelor's level (Institute of Applied Manpower Research, 1998).

In absolute terms the number of students opting for science courses has increased considerably since the sixties with the growth rate being about 5% in the nineties. However, in relation to other faculties in the liberal arts (arts, social sciences, commerce) enrolment in science has declined at the undergraduate level from 33.2% in 1971 to 21.7% in 1997; and at the postgraduate level from 26.1% in 1971 to 22.2% in 1997 (Table 7.1 and Fig.7.1). This percentage-wise drop of students opting for science largely reflects added opportunities for (the better) students in the faculties of engineering and technology, medicine and also agriculture. Moreover, some students in metropolitan areas now apparently prefer commerce to science. The shift from science is not easily perceived in the urban areas where demand for university education is very high. It is, however, apparent in the mofussil areas as illustrated by the case-study of the North Maharashtra University presented in a later section.

Table 7.1: Enrolment in higher education (liberal arts and science)

Enrolment	1971	1981	1991	1997
Liberal Arts (PG)	144666	254361	354216	460801
Science (PG)	37806	52809	71891	102617
% in Science (PG)	26.13	20.76	20.30	22.27
Liberal Arts (UG)	1492076	2041668	3285776	4871981
Science (UG)	495285	489415	756896	1058312
% in Science (UG)	33.19	23.97	23.03	21.72
Liberal Arts (PG+UG)	1636742	2296029	3639992	5332782
Science (PG+UG)	553091	542224	828787	1160929
% in Science (PG+UG)	32.57	23.61	22.76	21.76

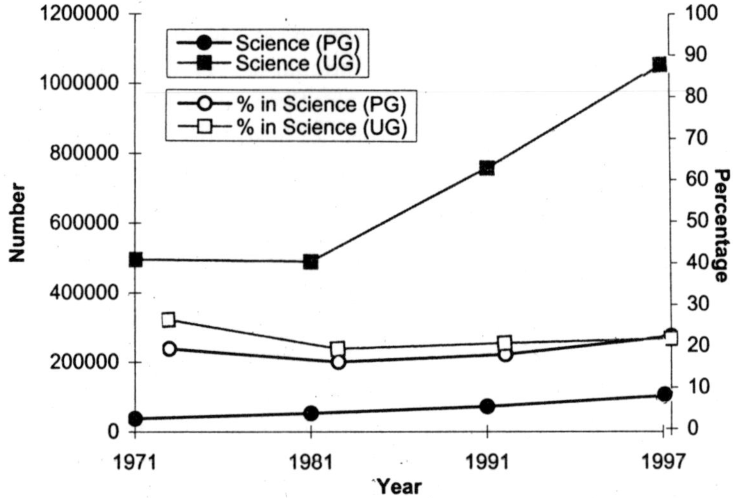

Fig 1 : Enrolment in Science in Higher Education

Except in the case of a few universities, undergraduate teaching is conducted almost entirely by the colleges affiliated to different universities. The subjects generally taught are physics, chemistry, mathematics, botany and zoology. Some colleges offer statistics, geology, geography and microbiology as well. A limited number of colleges have introduced electronics and computer science. In the 1980's and 1990's the percentage of students (within the liberal arts) offering science courses has remained fairly stable. However, there is a definite change in the preference of students for different subjects. While at the undergraduate level physics, chemistry, statistics continue to attract students there is a definite fall in the number of students wanting to study mathematics, botany, zoology and geology. The subjects in demand are the new ones like computer science, electronics and microbiology. At the Master's level the subject attracting most students are biotechnology, molecular biology and computer applications. Physics, chemistry and statistics have adequate number of applicants but not botany and zoology. For geology, geophysics and mathematics there are few takers, and these possibly drift in because there are no other alternatives.

The structure of the B.Sc. programme follows two patterns. According to the first pattern, which leads to a B.Sc. (General) degree, a student studies three subjects in all the three years of the course. Additionally he studies English during the first or second year. The second pattern, leading to a B.Sc. (Hons.) degree, requires the student to study three (or four) subjects in the first year (in addition to English), three during the second year, and only one during the third year (designated as principal subject). In universities following the first pattern the subsequent admission to the Master's programme may be in any of the three subjects studied in the B.Sc. class. In universities following the second pattern admission to the Master's programme can only be in the principal subject. The extent of preparation in a subject naturally differs with the two patterns, and consequently the standards at the Master's level also differ. Some technical universities (including the IITs) offer 5-year integrated programmes leading to an M.Sc. degree, with the option to the student to opt out after the third year with a B.Sc. degree. The postgraduate programmes leading to a Master's degree in science are generally of two years duration. In addition to the subjects taught at the Bachelor's level, Master's programmes are also available in subjects like geophysics, biochemistry, biotechnology, marine sciences, environmental science, energy studies and other inter-disciplinary areas. In some subjects (like Applied Geology), the duration of the M.Sc. programme may be of three years.

Course-work is an essential component of M.Phil programmes. A student is expected to take three advanced courses, including one on research methodology. A few universities have now introduced compulsory pre-Ph.D courses equivalent to those at M.Phil level.

The output of Indian science education, as far as number is considered, is not impressive. The total turnout of graduates, postgraduates and doctorates in the sciences, between 1950 and 1993, was approximately 3,451,000, 667,000 and 64,000 respectively. For 1993 the corresponding figures were about 160,000, 31,000 and 3,300 respectively (Rajagopal *et al.* 1994). Considering the enrolment for 1991 this output reflects an approximate 37% drop-out at the undergraduate level and 14% at the postgraduate level.

The North Maharashtra University: A Case Study

The North Maharashtra University, having jurisdiction over the Jalgaon, Dhule and Nandurbar districts of Maharashtra, was established in 1990. Earlier the colleges in the university area were affiliated to the University of Poona. The North Maharashtra University is a teaching-cum affiliating university with headquarters (and campus) at Jalgaon. At the beginning of 1999 the university had 114 affiliated colleges of which 69 were in the liberal arts and the remaining 45 were professional colleges. The liberal arts colleges offer programmes leading to the B.A., B.Sc. and B.Com. degrees. The number of colleges having the science faculty is 40. Of the professional colleges 23 offer undergraduate programmes. There are 22 colleges in the faculty of education, 10 of which offer programmes leading to diploma in education (Table 7.2). With the establishment of colleges offering undergraduate professional programmes there has been a steady decline in the number of students offering science subjects at the undergraduate level (Table 7.3). The fall in the number of students from over 10,500 in 1991-92 to less than 7000 in 1997-98 roughly corresponds to the number of seats available in the professional colleges (Table 7.4). It is evident that the best students are opting for the professional education but, unlike in the case of the larger cities, the vacancies created by the outflow of the better students to professional courses are not being taken by the less-endowed students opting for courses in arts and humanities. The decline in science education is, thus, not only in terms of numbers but also in terms of the quality of students opting for science subjects.

Another fact that has been noted is that even within the science faculty the preference is for a few application-oriented subjects like computer science, electronics and microbiology. At the honours level (third year of the programme) more than 50 per cent of the students opt for these subjects. Physics and chemistry have adequate students but there are few takers for subjects like geology, geography, mathematics, statistics, botany and zoology. In fact in these subjects, in many colleges, the seats are not filled.

Table 7.2: Liberal arts and professional colleges in North Maharashtra University

Liberal Arts		*Professional*	
Arts	17	Engineering (including Architecture	8
Commerce	2	Medicine (including Pharmacy)	7
Science	1	Ayurvedic	5
Arts and Commerce	10	Unani Medicine	1
Arts and Science	6	Law	2
Arts, Commerce and Science	33	Education	22
Total	69	Total	45

Source: Eighth Annual Report of North Maharashtra University (1997-98)

Table 7.3: Enrolment in science faculty, at undergraduate level, in North Maharashtra University

Year	*Number*	*Year*	*Number*
1991-92	10574	1995-96	06994
1992-93	10656	1996-97	07143
1993-94	08314	1997-98	06873
1994-95	07745		

Source: Dr. K.B. Patil (personal communication)

Table 7.4: Current intake for the undergraduate professional courses at the North Maharashtra University

Engineering	2000	Homeopathy	60
Medical	200	Agriculture	100
Ayurveda	240	Diploma courses	300
Pharmacy	300	Law	50
Architecture	30	Lalit Kala	50
		Total	3330

Source: Dr. K. B. Patil (personal communication).

Purpose of Science Education

At this stage it would perhaps be appropriate to delve into the purpose of science education. In the Indian context there are three major possibilities:

- To produce first-rate scientists capable of working at the cutting edge of modern science;
- To produce technicians for laboratories and industry; and
- To produce generalists who would show a better appreciation of the scientific method, and have a scientific ethos.

To the scientists, and to those concerned with applications of science, the primary objective of science education is obviously to produce scientists of high calibre who can undertake research at the cutting edge in all fields, and particularly in the thrust areas like space science, biotechnology, computer science and communications. To meet this objective the basic requirements are good infrastructure in the form of modern laboratories and libraries, and excellent human resources both in terms of faculty and students. Unfortunately, these are available only in a few universities, and in institutions like the Indian Institute of Science and the IITs. Unless the government provides massive funding for all universities, and establishes a few science universities, the objective of producing high-quality scientists, in large numbers, may never be fulfilled.

Many universities in India produce competent postgraduates and doctorates who end up as technicians in foreign laboratories (Manjrekar, 1999). Not that the objective of producing good technicians is to be looked down upon. Only this objective has to be met in a planned manner for our own country, taking into consideration the needs of our research laboratories and industries. The universities trying to meet this objective have to formulate their curricula accordingly. In fact this has already been done at some universities in the case of programmes in environmental science, energy studies and the like.

The fact of the matter is that the vast majority of our undergraduate students have little hopes of making a career as a scientist. In most cases they have been drifting into jobs in government or business in which their training in science is of little significance. Keeping this in mind the University of Delhi is contemplating a change in its B.Sc. programme. At a seminar on 'Science Education and Career Opportunities' (Centre for Science Education and Communication, 1997) it was concluded that science education should address "*the need of overall development of well-rounded persons who can be assets to an organised society*". Further, science education should aim at producing students capable of independently updating knowledge, thinking rationally, utilising acquired knowledge in problem solving, reflecting and forming opinion, putting in a systematic and responsible work effort, and communicating knowledge effectively.

Curricula Syllabi and Teaching Methodology

As mentioned time and again the bane of Indian higher education is the inflexible academic structure that places undue emphasis on the annual examination. This structure has done the most harm to the science subjects in which developments are rapid and the need for innovation the greatest. Even in the United States, whose education system is considered to be a model for flexibility and comprehensiveness (Srivastava, 1994), the need for frequent changes has been felt. Broadbasing of the programmes on offer, and variety in the courses available, have been the corner-stones of the system. In stark contrast we bind students to taking a set combination of subjects without having option of courses in these subjects.

This situation has to change and the cafeteria-type model has to be introduced at the earliest. Not only do the programmes lack variety but there is in most cases a deficiency in terms of content. The syllabi are out-dated and repetitive. As Modak (1996) points out they lack a conceptual basis and do not emphasise the basic tenets and lay stress on information. These deficiencies have to be removed. The suggestions offered by Modak (1996) and by the teachers of Delhi University (Centre for Science Education and Communication, (1997) indicate that the academic community has started thinking on these lines. However, with the affiliating system prevailing in most universities the process of syllabi-development is controlled more by the competence and interest of the teachers rather than by the needs of the students or other stakeholders. As in all democratic systems the Lowest Common Multiple prevails.

The way students and teachers look at syllabi is also important. The syllabi for different courses constitute the heart of the curriculum. They should be viewed as highways to academic excellence with the different items being signposts that indicate pathways to different areas that have to be explored by imaginative trends. Unfortunately both teachers and students tend to treat the syllabus as a road in a border-region where straying is not permitted. In many universities any deviation from the 'border-road' situation, in teaching or in examination, is met by shouts of "out-of-course". How can science improve in this situation?

In most of our universities and colleges the teaching of science is largely restricted to lectures and some practicals. Often the lectures are prosaic with practically no use being made of modern instructional technology. The practicals consist of very basic experiments. In many colleges, because of lack of resources, these are reduced to demonstrations by the teachers. The teaching methodology has to be radically changed so as to include lectures, tutorials, laboratory work, seminars, projects and group-writing with substantial use of information technology. At this stage one can do no better than to quote Jacques Delors (1996) "*Science teaching must avoid the pitfalls of a sterile academic approach and an ivory tower mentality, particularly in countries which especially need to make progress in technological fields. Conversely, however, the quality of science should not be sacrificed in the interests of immediate productivity, since what is at stake is universal, like science itself, and long range*".

The Constraints

Time and again concern has been expressed that the Indian university system has not been able to provide a steady flow of competent scientists who can help translate scientific achievement into technological development, or give India a secure position on the world scientific map. Prestigious institutes like the Indian Institutes of Technology and the Jawaharlal Nehru University were founded and developed to improve excellence. No doubt, the Indian Institute of Science and some departments in universities all over the country constitute islands of excellence but they seem to be lost in a sea of mediocrity. In fact, the general perception is that the standard of science education is steadily deteriorating. The time has come to seriously examine why the elite institutes have not been able to act as models or catalysts, and what has inhibited the development of healthy academic norms.

The failure of university science education to deliver the goods can be attributed to a number of factors.

First, the mushrooming of institutions of tertiary education: The number of universities has increased from 18 in 1947 to 240 in early 1999, and of colleges from about 600 to over 9000. The student strength has correspondingly grown from two lakhs to 60 lakhs. Because of the rapid and unplanned expansion quality has been a victim.

Second, the general neglect of education by the central government: At present the allotment to education is only 3.8% GNP against the minimum requirement of 6% GNP (a figure first recommended by the Kothari Commission in 1964, but possibly conservative according to present-day requirements). Of this the share of higher education is only 0.8%. The result is that one-third of the institutions are non-viable and most of the others unable to provide the necessary laboratory, library and other teaching facilities. We can no longer turn a blind eye to the fact that the condition of some of the state universities is pathetic.

Third, the neglect of universities so far as research funding in science and technology is concerned: No more than 6% of the Rs. 3300 crores spent on research funding (i.e. Rs. 200 crores) is given to the universities. Of this more than half is spent by a select few with the result that an amount of about Rs. 100 crores has to be shared by a majority of university personnel who constitute about 50% of the entire R&D manpower (University Grants Commission, 1995).

Fourth, the preference of the better students for engineering and medicine: The National Science Talent Search Awards Scheme, initiated in 1964, was enlarged in 1977 to the National Talent Search Award Scheme to include areas other than science. By the late 1980s only about 10% of the awardees were opting for science at the undergraduate level (Indian Academy of Sciences, 1989).

Fifth, the inflexibility of the system: The academic structure prevalent in Indian universities allows students to study only select combination of subjects, the most common being physics-chemistry-mathematics or botany-zoology-chemistry. There is generally no possibility of choosing a combination including both biology and mathematics, or opting for more than three subjects.

Sixth, the prevalence of an archaic examination system: In most Indian universities, students are evaluated on the basis of an annual essay-type examination that encourages memorising and discourages enquiry and analysis. The rejection by most universities, after a hasty, unplanned trial, of the semester system with continuous evaluation, has been a major set back.

Seventh, the general confining of undergraduate teaching to colleges: The teachers in colleges are poorly equipped and most of them not abreast with recent developments. Often in the colleges the laboratories are there only in name, and the libraries have only prescribed text-books. The standard of teaching in many colleges is depressingly poor and only in a few cases can it be said to be reasonably good. There is a perceptible gap between what a graduating B.Sc. student knows and what is required at the beginning of the Master's programme.

Eighth, the constraints on the teaching process: In most universities teaching is governed by a tightly-defined syllabus, which is revised only after long delays. Anything not included in the syllabus cannot be asked in the examination. The B.Sc. syllabus usually reflects what (reluctant) college teachers can teach rather than what is required. The University Grants Commission, after considerable effort, had model curricula prepared in 27 subjects, and circulated these to the universities in the early 1990's. However, an AIU survey shows that these have largely been ignored. Meanwhile, the gap between what is taught at the B.Sc. level and what is basic requirement for the M.Sc. programmes widens. The same can be said of our M.Sc. teaching and the requirements for research.

Last: The lack of a scientific ethos. This is hard to describe but is reflected in the generally routine nature of lectures, the (often) slip-shod handling of practicals, and the neglect of fieldwork.

The Positive Aspects

The status and future of higher science education in India has been discussed at the highest academic level (Indian National Science Academy, 1985; Indian Academy of Sciences, 1994). There is the realisation that there is considerable scope for improvement, and that innovative actions have to be taken if there is to be a narrowing of the gap between Indian science and the science of developed nations. The University Grants Commission initiated in the late 1970's and 1980's a number of programmes to improve the quality of teaching and research. These include:

i) Establishment of Academic Staff Colleges (ASCs) for imparting orientation courses (for new teachers) and refresher courses (for serving teachers).

ii) Starting of a Special Assistance Programme (SAP) under which selected departments are provided support at three levels, namely Department of Research Support (DRS), Department of Special Assistance (DSA) and Centre for Advanced Study (CAS).

iii) Setting up of Curriculum Development Centres (CDCs) (10 of which were in science) for developing model curricula at both undergraduate and postgraduate levels.

iv) Granting of autonomy to selected colleges (the Autonomous Colleges) so as to enable them to undertake innovations in areas like restructuring of courses, curricula development, the teaching-learning process, and the evaluation process.

v) Encouraging research by making provision for grants for major and minor projects, and by institution of research associateships, career awards, visiting associateships and fellowships for senior teachers.

vi) Setting up INFLIBNET, an inter-university centre for information and library networking.

vii) Introducing of a scheme for assisting the development of computer facilities and computer education. The computer centers established under the scheme provide facilities for software development, computation and analyses of research data, and also for teaching of MCA/M.Sc. (Computer Science) courses.

Programmes specific to science that have been promoted by the University Grants Commission include the establishment of the following:

i) A College Science Improvement Programme (COSIP) under which financial assistance is provided to predominantly undergraduate institutions for development of science teaching capabilities through curricula development and procurement of equipment, teaching materials and books and journals.

ii) A programme of the Committee for Strengthening of Infrastructure in Science and Technology (COSIST). Under this programme the Commission assists selected Science and Technology Departments in Universities to acquire sophisticated and expensive equipments necessary for research that will be internationally competitive.

iii) University Science Instrument Centres (USIC) for the training of experimental scientists and for generating interests amongst students in advances made in science and technology. These centres have the capacity to repair, develop and fabricate equipment. They also have, as a common facility for all science departments, sophisticated equipments required for advanced teaching and research.

iv) Setting up of autonomous inter-university centres for programmes including the Nuclear Science Centre, New Delhi (for accelerator-oriented research), the Inter-University Centre for Astronomy and Astrophysics (for Astronomical and Astrophysics research), the Inter-University Centre of Department of Atomic Energy, Indore (for use of frontline facilities of DAE) and the M.S.T. Radar Centre, Tirupati (for research in Atmosphere Dynamics).

The Council of Scientific and Industrial Research (CSIR), the Atomic Energy Commission and the different Departments of Government of India .(especially the Department of Science and Technology, the Department of Biotechnology and the Department of Environment and Forests) have been providing support to research projects of individual scientists in the universities through various schemes.

What Needs To Be Done

It is evident that what has been done for science education in the country is not sufficient or that it has not been done effectively. Perhaps both are true, for as Valiathan (1993) has pointed out "*knowing what to do and not caring to do it (properly) has cast a shadow on (our) national endeavours*". For this reason it may be necessary to re-try, on a selective basis, after effective planning, programmes that have been implemented and rejected in the recent past — e.g., examination reforms.

The bane of Indian science has been the separation of undergraduate teaching from (post) graduate teaching; and the isolation of scientists in the national laboratories from their colleges in the (neglected) universities. The situation has to change. Science can prosper only in an open environment characterised by interaction, cooperation and a free flow of ideas. This could be achieved by massive funding, especially of science departments in the universities, to remove obsolescence. A continued academic crusade has to be carried out for the establishment of permanent endowment funds in all the universities.

In recent years, at least two models of integrated teaching have been suggested which could be given a trial. These are meant for highly talented students. According to the first pattern, proposed in 1989, by a Working Group of the Planning Commission (see Indian Academy of Sciences, 1994) an integrated five-year M.Sc. programme should be introduced in select universities and institutions. In the first year the curricula will be common to all students and will concentrate on the foundations of all major subjects. The second and third year programmes will be in a selected subject and will follow the pattern of the B.Sc. (Honours) programme with a principal subject. After the third year a student would be awarded a B.Sc. (Honours) degree and could either leave or proceed for M.Sc. during the fourth and fifth years. The M.Sc. curricula would bring the student to the threshold of research.

According to the second pattern, proposed in 1995 by a Committee appointed by the University Grants Commission to suggest the structure of a postulated National Science University, the science teaching programme would include a four-year B.Sc. (Hons.) programme followed by a Ph.D. programme including course-work. On completion of course-work, the student would be entitled to an M.Sc. degree.

Both the patterns emphasise strong foundation courses in all sciences, flexibility in choosing combinations of subjects, and lay stress on the development of the faculties of investigative thinking and critical analysis.

A strengthening of undergraduate science could be achieved by replacing the B.Sc. (General) programme (3 subjects in the final year) by the B.Sc. (Honours) programme (principal subject in final year) where the former exists. This has to be accompanied by the implementation on a wider scale of programmes like COSIP, placing of greater stress on practicals and fieldwork, giving a retrial to the semester-system with continuous evaluation, a more effective functioning of the Academic Staff Colleges, and the grant of autonomy to a much larger number of colleges.

It is very disturbing that over one-third of students drop out before getting their Bachelor's degree. No country can afford such wastage. For the not-so-talented student, who does not aspire for a career as a research scientist, the introduction of an applied component in the final year of the B.Sc. programme would be relevant. It would be helpful to the student in securing employment as a scientific or technical assistant, or setting up a unit for himself. Applied or job-oriented courses that are offered by a few universities are fairly popular and useful. The University Grants Commission has taken up an ambitious programme of vocationalisation of courses under which a large number of vocational courses have been introduced at the undergraduate level. The development of this programme is to be carefully monitored.

Ways have to be found to introduce flexibility in the academic structure. The cafeteria-type credit system must be introduced, at least in a few selected universities, with the facility of transfer of credit from one university to another. This will allow the talented students to take the best available, and the most relevant, courses available at different places.

The postgraduate teaching in many universities is still being conducted according to the pattern of annual examinations. They should all be asked to switch over to the semester system with continuous evaluation. Because of the limited number of departments and students this should not be difficult. It would allow the adoption of a system of core (compulsory) and optional courses, and give the student an opportunity to specialise in a limited way. Closer interaction and collaboration between university departments and national laboratories is essential. The universities should enter into Memorandums of Understanding with national laboratories that allow exchange of teachers and scientists, use of equipment in laboratories by teachers, the participation of scientists in teaching and curricula development, and of course collaborative research. Central funding agencies (like CSIR, DST and DBT) have been funding research projects submitted by individual teachers in universities. No doubt good scientific contributions have resulted in many cases. However, these allocations have not always been on the basis of merit leading to heart-burning. The awards have also generated feelings of possessiveness and superiority in some and of alienation and frustration in others. The funding policy needs to be reviewed. It would, perhaps, be more productive if funds are given to departments with a group of good scientists rather than to individuals. Most importantly, there must be a much larger inflow of funds for the universities and colleges. As enumerated above, we have the programmes but these are not successful because the butter is being spread very thinly. Massive financial support is necessary to remove obsolescence, provide reasonable (if not excellent) facilities, and generate an enthusiasm for science.

To summarise if science education in the country is to become meaningful there is a need to undertake some radical measures without losing much time. These include:

A. General:

i) Infuse a much larger amount of funds at all stages and thus provide adequate infrastructure and human resources. The programmes of the UGC, presently given on selective basis, be implemented in all institutions.

ii) Modify the academic structure, especially at the undergraduate level, to provide more flexibility and promote innovative measures.

iii) Place stress on the understanding and use of modern information technology.

iv) Encourage quality by starting science universities that would undertake combined undergraduate and postgraduate teaching, as also high class research.

v) Place emphasis on laboratory work, fieldwork, group-learning and project work.

B. Postgraduate Teaching and Research:

i) Provide first-rate laboratory and library facilities.

ii) In the academic structure provide for core and optional courses that would enable the student to have a strong fundamental base, and to specialise in the area of his liking.

C. Undergraduate Teaching:

i) Discourage starting of new colleges and thereby stop the process of mushroom growth and dissipation of scarce resources.

ii) Introduce cafeteria-type approach for courses or offer with a credit-based modular system for attaining requirements for a degree.

iii) Introduce examination reforms emphasising continuous internal assessment.

iv) Make learning student-centred rather than teacher-centred, both in terms of teaching-learning methodology and faculty-recruitment.

Conclusion

In the post-independence era science and technology have been the cornerstone of India's developmental policy. Maddox (1993), while reviewing the status of science in India, writes, "*Never can there have been such a determination to attain improvement by science and technology as in India since 1947*". It is, therefore, paradoxical that our policy-makers (after Nehru) should have given short shrift to education in general and science education in particular. A steady deterioration in standards is a natural consequence. This, however, does not mean that we have failed totally. Today our science is like a centipede with a head of excellence, separated by segments of varying quality from a tail of utter mediocrity. It is time to act in a manner by which that the centipede curls up, into am ball of quality. If this is to be achieved science education must be accorded priority by the planners and policy makers. There has to be a loosening of purse-strings. But that will not be enough. What is required now is a change in attitude. There has to be massive funding, dedication, recognition of creativity and a resolute commitment not only to survive and succeed but also to excel in the global context.

References

Alam, M., (1991), Higher Education in Medieval India, in Moonis Raza (Ed.), *Higher Education in India: Retrospect and Prospect*, AIU, New Delhi, pp.10-21.

Association of Indian Universities, (1998), *University Institutions in India*, AIU, New Delhi.

Centre for Science Education and Communication, (1997), *Science Education and Career Opportunities: An Exercise in Looking Ahead*, CSEC, University of Delhi, Delhi.

Delors, Jacques, (Editor), (1996), *Learning: The Treasure Within*, Report to the UNESCO of the International Commission on Education for the Twenty First Century, UNESCO Publishing, Paris, 266pp.

Indian Academy of Sciences, (1994), *University Education in India*, Academy Papers 1, IASc, Bangalore.

Indian National Science Academy, (1985), *Issues in Higher Education in Science*, INSA, New Delhi.

Institute of Applied Manpower Research, (1998), *Manpower Profile, India, Yearbook 1998*, IAMR, New Delhi.

Jain, N.K., (1982), *Science and Scientists in India*, Indian Book Gallery, New Delhi.

Maddox, J., (1993), India's Great Ambition to Succeed, *Nature*, 366: 611-614.

Manjrekar, J., (1999), Higher Education in Science: A Matter of Training Technicians, *Current Science*, 76(1): 7-8.

Modak S.P., (1996), Science Education in Indian Universities: Proposal for a 5-year Integrated Course in Life Science, *Current Science*, 71(12): 960-967.

Rajagopal, N.R., Sehgal, Y.P., Das, S.R., and Sudhir Kumar, (1994), Scientific and Technical Manpower in India - An Analysis of Trends, *CURIE*, 1: 24-35.

Srivastava, P.N., (1994), 'Science in India' *Presidential Address, 81st Session, Indian Science Congress, Jaipur*, ISCA, Calcutta.

University Grants Commission, (1993), *Annual Report for 1992-93*, UGC, New Delhi.

University Grants Commission, (1995), Report of Srivastava Committee on *National Science University: Concept and Structure*, UGC, New Delhi.

Valiathan, M.S., (1993), *Presidential Address, 68th Annual Meeting of the Association of Indian Universities*, AIU, New Delhi.

8

The Dilemma of Research in Indian Universities*

Introduction

There is general acceptance of the fact that the quality of research being carried out in most Indian universities falls short of international standards. This is attributed to a number of factors including lack of infrastructure, financial constraints, inadequate planning, administrative apathy, shortage of committed students of high calibre, and inadequate or inappropriate supervision. While these constraints are real, and cannot be wished away, it is also necessary to address certain other basic issues that reflect the overall ethos of research in Indian universities. These include an understanding of what constitutes research, the nature and type of research being undertaken by universities, and appropriate criteria and procedure for its evaluation. It is proposed to review these aspects in this short presentation.

What is Research?

The scepticism about the quality of research being conducted by our universities is, at least in part, due to some of the products that are passed onto less-knowledgeable bureaucrats and unsuspecting laypersons as being the result of 'research activity'. These include articles in newspapers and magazines, preliminary findings of surveys and results of routine testing and analysis. It is, therefore, necessary to clearly define what constitutes research. It has to be understood that research leads to the generation of new and meaningful data, to the development of new ideas, hypotheses and concepts, and to novel and relevant interpretations. The University Funding Council of UK, for its Research Assessment Exercise (RAE), conducted in 1989, defined research as follows: *"Research, for the purpose of the Council's review, is to be understood as original investigation, undertaken in order to gain knowledge and*

* Keynote Address at the AIU Seminar on '*Supervision of Research*' organised by the Goa University and the National Institute of Oceanography at NIO, Dona Paola, Goa, August 17-18, 2000.

understanding. In the humanities it includes scholarship that leads to new or substantially improved insights, in science and technology it includes the use of existing knowledge in experimental development to produce new or substantially improved materials, devices, products and processes, including design and construction. It excludes routine testing and analysis if materials, components and processes – e.g. for maintenance of national standards – as distinct from the development of new analytical techniques" (Jones, 1989). Jenkins (1995) pointed out that for the RAE of 1996 the development of teaching material has also been excluded from the definition of research.

Nature of Research

The research undertaken in the universities can be broadly classified into two types:

- *Basic (or fundamental) research* undertaken in a free state of inquiry solely to acquire knowledge.
- *Applied (or developmental) research* undertaken to acquire knowledge or resource that has practical application to problems of society.

Basic research is pursued in practically all disciplines, and especially so in the departments belonging to the faculties of arts, social sciences and natural sciences. It contributes to the intellectual development of the faculty and students though there may not be any immediate benefits. In the case of basic research the initiative is generally taken by individuals or research groups, not by the institution. The nature of research undertaken, and its quality, is based on tradition, the ability of the faculty and the available facilities. Applied research is undertaken largely in the laboratory-based science and technology departments, some social science departments and central facilities. The type of research undertaken reflects the needs of society. While funding for basic research generally comes from the university and government agencies, applied research may receive money from industry and business.

During the nineteenth century, and the greater part of the twentieth century, research was concentrated to disciplines and the specialised areas within the disciplines. This led to the development of knowledge but also led to its segmentation. However, with the blurring of boundaries between different subjects, and the need to examine subjects from different viewpoints, the emphasis is now shifting to inter-disciplinary and multi-disciplinary approaches. A holistic approach has now become necessary in many areas including biotechnology, energy studies, environmental studies and economics. A further reason favouring the inter-disciplinary approach is that research topics are increasingly being determined by the problems of society. With increased interaction between the universities and industry the latter is funding research to a greater extent. The research is undertaken for specific purposes, oriented towards production, and is therefore in many cases confidential. This is contrary to the traditions of universities and academics that have traditionally believed in publishing the results of their work as soon as possible. It is natural that individuals prefer to work in areas of their own liking, and undertake contractual work only because of the funds it provides. In the universities we find that there is continued debate or discussions on various aspects of research. They are on such issues like basic research versus applied research, quantitative research versus qualitative research, discipline-specific research versus inter-disciplinary or multi-disciplinary research, voluntary research versus contract research, and creative research versus research for circulation (Ferrer, 1999).

Bennich-Bjorkman (1997) in a critical study on the organisation of innovative research in universities, points out that research contributions need to be creative, and in order to be so classified, they should provide new concepts and theories that furnish fresh interpretation of society and nature, or provide new solutions to old problems, or pose new questions, or rephrase problems in new terms. He points out that several scholars have suggested that to merit the label 'creative' the contributions should be, amongst other things, novel and relevant (valuable). Based on a combination of these two requirements research contributions can be classified as:

- *Creative* for contributions that are both novel and relevant
- *Original* for contributions that are novel but not relevant
- *Cumulative* for contributions that are relevant but not novel
- *Replication* for contributions that are neither relevant nor novel.

Bennich-Bjorkman (*op. cit.*) states: *"Progress, then is made by research contributions of either a creative or cumulative kind. However, original work which is bereft of the quality of relevance does not constitute genuine progress"*. In defense of originality one can, however, say that what is not relevant today may become relevant in the near future. Original contributions, thus, have the potential of becoming creative. Contributions from universities are generally cumulative or replications. Original contributions are few and creative ones still less. Unfortunately, the research contributions from many universities are replications and a product of what is euphemistically known as 'parallel research'. No wonder that many theses lie unpublished on the shelves of university libraries with the results never seeing the light of day. The requirement of basic research, namely excellent infrastructure, highly qualified and motivated academic personnel and administrative support, are available in only a few Indian universities. By and large most Indian universities would be better off concentrating on applied research.

Traditionally, teachers in universities have enjoyed complete freedom regarding the choice of topic of research. There is likely to be resentment if any 'directions' are given in this respect. Hence, orientation of the research supervisors is important. The promotion of applied research in a university has to be carefully planned. A possible strategy for the promotion of an applied research ethos could include:

- Involving undergraduate students in surveys that identify societal problems and generate background data;
- Assigning to Master's and M. Phil. students, as a compulsory part of their curriculum, problems involving preliminary research on topics of known societal interest; and
- Identifying (and allotting), for Ph.D. programmes, topics related to society's needs that require focussed studies, including use of advanced technologies/sophisticated software/conceptual analysis.

Applied research should logically culminate in 'participatory research' wherein there is a convergence of traditional knowledge and frontier research. Here the researcher in the university works with the common man, on the latter's problem, making use of his traditional knowledge and home-developed skills (Krishnakumar, 2000). During the course of applied/participatory research a situation may develop when it becomes necessary to look into fundamental issues. A return to basic research becomes essential completing the research cycle.

Creative research is usually produced by universities and departments that have a tradition and culture of productivity. In this respect Bennich-Bjorkman's study provides two important conclusions. First, for a Department to become excellent in research it must develop a culture which encourages intellectual and scholarly exchange, forges social bonds and nurtures a genuine sharing of interest. Secondly, that such a culture has to develop spontaneously and cannot be bureaucratically imposed. The quality of scholarship that exists and the relations that are already in place play a definitive role in promoting the spirit of excellence.

Striving for Excellence: The Supervisor's Role

While striving for excellence in research in the universities one may examine two contrasting models – the German and the American. In Germany research was introduced as an important activity of the universities in the early nineteenth century. Research schools were built around a professor and his research interest. The student worked on his mentor's project and on his dissertation simultaneously. In this system the individual's effort is the dominating factor with the supervisor playing a facilitator's role by providing the guidance. Talent is (or was) developed individually and independently. Research is an activity for the select few. In contrast in the United States coursework is an important part of a doctoral programme. There are many interactions in the form of discussions and seminars. The professional dimension of research is emphasised, and one is 'trained for' and not 'born into' research. Which model is to be followed is for each institution to decide depending upon its tradition and culture. However, in an era in which there is intense specialisation, yet in which a holistic approach is being advocated (partnership and networking are key words). The American system promises to be more productive.

Interestingly, as regards supervision of research in Indian universities, the approaches adopted in the faculties of Science, Technology, Agriculture and Medicine, on the one hand, and in the faculties of Arts, Social Sciences and Law, on the other, appear to be different. In the case of the former group the topic allotted to a doctoral student is generally a part of a larger (long-term) project undertaken by the supervisor. He is deeply involved in the project and contributes substantially in terms of ideas and project design. A number of students work together as part of a research group. The American model is thus more appropriate. In the case of the latter group the relationship between the supervisor and the student is less well defined. Students choose their own topic for research, and often the interest of the supervisor on the theme of research is only marginal. The interaction between student and supervisor is less frequent that in the case of science and technology, and the supervisor's role may be restricted to providing guidelines and suggestions. The German tradition, that favours individual initiative and interest, possible provides the patter for research in the arts and social sciences. Productive and meaningful research requires a strong foundation and a clear grasp of the fundamentals of a subject. Coursework, including instructions on research methodology, and fundamental ideas and principles of a discipline, should be an essential ingredient of doctoral studies in all disciplines.

The average university department in India does not have facilities required for research work of international standard. Under these circumstances it is necessary for them, and especially the departments of disciplines in which experimental work is necessary, to enter into collaboration with other institutions like national laboratories. This would grant the research workers in the university access to sophisticated equipment and also literature. The arrangement should be useful to scientists in the laboratories also for they would get the chance to supervise research and interact with fresh, highly-motivated students. Likewise, universities need to develop linkages with 'the world of work' – industries and business houses. Thus while business and industry can give the much-needed financial support the universities can, in return, provide the information base and expertise for the solution of industries' problems. Silicon Valley provides an unparalleled example of what can be achieved if the 'world of knowledge' and 'the world of work' act in unison. Supervisors, in their capacity of project leaders, have the responsibility of taking the necessary steps to develop the required linkages.

Evaluation of Research

All universities have a commitment to research, and most departments on a university campus consider the conduct of research as being their most important function. The evaluation of the research contribution of a department, or a university as a whole, is not easy because of the inherent difficulty in distinguishing between the contributions of an individual from that of the academic unit. Ramsden (1994) points out that in many institutions the distribution of research output is heavily and negatively skewed – most papers are produced by a small number of academics with many faculty members producing little or nothing. Lotka's Law, stating that the number of persons producing n papers is approximately proportional to $1/n^2$, commonly prevails. Moreover, contributions to fundamental research are generally not noticed while the results of applied research often receive considerable publicity and this clouds public perception, and even the perception of academics. It will be illogical to expect the same research productivity from a small department in a university as from a centre for advanced studies in the same subject in another university. Likewise it would not be correct to expect the matching productivity from a university department and a national laboratory.

Evaluation, unfortunately, invokes comparison and this often affects the academic ambience, especially when there are researchers working in the same discipline (say geology) but different sub-disciplines (eg. mineralogy, petrology, geotectonics and palaeonology). Likewise it is difficult to compare the research outputs of different faculties (arts, science, social sciences, engineering, medicine) or different subjects in the same faculty (mathematics, physics, chemistry, botany, zoology, biotechnology).

A variety of indicators are being used to evaluate the quality of research. These include publications, research-support received, peer opinion, overall research activity, and honours and awards received. Ideally, an appropriate mix of all these should be used while evaluating a department, but this may not always be possible. Perhaps, one may also have to consider not only the quality of research but also the way the institution manages the research environment, and the way research impinges on both post-graduate and under-graduate teaching (Piper, 1993). Some of the indicators are briefly reviewed in the sub-sections that follow.

Publications

An assessment of publications is possibly the most straight-forward way of measuring the research output of an institution. Various types of bibliometric studies have been proposed, and these together have given rise to the field of *Scientimetrics.* A research journal of the same name, established in 1978, has published, till the end of 1999, 1062 papers in this area (Persson, 2000). Harris (1990) recognised four types of measures that could be the basis of evaluating research publications–quantity, impact, quality and importance. *Quantity* appears to be the simplest of these for it involves only the counting of the number of publications produced. *Impact* is a measure of the influence of a publication on fellow workers and can be evaluated by noting the number of times it is cited by other researchers. *Quality* and *Importance* are subjective, value-based, measures that cannot be estimated by bibliographic means, but require peer evaluation (see Ramsden, 1994).

In evaluating publications weightage has obviously to be given to the nature and type of publication. *The Publication Count*, i.e., the numbers of papers published, cannot alone be the measure of research output, for this would encourage the piecemeal publication of results, publication in journals with lenient refereeing norms, and multi-authored publications. The quality of the publication has to be the primary consideration in evaluation. Hence, it is necessary to adopt, while evaluating the merit of a publication, 'weights' like the reputation of the journal, nature and length of publication, the number of authors and the notice the publication has received from other workers. It would be appropriate to consider only the contributions that have appeared in refereed research publications. *Citation Index* and the *Garfeld (Impact) Factor* of the journal in which a paper is published are often considered to be the most important indicators. Abstracts of papers submitted to seminars and symposia, and contributions appearing in news magazines and newspapers need to be disregarded. The latter may not appeal to some teachers in the social sciences and languages (for example, to poets) and in special cases there may be a need to refer some publications to a panel of experts. Further, credit will also have to be given to unpublished research reports prepared as part of consultancy services, to edited research volumes and to authored standard text-books. An assessment method that takes into account publications/contributions of various types is often necessary.

Citation Index: It is logical to assume that a work of good quality will be taken note of by subsequent workers and consequently referred to in their publications. As the Journal Citation Reports (JCR) notes: *A citation is the formal acknowledgement of 'intellectual debt' to previously published research, publicly recorded in the references listed by contemporary authors"* (Institute for Scientific Information, 1994). It adds that the citation data is unobtrusive, quantitative and objective. Hence the number of times a work is cited (the number of citations) is a widely-used measure for evaluating the quality of research. However, several arguments have been advanced against the use of citations as a measure of quality. These include:

- A citation does not differentiate between a complimentary and a non-complimentary reference. A work that is referred to in critical terms may, therefore, score a point or points. However, most workers tend to disregard a trivial paper, or a paper that presents outlandist views, and hence this should not be a major difficulty.
- Some research workers may have a bias for or against a certain individual or institution leading to non-citing or over-citing of their papers. However, such a bias eventually tends to even out and is, therefore, not significant.
- There may be omission of reference to papers owing to ignorance of their existence, preferential citing of publications of eminent workers, non-citing of even significant work of little-known workers and 'plagiarism' of citations (Johnes and Taylor, 1990).

- Citations do not distinguish between major works, (like monographs and lengthy research papers), review papers and short communications (including letters).
- Publications in languages other than English are less accessible to researchers, and therefore not cited.
- Citation to multi-authored papers is recorded under the first author's name only. No credit is given to other authors. In the case of publication by a group, the group leader often puts his name last. The group may publish a number of papers but the group-leader may not receive any credit though he may be the 'brain' behind the research project.

In spite of the above-mentioned deficiencies the use of citation, as a measure of research quality, has fairly wide support largely because it has a statistical base. Citations can provide a more authentic picture of research quality if each citation could be assigned a weight based upon the impact factor of the journal and the area/sub-discipline of the paper. They cannot, however, form the sole, or even the most important factor, in evaluation. As the JCR states, "*The quantitative citation data it (JCR) reports are intended to complement, not replace, traditional qualitative and subjective inputs, such as peer surveys and specialist opinions*" and "*Citation data are not meant to replace informed peer review*". (Institute for Scientific Information, 1994).

Impact Factor: The Impact Factor, also referred to as Garfield Factor, reflects the number of citations on articles published in a journal. For example in the case of JCR it reports on the average number of current citations of articles a journal published in the previous two years. The eminence of a journal is reflected in its impact factor score. In turn it means that an article published in a journal having a high impact factor is of good value. The impact factor is field- (discipline) and sub-field related and attempts have been made to normalise the impact factor of different journals, across fields (Vinkler, 2000). Incidentally, the impact factor may vary considerable even amongst journals of very good reputation. The Impact Factor for Current Science, India, for 1993, was only 0.376 compared to 22.326 for Nature, UK. The country of publication of the journals and their availability to readers worldwide could have been a contributing factor to the large difference.

Publication-based Evaluation: Citation Indices and Impact Factors are not available for all subjects. Further, they do not differentiate between different categories of publications like research papers, review papers and shorter communications, nor do they consider non-journal publications like monographs and books. Hence it is necessary to have a publication-based methodology by which the work of a researcher, research-group, department or institution can be evaluated. Such a methodology is presented below.

A classification of publications/research contributions that could be utilised for evaluation is:

1. Monographs
2. Research papers in international journals
3. Research papers in national journals
4. Review papers in international journals
5. Review papers in national journals
6. Authored books of post-graduate level
7. Edited research volumes
8. Chapters in refereed, edited books of postgraduate level
9. Short communications in international journals
10. Short communications in national journals
11. Papers in 'Proceedings' of Seminars
12. Papers/review papers in University-level journals
13. Project/technical reports (unpublished)

Ramsden and Moses (1992) proposed as an indicator of research performance of academic staff an index of Research Productivity (IRP). It is the five year sum of (3 x the number of single or multi-authored books) + (the number of papers published in refereed journals) + (the number of edited books) + (the number of chapters in edited books). The research productivity of any academic unit would then be the total of the index of research productivity of its academic staff. In the case of multi-authored publications there is difficulty in assigning credit to the individual authors. Giving credit only to the first author, or giving full credit to all authors, will introduce bias in the publication count. Under the circumstances it is best to divide the credit equally among all the authors. Thus a researcher is entitled to one credit for all single-authored papers, half (0.5) credit for paper with a single co-author, and one third (0.33) credit for a paper with two co-authors. In case an author changes his or her institution the credit should go to the institution where the work was undertaken.

Considering the fact that in India the standard of research publications vary considerably a modified Index of Research Productivity (IRP) has been suggested (Powar, 1996) and this is suitable to the Indian research environment. The IRP is described as the five year sum of (4 x sum of the number of research monographs and postgraduate level books)+ (3 x sum of research and review papers in international journals and chapters

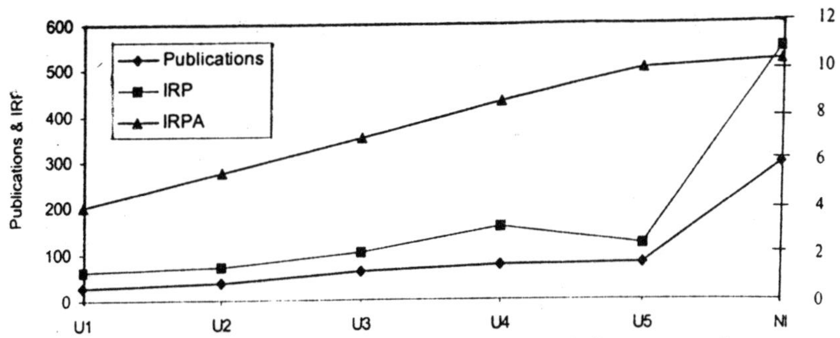

Fig 1: Number of Publications, IRP, IRPA for 5 University Departments of Geology and a National Institute for the years 1990 to 1994

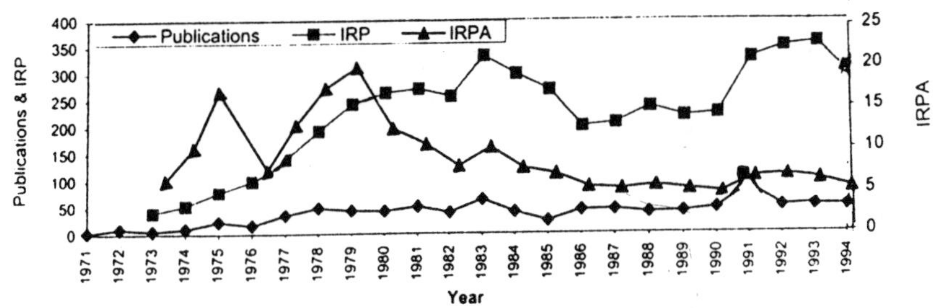

Fig 2: Total Publications, IRP & IRPA for a National Institute in Geology

Weightage Groups:

Group I

1 Monographs
2 Authored Books
3 Chapter in Edited Books

Group II

4 Research Papers in International Journals*
5 Review papers in International Journals

Group III

6 Research Papers in National Journals
7 Review papers in National Journals
8 Edited Research Volume
9 Short Communication in International Journals

Group IV

10 Short Communication in National Journals
11 Papers in `Proceedings' of Seminars
12 Papers in University-level Journals
13 Unpublished Reports

* Journals included in the Science Citation Index Only

IRP = Sum of Last Three Years of (4[I]+3[II]+2[III]+1[IV])

IRPA = IRP of Current Year/No. of Scientists two years ago

in refereed books of postgraduate level) + (2 x sum of research and review papers in national journals, edited research volumes and short communication in international journals) + (sum of short communications in national journals, Proceedings of seminars, papers/review papers in university level journals and unpublished project/technical reports). For the purpose of computing the IRP a rather restricted definition of `international journal' is recommended. The term should cover only those journals that are included in the Journal Citation Reports of the Science Citation Index, the Social Sciences Citation Index and the Arts and Humanities Citation Index. While calculating the index of Research Productivity of individuals only partial credit is to be given to each author in the case of multi-authored publications. For this purpose apportioning of credit should be done as discussed in the previous paragraph. The total of the IRP of all academic staff is the Index of Research Productivity of the academic unit (department/school/university). In view of the fact that different academic units vary in terms of the number of academic staff an additional parameter, the Index of Research Productivity per Academic (IRPA), may be obtained by dividing IRP with the average number of research staff on rolls during the five-year period under consideration. Two examples are given below to illustrate the use of IRP and IRPA for evaluating the research in institutions.

In the first example (Fig.8.1) the total publications, IRP and IRPA of six academic units, for the period 1990-1994 are shown. Five of the academic units are Departments of Geology in Indian universities that have received substantial research funding from the University Grants Commission under its Special Assistance Programme. The sixth unit is a national research institution funded (in substantially larger measure) by the Department of Science and Technology of the Government of India. It is worth noting that there is not much difference in IRPA of the two — best university departments and the national institute. It should be possible to introduce greater sophistication to this exercise. The IRPA could be divided by say the expenditure in lakhs to get an index that will reflect value (return) for money spent. In the second example (Fig. 8.2), the number of publications, IRP and IRPA for a 25-year period (1971-1994) for the national institute are shown. The figure reflects the growth and development of the institute in terms of research productivity.

Research Support

Research workers in universities depend to a considerable extent on external agencies for research funding. The dependence is much greater in the case of science and engineering departments, but other disciplines also require a measure of financial assistance. The funding agencies on their part scrutinise the research proposals for their quality and suitability. The quantum of funds made available is, therefore, taken to be an index of research capability. As the quantity of funds required, and available for dispensation, differ with disciplines and areas, the funds attracted cannot be used to compare the quality of research across disciplines within the same institution. For example, during 1993-94 the distribution of research grants given by the Central Government was as follows: Sciences 51.99%, Agricultural Sciences 16.21%, Engineering and Technology 25.80% and Medical Sciences 6%. Within the allotment for Science, the Biological Sciences received 59.67%, Chemical Sciences 11.88%, the Physical Sciences 11.78%, the Earth Sciences 13.01% and the Mathematical Sciences 3.66%. (Sharma and Sharma, 1999) Research allotment, at best, can indicate the relative merits of departments of the same subject in different universities.

The obvious criticism of using research funding as a criterion of research quality is that this funding is a measure of input rather than of output. Apart from the suitability of a proposal the decision to extend support may be influenced by reputation and presentation. Projects with massive research funding have been known to not yield anything worthwhile while poorly supported projects have produced outstanding results.

Peer Opinion

The opinion of peers, obtained after a review of different aspects of research activity, is often the basis for judging the quality of research of an individual or an academic unit. Its advantage is that it can take into account such aspects as quality and impact. Its main defect is that it can be highly subjective in nature. Opinions may be influenced by such considerations as the reviewer's research interests, his affiliation and even personal relationships. The subjectivity can be reduced by having the review conducted by a panel of peers rather than by an individual. The choice of reviewers is crucial to the success of the exercise. They should preferably be senior persons who have nothing to gain or lose from the review, who are known to be objective and impartial, and who are fully conversant with the latest developments in the area of research. Self-appraisal and the preparation of a well-thought report on activities, achievements and future prospects is an essential prelude to peer evaluation.

Awards and Honours

Awards and honours received for research work reflect the positive opinion of peers regarding the research contributions of an individual. These include :

- Medals and prizes awarded by national academies, academic societies, educational trusts and government agencies,
- Nominations by academic and research bodies for delivering endowment and national lectures,
- Election to fellowships of national and state academies, and
- Prizes for excellence of papers published by research journals, or presented at seminars and conferences.

Most of these awards and honours are bestowed for continued excellence. They are based on criteria that have already been considered, like publication and peer opinions, and therefore do not really act as additional performance indicators. They only substantiate conclusions regarding excellence already recognised from other measures.

Conclusion

Research is one of the two basic functions of a university, and every effort must be made to achieve excellence. It is the responsibility of university managers to provide adequate research facilities to its faculty and also help in creating a proper ethos. The nature of research to be encouraged depends upon a number of factors, including the traditions of the university and the expectations of society. However, there has to be a conscious effort to cultivate excellence. The role of the teacher as co-worker, supervisor and mentor is crucial, and cannot be over-emphasised. Research, being one of the two key functions of a university, must be carefully evaluated. The results will not only give an idea about the ability and commitment of the faculty, but will also provide a basis for short and long-term planning, and for identification of areas that deserve support.

References

Bennich-Bjorkman, Li., (1997), *Organising Innovative Research: The Inner Life of University Departments*, Pergamon/IAU, Paris.

Ferrer, F., (1999), Some Thoughts on Trends in Educational Research, *Prospects*, 111: 409-422.

Harris, G.T., (1990), Research Output in Australian University Economics Departments — An Update for 1984-88. *Australia Economics Papers*, 29:249-259.

Institute for Scientific Information, (1994), *Science Citation Index, Journal Citation Reports*, I.S.I. Philadelphia, pp.6-7.

Jenkins, A., (1995), The Research Assessment Exercise, Funding and Teaching Quality, *Quality Assurance in Education*, 3: 4-12.

Johanes, J. and Taylor, J., (1990), *Performance Indicators in Higher Education*, SRHE and Open University Press, Buckingham.

Jones, P.K., (1989), Report on the 1989 Research Assessment Exercise, University Funding Council, London.

Krishnakumar, A., (2000), "We are Pioneers in Participatory Research": Interview with Dr M.S. Swaminathan, *Frontline*, 17(17): 83- 87.

Persson, O, (2000), A Tribute to Eugene Garfield – Discovering the Intellectual Base of his Discipline, *Current Science*, 79(5): 590-591.

Piper, D.W., (1993) *Quality Management in Universities*, Australian Government Publication Service, Canberra.

Powar, K.B., (1996), *Accreditation in Higher Education – An Indian Perspective*, Viva Books Private Ltd., New Delhi.

Ramsden, D.W., (1994), Describing and Explaining Research Productivity, *Higher Education*, 28: 207-226.

Ramsden, P. and Moses, L., (1992), Associations between Research and Teaching in Australian Higher Education, *Higher Education*, 23: 273-295.

Sharma, M. and Sharma, T.C., (1999), *Funding of Research and Development in Science and Technology in Indian Universities*, AIU Occasional Paper 99/1.

Vinkler, P., (2000), Evaluation of the Publication Activity of Research Teams by means of Scientometric Indicators, *Current Science*, 79(5): 602-612.

9

Autonomy of Indian Universities*

Introduction

Traditionally, universities have been considered to be highly privileged institutions that enjoy almost complete freedom of thought and actions and are accountable only to themselves. Hence the perceived 'ivory tower' existence. However, over the years there has been a continued erosion of the freedom, rights and privileges of universities. Today, the popular perception (at least amongst academics) is that the universities have lost their autonomy and largely function under a variety of constraints that makes it difficult to provide quality education. It is also felt that unless the Indian universities, and the institutions affiliated to them are allowed to function independently, it will be difficult for them to keep up with the developed (and even some of the developing) countries as regards the quality and relevance of the education imparted. A number of suggestions have been made in earlier years to restore academic autonomy, and to an extent administrative and financial autonomy also, to the academic institutions. An important recommendation is that autonomous status be granted to as many institutions as possible. It has evoked reactions, both positive and negative, from the academic community. In this article, an attempt is made to evaluate the present status of Indian universities as regards autonomy and to suggest ways by which it could be enhanced.

Autonomy, Accountability and Academic Freedom

Autonomy may be described as the power to act without external control. It is to be viewed as an organisational or managerial requirement for the fulfillment of responsibilities (Sarup, 1993). Autonomy and accountability are mutually complementary. An individual or an institution cannot be held responsible for (lack of) performance if it has

* Paper presented at the National Seminar on '*Educational Reforms*' organised by the Department of Culture, Govt. of India to commemorate 'Fifty Years of Indian Republic', at New Delhi on March 14-15, 2001.

not been given the requisite freedom to act. If a university is to be held accountable for the quality of its education, or the preparedness of its product (students), then it has to be given autonomy regarding essential matters like selection of staff, content of curricula, minimum standards to be achieved, and apportioning and utilisation of funds allotted to it. It is necessary to attain a balance between accountability and autonomy for, as Berdahl (1990) points out, "*too much autonomy might lead to universities unresponsive to society; too much accountability might destroy the necessary academic ethos*".

A related issue that is often raised while discussing the performance of teachers is that of 'academic freedom'. As Tight (1988) points out "*academic freedom refers to the freedom of individual academics to study, teach, research and publish without being subject to or causing undue interference*". It does not confer upon the academic community unfettered rights of action and behaviour. The concept of academic freedom enjoins that the teacher be allowed to express his views freely and openly, even though they may be at variance with the 'official' view, without fear of being penalised. However, the academic freedom does not extend to, for example, neglecting teaching assignments in favour of research interest. Academic freedom is a privilege that carries with it the responsibility of ensuring that it is used only for the welfare of the academic community and the good of the parent institution.

Autonomy of Indian Universities

About fifty years ago the Indian universities enjoyed considerable autonomy and the authority of the Vice Chancellor was not questioned. Over the years the autonomy has been considerably eroded largely because of financial restrictions and political interference in matters which should normally be considered to be the internal concern of the universities. To that extent the right of the government and society to hold the authorities of the universities responsible for happenings in the universities is reduced.

The concept of university autonomy has long been debated. Ashby (1966, p. 293) points out that "*the question as to what constitutes autonomy in universities is anything but unambiguous, and the patterns of autonomy which satisfy academics in different countries are very diverse*". The Gajendragadkar Committee Report (UGC, 1971, pp. 9-10) states, "*The concept of university autonomy is often misunderstood. It is not a 'legal concept', not even a 'constitutional concept'. It is an ethical concept and an academic concept. This concept does not question that, in a democratic society like ours, legislatures are ultimately sovereign, and have a right to discuss and determine the question of policy relating to education, including higher education..... The concept of university autonomy, however, means that it would be appropriate on the part of democratic legislatures not to interfere with the administration of university life, both academic and non-academic. The claim for autonomy is made by the universities not as a matter of privilege, but on the ground that such an autonomy is a condition precedent if the universities are to discharge their duties and obligations effectively and efficiently*".

Berdahl (1990) differentiates between two types of autonomy, substantive and procedural. Substantive autonomy is the power of the university or college in its corporate form to determine its own goals and programmes (the 'what' of academe). Procedural autonomy is the power of the university in its corporate form to determine the means by which its goals and programmes will be pursued (the 'how' of academe). It may be argued that government has the right, in consultation with academe, to impinge upon substantive autonomy in the interest of the people. The procedural autonomy of universities must, however, be safeguarded. A sharing of concerns by the universities and governments and a mutual understanding as to who will make which kinds of decisions is essential.

The erosion of autonomy of universities is due to two types of actions. First, the deliberate assumption of powers by the government through acts of legislature and even ordinances, and second, the extremely conservative interpretation of rules and guidelines by the bureaucracy, or the liberal use by it of provisions (in Acts) that have been provided for use in exceptional cases. Thus Acts have been passed that enable the government to give directives to the university, ordinances have been promulgated to provide that a Vice Chancellor shall hold office at the pleasure of the Chancellor or to curtail his term of appointment. Guidelines issued by the University Grants Commission have been treated by bureaucracy as directions with the strictest interpretations, and permissions for starting new colleges given indiscriminately without consulting the universities. It must, however, be admitted that Vice Chancellors and university bodies have, on occasions, given the government a reason to intervene by taking actions that placed a liability on the government. The crux of the matter is that accountability is inextricably linked with autonomy and if the universities are to be held accountable for happenings in the area of higher education then they must be given a reasonable amount of autonomy and a conducive environment in which to perform.

Role of Statutory Councils

The erosion in the autonomy of the universities is to an extent due to the actions of the numerous statutory councils that have been established to regulate the quality of professional education. These Councils have today become centres of authority. The University Grants Commission, established under the University Grants Commission Act, 1956, has the general duty of taking "in *consultation with the universities and other bodies concerned, all such steps as it may think fit for the promotion and coordination of university education and for the determination and maintenance of standards of teaching, examination and research in universities*". The functions and responsibilities of the universities are defined in the respective Acts of Parliament or State Legislature. The different statutory councils, established under Acts of Parliament, have been assigned functions and responsibilities generally relating to maintenance of standards that overlap those given to the universities. This often leads to situations in which the decisions of the Councils and the universities are at variance. The legal position is that Central Acts take precedence over the Acts of the States; and in case of overlap the provisions of the later Act supercede those of the earlier Acts. The net result is that the universities have lost their autonomy to a great extent.

The Association of Indian Universities recently undertook a survey (Association of Indian Universities, 1999) to assess the role and functioning of the various statutory councils and the impact of their decisions on autonomy of universities. In this context it may be mentioned that the statutory bodies are of two types: (a) those with both funding and regulatory powers relating to education, for example, the All India Council for Technical Education (AICTE) and National Council for Teacher Education (NCTE); (b) those with regulatory powers relating to education, that devolve largely from the need to maintain standards in the professions, including the Pharmacy Council of India, Indian Nursing Council, Bar Council of India, Dentists Council of India, Medical Council of India, Distance Education Council, Central Council for Homeopathy, Central Council of Indian Medicine, the Rehabilitation Council of India and the Veterinary Council of India. The consensus that emerged from the survey was that Councils tend to take unilateral actions without consulting the universities and without taking into account the decisions taken, and the notifications issued by the Councils often transgress upon the academic, developmental, and administrative autonomy of the universities. Particularly disturbing have been some decisions of the AICTE, the NCTE and the Councils controlling medical education of different categories. The notifications issued by the

Councils mainly relate to grant of permission to start new courses, fixation of norms and standards relating to academic infrastructural and viability requirements; prescribing of qualifications for teaching and other supporting staff; grant of admission; prescribing of minimum criteria for eligibility including those covering subjects to be offered, practical training and attendance, change in intake, curriculum and examination pattern. The autonomy and functioning of the universities is compromised because of delays in grant of approval to courses/ programmes, lack of transparency in the decision-making process, and indiscriminate grant of approval to start institutions and programmes without consulting the universities.

The consensus that emerged from the survey is that the Councils should confine themselves to the formulation of broad guidelines and leave the actual implementation of the guidelines to the universities. To be more specific:

- the Councils should have a better, and more realistic, appreciation of their roles and expectations of the academic community,
- the Councils should focus on broad policies and guidelines and leave it to the universities to take necessary action thereon,
- the Councils should work in consultation with the universities,
- the universities should be allowed to finalise details relating to intake, admission procedure and other matters, in accordance with local requirements, so long as the decisions are within the broad guidelines of the Councils, and
- the universities should be allowed to frame detailed syllabi, decide upon the mode of evaluation, and lay down policies for development of infrastructure within the framework of the guidelines of the Councils.

The Affiliation System and Autonomous Colleges

Many of the ills of Indian higher education can be attributed to the system of affiliation. Most conventional Indian universities are teaching-cum-affiliating; and some of the larger universities have more than 300 colleges affiliated to them. The colleges have common syllabi and the students appear for a common examination usually conducted at the end of the year. For many universities the conduct of examinations has become the most important administrative function. This limits the autonomy of the institution and the individual teacher, and teaching has to be along prescribed lines.

The affiliating system was devised to regulate and standardise the quality of education. But with the tremendous increase in the number of institutions the system has become counter-productive. Because of it some sub-standard colleges serenely ride piggy-back on the reputation of the mother institution. The affiliating system is a drag on the better institutions that would otherwise regularly revise and update their curricula and introduce innovative programmes. In order to allow the growth of colleges that have the desire to move ahead the concept of autonomous colleges was introduced about a decade back. It allows the college to have autonomy as regards academic matters. However, not many institutions have sought the autonomous status, their present number being about 120. Managements, teachers and students all look upon this innovation with suspicion. There is clearly a need for dialogue amongst all concerned so that a conducive environment can be created. Many educationists feel that the programme of granting autonomy to the colleges needs to be vigorously pursued, even to the extent of making every college autonomous and responsible for itself (Powar, 1997).

Realising the difficulties faced by good institutions in revising syllabi, evolving methods of teaching and learning, or introducing innovative programmes, the concept of autonomous colleges was adopted in the National Policy on Education, 1986. It was visualised that by the end of Seventh Five Year Plan (1990) there would be about 500 such autonomous colleges. But as of today there are only some 120-odd colleges. The functioning of the autonomous colleges has been studied at NIEPA (Sudha Rao, 1999, Sudha Rao *et al.*, 1999). The study yields a positive picture. Most of the colleges have been successful in remobilising community support, have undertaken meaningful extension and some research activities, restructured their courses, introduced examination reforms (including semester system, internal assessment, continuous evaluation), ensured accountability of teachers, and implemented UGC guidelines regarding administration and management. However, Thangamuthu (1993) has drawn attention to the lop-sided spatial distribution of the colleges (practically all of them are in the southern states of India and are privately managed). The government colleges (or the governments) are evidently lukewarm to this innovation. It has to be studied why most colleges are unwilling to apply for autonomous status. One reason that is often cited is the unwillingness of teachers to shoulder extra responsibility. Thangamuthu is of the view that the teacher unions feel that the autonomous colleges would become elitist institutions and thus help perpetuate inequity. Another fear is that autonomy gives undue strength (power) to the managements. Whatever the reason the reluctance of colleges to take up autonomous status must be researched into, otherwise an excellent innovation could become ineffective (Powar, 2000).

Conclusion

It is unfortunate that in the fiftieth year of the Republic the Indian higher education system is in a state of inertia. Many of its ills are directly attributable to the centralisation of the decision-making process. It is essential the universities be granted autonomy to take crucial decisions that are necessary for them to meet stated objectives. More precisely the autonomy that they enjoyed in the past but which has eroded over the years has to be restored. Flexibility and quick decision-making is essential in the modern world. If the autonomy is not restored the universities will not be able to deliver education of required quality and relevance. However, it has to be emphasised that the autonomy will have to be complemented by accountability.

References

Ashby, E., (1966), *Universities, British, Indian, African,* Harvard University Press, Cambridge.

Association of Indian Universities, (1999), *The Diminishing Autonomy of Indian Universities*, AIU Report No. 1/99, AIU, New Delhi.

Berdahl, R., (1990), Academic Freedom, Autonomy and Accountability in British Universities, *Studies in Higher Education*, 13(2): 169-180.

Powar, K.B., (1997), *Higher Education in India Since Independence: Retrospect and Future Options*, AIU Occasional Paper, 97/1. AIU, New Delhi.

Powar, K.B., (2000), *Reforms and Innovations in Higher Education in India: The Relevance and Role of Research*, AIU Occasional Paper 2000/1. AIU, New Delhi.

Sarup, A., (1993), University Autonomy and Accountability, *Journal of Higher Education*, 16(2): 163-171.

Sudha Rao, K., (1999), *Management of Autonomy in Autonomous Colleges*, NIEPA-Vikas Publishing House, New Delhi.

Sudha Rao, K., Mathew, G., and Samanray, S.K., (1999), *Autonomous and Non-autonomous Colleges: Selected Case Studies*, NIEPA-Vikas Publishing House, New Delhi.

Thangamuthu, (1993), Autonomy for Colleges: The Vision and the Reality, *Journal of Higher Education*, 16(2): 273-282.

Tight, M., (1988), So What is Academic Freedom? in Tight, M., (Editor) *Academic Freedom and Responsibility*, Open University Press, Milton Keynes, U.K.

University Grants Commission, (1971), *Report of the Committee on the Governance of Universities and Colleges (Gajendragadkar Committee Report)*, UGC, New Delhi.

10

Accountability in Indian Higher Education*

Introduction

Traditionally a university has had a special place in society, commanding respect and enjoying a considerable measure of freedom. This is especially true for India where learning is held in high esteem and a teacher accorded reverential treatment. Until a few decades ago a very small proportion of youth, mainly from privileged families, entered the portals of a university, and the money contributed for its maintenance by the public exchequer was relatively inconspicuous. Society did not expect much in terms of returns and the universities led an 'ivory tower' existence being largely unconcerned about their surroundings. The situation has, however, changed. The common man has realised that the professional skills and knowledge gained through university education provide means for possible upward economic and social mobility. Moreover, the government is acutely conscious of the fact that it provides the bulk of the finance required by the universities and has hence started exerting controls and making demands. We now have a situation wherein the actions and performances of universities are being closely scrutinised both by the government and the people. The academic community has (grudgingly) accepted the fact that the people have a right to know and judge its performance. The Gnanam Committee Report (UGC, 1990, p. 224) acknowledges, "*It (society) is entitled to demand that the members of the academic community individually and collectively be made accountable in concrete, visible terms*". However, mere acceptance of the concept of accountability does not mean much. Ways and means will have to be found by which the system of accountability can be implemented effectively and fairly.

* Background paper for the AIU Annual Seminar on '*Accountability in Higher Education*' organised at University of Poona, Pune on November 12, 1994.

What is Accountability?

In the simplest form accountability means the requirement to demonstrate reasonable actions to some external constituency or agency (Berdahl, 1990). In the case of the universities this external constituency is, broadly speaking, 'society', and more specifically 'government'. In view of the (usually) complex relationship between governments and universities the process of demonstrating and judging accountability can be both difficult and frustrating. It is necessary to appreciate the fact that the main purpose of an accountability system is not to demonstrate that things are being done (or not being done) but to facilitate the process of improvement of performance. The accountability system should not result in a feeling of failure but should generate a sense of responsibility.

Accountability has two aspects — moral and legal or contractual (Wagner, 1989). Moral accountability is based upon a sense of responsibility, a feeling that one is responsible to one's clients (students and parents), to colleagues and to oneself. Legal accountability is being responsible to one's employer in terms of fulfillment of terms of employment. It is possible to satisfy legal responsibility yet not live up to moral responsibility. A teacher may take his classes according to schedule but in a disinterested manner, fulfilling the requirements of legal accountability but not of moral accountability. An official may, likewise, 'work' eight hours a day, merely forwarding files to his superior without contributing to decision-making. An accountability-evaluation system must be able to shift the emphasis from legal accountability to moral accountability.

In view of the practical implications it is necessary to analyse the meaning (and concept) of accountability. Wagner (1989) discusses two alternatives. Firstly, accountability may be taken as an obligation to give an account (of one's performance) in the form of a report or some other form of exposition. Secondly, it may mean being answerable for one's actions. Governments would probably prefer the latter alternative. In fact both forms of accountability are being practised in our universities to a limited extent. Annual reports and budgets are presented to senates and courts for their approval. And university managements are often grilled on actions and decisions during 'interpellation' in the 'question-hour' of senate meetings.

If the main purpose of an accountability system is to ensure 'minimum performance' and enhance the quality of higher education then accountability-assessment procedures will have to be more rigorous, and the report will have to include recommendations on corrective action.

The Domains of Accountability

The accountability of a university can be discussed with respect to its administrative, academic and finance-related actions. Corresponding to these we have three types of accountability — administrative, academic and financial. Administrative accountability relates to the managerial functions that are necessary for the smooth functioning of the university and its various sub-systems. Academic accountability is concerned with the implementation of academic programmes and the achieving of minimum standards of education. Financial accountability deals with the procurement of funds and efficient utilisation of resources. In all these domains of accountability it should be possible to identify expected levels of attainment. A university should be able to achieve the following:

A. *In Administrative Matters*

- adhere to reasonable norms of administrative efficiency as regards correspondence, movement of files and solving of routine problems,
- take timely decisions at appropriate levels,
- adhere to a pre-determined schedule of meetings of various bodies and committees,
- conduct examinations and declare results according to pre-determined and pre-announced schedule,
- provide adequate student-support services like students' hostels, canteens, and sports facilities,
- adequately maintain the university campus and provide basic facilities to residents, and
- strictly adhere to norms while making appointments to faculty positions or admitting students.

B. *In Academic Matters*

- start academic terms on time, conduct regular teaching activities, and complete pre-determined, minimum days of actual teaching,
- monitor quality assurance activities including updating and revision of curricula,
- provide adequate laboratory and library facilities,
- provide basic research facilities to faculty members and research scholars, and

- promote human resource development programmes such as the orientation and training of teachers and preparation of students for various competitive examinations.

C. *In Financial Matters*

- prepare in time budget estimates on the basis of a careful evaluation of essential and developmental requirements of various departments and units,
- monitor income and expenditure and ensure that expenditure is phased out over the entire year,
- ensure that orders are placed and expenditure incurred according to set procedures and norms,
- ensure that expenditure statements are presented and audited in time,
- ensure that external audit is conducted annually and the suggestions/observations are acted upon,
- ensure that mandatory deductions such as those of provident fund and income tax are made regularly and the deducted amounts remitted to the designated fund or authority, and
- ensure that surplus funds or endowment funds are invested according to sanctioned norms and procedures in order to get maximum returns.

Conclusion

In keeping with the demands of the times, and the mood of the government, the universities will have to face the question of accountability squarely. There are some areas and segments in which improvements are urgently required, and these are possible. In others the shortcomings are a part of the national malaise. It is necessary to analyse and determine what can be done under the prevailing conditions. Norms of determining minimum performance in essential areas need to be drawn up. The performance of a university, however, cannot be judged only on the basis of attainment or non-fulfillment of minimum norms. A university is a highly complex organisation charged with a variety of responsibilities, many of them not well-defined. Its contribution to social, economic, scientific and technological development through research, to national integration through cultural activities, to development of sportsmanship and camaraderie through sporting activities, and to moral development and character-building through value-education programmes cannot be measured in tangible terms. A holistic approach may ultimately prove to be most realistic.

References

Berdahl, R., (1990), Academic Freedom, Autonomy and Accountability in British Universities, *Studies in Higher Education*, 15(2): 169-180.

University Grants Commission, (1990), *Towards New Educational Management*, (Gnanam Committee Report), UGC, New Delhi, pp. 384.

Wagner R.B., (1989), *Accountability in Education: A Philosophical Enquiry*, Routledge, London, pp. 156.

11

Environmental Studies in Indian Universities*

Introduction

In recent years there has been a growing concern in India regarding the steady deterioration in the country's environment. Unplanned development, rapid industrialisation and unprecedented growth in population (with its accompanying poverty and deprivation) are recognised as being the main causes of environmental degradation. The government both at the centre and in the states are seized of the problem and have passed legislations to preserve ecology and prevent pollution. However, bureaucratic indifference and general public apathy have not helped the cause. A number of voluntary (non-government) organisations and individuals have raised their voices and expressed concern about unplanned development. Some commendable efforts have also been made to assess the current state of the country's environment, spread awareness amongst the masses, and implement programmes of eco-protection and eco-restoration. The efforts are, however, far short of requirements. The universities and other institutions of higher education have contributed in bits and pieces but their efforts have been largely uncoordinated. It is not illogical that many expect the universities, as generators, repositories and transferors of knowledge, to make a larger and more meaningful contribution.

Global Concern: Historical Perspective and Imperatives

Global concern regarding the steadily deteriorating state of the environment was first seriously manifested in the form of the United Nations Conference on Human Environment, held in Stockholm, in June 1972. It focused attention on the dangers posed to the quality of human life, and to survival itself, by continuous degradation of ecological assets and by pollution due to industrial effluents. It tried to find ways by

* Updated version of background paper for the AIU National Seminar on '*Environmental Challenges and the Universities*', University of Delhi, Delhi,, December 20, 1993.

which the precious environment could be preserved. The conference highlighted the divergence in the viewpoints of the developed and developing nations. As Sandbrook (1992) pointed out it was "*a dialogue of the deaf between the rich and the poor*". For the rich developed nations, the main concern was the cleaning up of the "*effluence of affluence*". They advocated that the cleaning up be taken up by all nations simultaneously so that the additional cost of cleaning operations should not place any country at a disadvantage in a competitive international market. For the developing world, seeking the fruits of industrialisation, pollution was relatively unimportant, the first priority being the alleviation of poverty. As Indira Gandhi tersely pointed out "*of all the pollution we face the worst is poverty*". The Stockholm Conference opened the eyes of the North to the problems of the South. It also saw the adaptation of rules and regulations to cover environmental ills — at least in the developed countries. More importantly it led to the establishment of the United Nations Environment Programme (UNEP).

The World Commission on Environment and Development (Brundtland Commission) was established in December 1983, and it presented in 1987 a remarkable report Our Common Future (World Commission on Environment and Development, 1987) which "*tried to balance the arguments concerning north/south responsibility and suggest ways forward*". It concluded that "*if we continue to use up natural resources as we do at present, if we ignore the plight of the poor, then we can (only) expect a decline in the quality of life (op.cit)*". The Brandtland Report suggested that the concept of sustainable development should become an acceptable principle of both national and international development and policies, and that national governments should begin a systematic integration of economic and environmental considerations. Sustainable development was described as "*development that seeks to meet the needs and aspirations of the present generation without compromising the ability to meet those of future generations*".

The very significant conclusions of the Brundtland Report were extensively discussed and a debate in the United Nations, in 1989, led to the UN Conference on Environment and Development, better known as 'Earth Summit 92', at Rio de Janeiro, Brazil, in June 1992. At this conference a comprehensive and far-reaching programme for sustainable development was agreed upon in the form of *Agenda 21* comprising of 38 chapters. Chapter 36 envisages the United Nations undertaking a comprehensive review of its educational programmes including training and public awareness. It calls upon countries to support university and other tertiary activities and networks for environment and development education; establish national or regional centres of excellence in inter-disciplinary research in environmental and developmental sciences; promote cooperative research and information sharing and dissemination; and promote all kinds of adult and continuing education programmes in environment and development. It recommends that programmes at post-graduate level should include specific courses aiming at further training of decision-makers.

At Rio it was clear that all countries are today committed to the protection of the environment and to the principle of sustainable development.

The road beyond Rio has been far from smooth. There is dichotomy in North-South thinking on almost all-important matters related to environment. Five years after Rio (Rio + 5), at a meeting of the Commission on Sustainable Development, held in April 1997, representatives of different countries virtually agreed to disagree about everything previously agreed to. Doubts are today being expressed about *Agenda 21* itself. Mercifully, however, there is unanimity about the importance of environmental education and the need to promote it enthusiastically.

Role of Universities

The universities have an important role to play in generating public awareness, protecting the environment and promoting sustainable development. As John Berry (1993) succinctly puts it "*.... universities are the best source of expertise to conduct the necessary research and guide the development of policy framework. They are also the training ground for the next generation of society's leaders who need to be educated regardless of their discipline, with a broad and sensitive understanding of the issues*". This is particularly true for India where the universities are charged with the responsibility of undertaking teaching, research and extension activities. The role of universities was discussed at a conference on 'University Action for Sustainable Development' held at Dalhousie University, Halifax, Canada in December 1991, and which was attended by 33 Vice Chancellors and Presidents from 10 countries. The Declaration issued at the end of the conference emphasises that "*universities and their graduates must be significant actors if (human) demands (upon the planets) are to be shaped into sustainable and equitable forms necessary for a wholesome future environment*". The Halifax Declaration (IAU/UNU/AUCC/DU, 1992) asked the universities to:

- "Ensure that the voice of the university is clear and uncompromising in its ongoing commitment to the principle and practice of sustainable development within the university, and at the local, national and global levels,
- Utilise the intellectual resources of the university to encourage a better understanding on the part of society of the inter-related physical, biological and social dangers facing the planet Earth,
- Emphasise the ethical obligation of the present generation to overcome those current malpractices of resource utilization and those widespread circumstances of intolerable human disparity which lie at the root of environmental unsustainability,
- Establish whatever programmes are necessary within the university to generate the capability and the capacity necessary to develop appropriate environmental technologies and practices as well as to diminish environmental illiteracy and enhance ethical awareness on the part of faculty, students, and the public at large,
- Cooperate with one another and with all segments of society in the pursuit of practical, effective revision and reversals of those current practices which contribute to environmental degradation, to South-North disparities and to inter-generational inequity,
- Employ all channels open to the university to communicate these undertakings to UNCED, to governments and to the public at large".

Society in India, and especially in its rural areas, looks up to the academic community to provide information and guidance. The universities should, therefore, not hesitate to assume the responsibility of making objective assessments, suggesting remedial measures, contributing to attitudinal and policy changes, and more generally in educating the masses in matters relating to the environment. It is perhaps relevant that the Supreme Court, in a judgement passed in November 1991, asserted that the universities and colleges should consider the feasibility of making environment a compulsory subject at each level of college education.

The Indian universities can play an important role in meeting environmental challenges by undertaking the following activities:

A *In Teaching*

a. by 'greening' of undergraduate programmes by incorporating in the syllabi topics on natural environment, socio-cultural environment, demography and human development,

b. by introducing at the Master's level environment-specific courses/papers in each subject e.g., environmental management, or environmental legislation,

c. by starting, specialist courses leading to qualifications in environmental aspects, e.g., Master's in Environmental Sciences, or Environmental Management or Environmental Engineering,

d. by developing 'certificate' and 'diploma' programmes on different aspects of environment, especially for the lay-public, and

e. by designing short courses on environment management and conservation of resources, essentially for managers.

B *In Research*

a. by undertaking, at M.Phil and Ph.D levels, research on environmental problems emphasising the inter-disciplinary approach,

b. by undertaking surveys aimed at obtaining multi-faceted information on areas that are relevant to sustainable development,

c. by encouraging consultancy services related to pollution-control and eco-protection or eco-development, and

d. by developing data banks on natural resources, eco-systems, industries for future use.

C *In Extension*

a. by undertaking programmes aimed at raising public awareness about the environment, and

b. by involving its students, through NSS and similar activities, in programmes of eco-development like aforestation and water-conservation.

It may hardly be emphasised that environment-friendly atmosphere must exist on the university and college campuses. Sound environment policies and practices, on the part of the administration, will go a long way in influencing and motivating all sections of the university community — students, teachers and administrative staff.

Status of Environmental Studies in Indian Universities

Teaching programmes on the environment were initiated in India, in 1976, when the Jawaharlal Nehru University started a Masters programme in Environmental Science. The University of Madras introduced, in 1984, a course in Environmental Toxicology. The Bharatidasan University started the second Masters programme in

Environmental Science in 1984. The Pondicherry University joined in 1987 with a Masters programme in Ecology and Shivaji University started a Masters programme in Environment the same year. Awareness of the need to teach Environmental issues quickly spread and by 1992 five universities were offering Masters programme in Environmental Engineering, fourteen in Environmental Science, two in Ecology, and two in Environmental Management. In addition many universities had special papers on environmental aspects in at least one subject in the science faculty (Powar, 1994). Today about 50 universities are offering Masters programme in environment including environmental science, environmental engineering, environmental management, ecology, forestry and wildlife (see Sharma, 2000). Approaches, curricula and thrust may differ depending upon the expertise available in the university. As Sharma (*op. cit.)* points out there are three approaches towards environment education at the tertiary level. These are the:

- *Holistic approach* wherein all aspects related to environment are included in the curricula e.g., programme in Environmental Studies;
- *Stream approach* wherein the curricula is restricted to a broad sub-area of Environmental Science or Environmental Engineering; and
- *Sector approach* wherein activities are confined to that aspect of the environment in which the department has expertise, e.g., Environmental Geology.

While the sectoral approach can be adopted by every department of a university the stream and holistic approaches require an 'umbrella type' organisation in which inter-disciplinary teaching and research is called for.

It is heartening that research on environmental aspects is being taken up in universities on a large scale, and that most research projects underway have an inter-disciplinary base and adequate financial support is available from government agencies. The environmental scenario in the universities is encouraging.

Conclusion

As human society begins the third millennium AD, one of its major concerns is that of protecting the natural environment. The problem has, however, to be viewed in the context of meeting the immediate needs of a steadily increasing population, through developmental programmes that inevitably scar the environment. Evidently the only alternative appears to be the adoption of programmes of eco-restoration and sustainable development but these are not easy to implement. They would require a coordinated effort on the part of all sections of society. The universities have a crucial role to play by educating people at all levels, conducting research, making objective assessments and advising on policy matters. The problems are many and will have to be tackled with a sense of urgency. A concerted effort with a mission-mode is called for and there is confidence that the universities will take up the challenge.

Reference

Berry, J, (1993), Canadian Universities: Responding to the Challenges of the '90s, *ACU Bull.Curr Doc., No.107*, pp. 2-8.

IAU/UNU/AUCC/DU, (1992), Universities and Sustainable Development: The Halifax Declaration, *ACU Bull Curr.Doc. No.104* (June 1992), pp. 18-19.

Powar, K.B., (1994), Environmental Issues and Universities in Powar, K.B (Editor), *Environmental Challenges and the Universities,* AIU, New Delhi.

Sandbrook. P, (1992). From Stockholm to Rio, in *'Earth Summit' '90.* Regency Press Corp., London, pp. 15-16.

Sharma, C.B.S.R., (2000), Higher Education in Ecology and Environment in India, in Pathan, A.M. and Thigale, S.S. (Editors), *Contributions to Environmental Geosciences*, Aravali Books International, New Delhi, pp. 219-244.

World Commission on Environment and Development, (1987), *Our Common Future*, Oxford University Press, Delhi.

12

Internationalisation of Indian Higher Education*

Introduction

The process of globalisation, which has been accelerated by the advent of free-market economy, and by the remarkable developments in communication technology, has changed the character of higher education in many countries. It has led to internationalisation of higher education, which has been defined by Knight and de Wit (*cf.* de Wit, 1999) as *"the process of integrating an international/intercultural dimension into the teaching, research and service functions of the institution"*. It is to be understood as being a response to globalisation and incorporates both international and local events. Internationalisation of higher education is reflected in increased student mobility, in universities offering off-shore programmes and establishing foreign campuses, and in twinning arrangements between institutions covering teaching, training and research.

Internationalisation of higher education is today being promoted in all countries because of the academic, social, political and economic advantages that accrue from it. It promotes values and culture, generates goodwill, enriches the teaching-learning process and thereby enhances the quality of education, encourages competitiveness and helps generate financial resources. One may add that internationalisation of higher education is now a fact of life that cannot be neglected (Powar and Bhalla, 2000).

Promotion of 'Internationalisation'

Meaningful internationalisation of Indian higher education can be achieved by:

- Encouraging student inflow from both developed and developing countries.

* Paper presented at the AIU Roundtable *on 'Internationalisation of Indian Higher Education'* organised at the University of Mysore, Mysore on February 26-28, 2001.

- Making available academic programmes overseas and establishing off-shore campuses.
- Establishing institutional linkages.

In this respect the Indian universities can learn from the experience of universities from developed countries, particularly the United Kingdom and Australia. There is a need to:

- advertise and promote (e.g. through educational fairs) the 'educational wares' of Indian universities to attract international students,
- offer through off-shore centres programmes leading to diplomas and degrees in the professional areas for students in the under-developed and developing countries,
- offer 'virtual programmes' in specialised areas via the internet,
- promote student mobility by adopting credit-transfer mechanisms, and emphasising the importance of international experience in higher education,
- add international components to existing academic curricula, and develop special academic programmes for international students, and
- establish institutional linkages with universities abroad.

Encouraging International Students to Study in India

The most obvious manifestation of internationalisation is the presence of international (often referred to as 'foreign') students on university campuses. They contribute a great deal to the academic and cultural environment of a campus. As Altbach (1989) states, "*Foreign students are amongst the most visible aspects of the internationalisation of higher education. They are a concrete manifestation of the ways in which the knowledge network functions*". He adds, "*Foreign students and scholars are one of the most important elements of the international knowledge system.... They are the 'carriers' of knowledge across borders. ...They are the embodiment of the cosmopolitan culture....(and they) are one of the most visible and important parts of the world wide exchange of ideas*". And further, "*Foreign students and scholars are a key part of academic life....(They) constitute an important academic resource in that they provide valuable expertise and a cross-cultural perspective*".

Young people, from different countries, may have varying reasons for wanting to go abroad. Students of developing countries aspire to join foreign universities in order to avail of advanced facilities for enhancing their knowledge and skills. Their preferred areas of study are science, engineering, medicine and management. Students of the developed countries largely seek to learn a language, or study social conditions, or have an insight into the arts and culture. However, all students wish to broaden their vision, develop friendships, learn about history and culture, and generally imbibe the spirit of internationalism.

The Indian Approach

Traditionally, India has welcomed the presence of students and scholars in India. Though many international students are to be seen on the campuses of our metropolitan universities, India has not adopted any well-defined policy regarding them. The Indian government has been supporting the education of international students in a selective way through the award of scholarships administered by the Indian Council for Cultural Relations. Self-financing students can seek admission to programmes in the liberal arts, and to a limited extent to some professional courses. However, there is the need to take active steps to promote international education. India should take advantage of the high academic reputation enjoyed internationally by some of its institutions of higher education and should open them to students of other countries, to a greater extent, for the following reasons:

- India has the second largest network of higher education in the world and the third largest reserve of scientific and technical manpower. It can be a haven for students of the developing countries who would prefer to come to India because the education and maintenance costs are low compared to the western countries, English is the medium of instruction in higher education, the cultural environment is similar to that in their home countries, and the higher education that they would receive in India is relevant to the needs of their countries.
- International students of today turn out to be most effective ambassadors of our culture, ideals and thoughts. National interest can be effectively served by having persons in decision-making positions, in other countries, who during their sojourn in India have learnt to appreciate our ways and methods, and have developed personal relationships with our citizens.
- With an increased base of individually supported international students there will be a positive incentive for our institutions to maintain and improve standards of performance.
- International students, if charged differential fees (equivalent to the actual cost of education, or a little higher), will help in generating financial resources required for maintaining and improving infra-structural facilities of our educational institutions. The additional funds can be used to partially offset the fees being charged to Indian

students. The international students will contribute to our national economy through other spending during their stay.

- The presence of international students on our campuses will broaden the horizons of Indian students by exposing them to their counterparts from other countries. The international students will promote cultural and intellectual enrichment and foster mutual understanding.
- Providing admission to international students means an opportunity for Indian students and faculty to interact with bright and innovative students from a different background, and this could contribute to the development of arts, culture, humanities, sciences and technologies.
- Internationalisation of our higher education institutions will be in keeping with the growing internationalisation of higher education worldwide.

International Students in India: Present Position

Presently international students from about 100 countries are pursuing various undergraduate, postgraduate and research programmes in India (*see* Powar *et al.*, 1997: Powar and Bhalla, 2000). These students can be categorised as follows:

- Government of India supported students,
- Self-financing students,
- Students sponsored by foreign governments and/or funding agencies such as the World Bank, Asian Development Bank, United Nations Development Project, African Development Bank,
- Casual students and students coming under inter-university bilateral agreements, and
- Children of Non-Resident Indians and expatriate Indians.

The countries that provide international students to India can be broadly grouped as:

- The developed countries that are technologically advanced and economically strong, and have good facilities for higher education and training (e.g. USA, UK, Canada, Australia, countries of the European Union, Japan), but send students for studying sociological, economic and cultural aspects (as also Music, Visual Arts, and Performing Arts), and
- The less-developed and developing countries (SAARC countries and the countries of Southeast Asia, Western Asia and Africa) where facilities for education, not only in the professional courses such as

engineering, medicine and management, but also in science, humanities, social sciences, commerce and law, are inadequate.

The students from developed countries come to India largely for programmes in India Studies and Performing Arts, and include Government of India scholars and self-financing students. The number of such students is, however, quite small. It is the non-resident Indians (NRIs) and expatriates from USA, Canada, UK and other countries, who come to India in larger numbers as self-financing students in private medical and engineering colleges. It is not because the facilities for education in these disciplines are not available in the countries in which they live, or of which they are citizens, but because education in these disciplines is cheaper in India than in the countries of their residence. Moreover, getting admission to these professional courses in Indian institutions is easier because of reservations for NRIs.

International students from developing countries come for higher education in India in practically every discipline: from humanities, social sciences, law, commerce and science to engineering, technology, medicine, management studies and agriculture. It is the students from the developing countries that constitute the majority (about 95%) of international students seeking higher education in India.

Information related to the number of international students studying in Indian universities during the period 1992-93 to 1998-99 has been given by Powar and Bhalla (2000). It represents data collected by the Association of Indian Universities. Shortage of returns on information could account for the numbers being less by about 10-15%. It reveals that:

- More than 95% international students in India come from the developing countries of Asia and Africa. The countries sending the most students are Bangladesh, Nepal and Kenya (about 500 each), followed by Sri Lanka, Sudan, Ethiopia and Mauritius (over 250 each).
- There was a steady increase in the number of international students coming to India during the early 1990's with a peak of over 13,000 being achieved in 1993-94. A noted decrease occurred in 1995-96 and by the end of 2000 the number had approximately halved.
- During the 1990's there has been a significant decrease in the number of students from Western Asia, South Asia and Northern Africa. The countries from which decreasing number of students are being received are Kenya, Jordan, Kuwait, Afghanistan, Iran, Somalia, Malaysia, UK and Sudan.

- During the same period the only countries that have contributed an increased number of students are Indonesia, Uganda and Mauritius.
- International students prefer to join educational institutions located in and around the metropolitan cities like Delhi, Mumbai, Chennai and Pune, except when they are admitted to professional courses offered by colleges located in smaller towns.
- The international student population in India is not equally distributed throughout the country or in various disciplines. The students prefer the western (especially Maharashtra) and southern parts of India.
- The fall in number of students is reflected in a substantial drop in number in some universities, e.g. in Dr Babasaheb Ambedkar Marathwada University from 1003 in 1992-93 to 51 in 1998-99 and the Manipal Academy of Higher Education from 1477 in 1993-94 to 85 in 1998-99.
- The only university that has registered an increase is the University of Delhi, where the number has risen from 872 in 1992-93 to 1402 in 1998-99.

Suggested Measures for Facilitating Student Inflow

The data presented in the previous section presents a discouraging picture. It is disappointing that while most developed countries are attracting increasing number of students from the developing countries the number of international students in India is going down. In order to make Indian universities more attractive to international students a variety of improvements are necessary, and some of them are enumerated below.

Developmental

Strengthening of Infrastructure

Universities and institutions which decide to enrol international students on their campuses need to build up a good infrastructure in the form of good lecture halls, well-equipped laboratories, adequate library resources, facilities for sports, amenities for social and cultural life, recreation facilities and, above all, special hostel facilities. For institutions offering specialised, short-term programmes for a group of foreign students from the developed countries, it would be advisable to develop a separate complex with classrooms, sectional library and computer unit, so that the international students can study in an environment comparable to that obtained in their home countries.

Administrative

Streamlining Admission Procedures

In order to attract international students, the procedure of making admissions of international students has to be simplified. They should not be made to proceed from one office to another, or to stand in long queues. There should be a single window system.

Creating Additional Seats

It is the considered opinion of many that our higher education institutions should not take international students at the expense of local students. It should be possible for every institution to create a certain percentage of additional seats, say 10%, for which no extra academic staff is required. According to Lavakare *et al.* (1995), if 10% additional seats are created in an IIT for international students, about Rs 3.6 million may accrue in foreign exchange which would constitute about 15% to 17% of its annual budget.

Charging Economic Fees

Most developed countries have adopted a system of differential fees for international students. The fee amounts to at least the actual unit cost of education, and usually even more. In India, the cost of higher education is heavily subsidised, usually by the state, and international students are subsidised to the same extent as the local students. If international students are to be inducted into the higher education system, a reasonable fee structure based upon the unit cost of education has to be worked out.

Providing Incentives to Institutions

In order to offer sufficient incentive to higher education institutions, it is recommended that the central and the state governments should permit the institutions to utilise the money earned as fees for the development of the institutions in any manner they like without that amount being deducted from their budget.

Academic

Internationalisation of the Curriculum

The highest priority has to be given to the modernisation of the curriculum. This implies not only the incorporation of the latest in terms of knowledge and skill components but also the diversification of the contents to give an international dimension to the programme on offer. It is necessary that, at least at the Master's level, the curricula contain information on different regions of the world, especially Europe, Africa and Southeast Asia.

Establishing Linkages with Institutions in other Countries

It should be realised that, by definition, international education is a two-way process. For the successful internationalisation of an institution it is necessary to establish partnerships with institutions in both the developed and the developing countries with a view to facilitating faculty and student exchanges and undertaking joint research projects. Students and scholars from foreign universities constitute an important academic resource by providing a cross-cultural perspective.

Making Provision for English Language Courses

Students coming from Arab countries, Iran, Afghanistan, countries of the CIS, Thailand, Korea, China, Japan, more often than not have inadequate knowledge of the English language. It is necessary that, for enabling such students to keep pace with the regular courses and averting their dropping out, special English classes for international students are conducted for the first few months, or even the first year. This can be done in a systematic manner if an English Language Cell is created as a part of the International Centre, and the necessary academic staff is provided.

Academic Restructuring

It has to be appreciated that internationalisation of education does not only mean making available full-time degree and diploma programmes. It also includes giving an opportunity to students to have an international experience by way of short-term visits. In fact, most student mobility programmes visualise a visit of one semester or one year. To facilitate this Indian universities need to make their academic structures more flexible and internationally-oriented. It is essential that the universities introduce examination reforms, adopt credit-based system of grading, and adopt credit-transfer mechanisms. As of today a foreign student can come to India for a semester and get credit for his work, for foreign universities do recognise the work put in elsewhere. On the other hand, a short-term study by an Indian student does not gain any credit for him, for his efforts cannot be recognised under the structure of Indian universities.

Governmental Action

Policy Formulation

Unlike some of the advanced English-speaking countries, particularly USA, UK, Canada and Australia which have made concerted efforts to attract international students, India has done little to market its education. It is necessary to finalise a national policy and adopt consistent strategies that would encourage Indian institutions in the matter of admitting international students. Properly implemented, a policy encouraging international students to come to India will surely achieve the dual objectives of furthering good relations and generating financial resources. It is encouraging that the government is seriously examining ways and means to facilitate the promotion of Indian higher education abroad. For this purpose it is in the process of constituting a Committee for the Promotion of Indian Education Abroad (CoPIE).

Simplification of Visa Procedures

Many international students complain of the difficulties they are to face in obtaining visa and particularly in visa-extension. Within the existing legal framework it should be possible to simplify procedures relating to registration, entry-test requirement and issue of No Objection Certificates. A more liberal interpretation of legal requirements would be helpful. In substance, the Government of India should look into these problems and should take steps to see that the entry of international students is simpler with decisions taken in time. In order to create a hospitable environment the possibility of liberalising internal travel formalities could be considered by the Ministry of Home Affairs.

Open-door Policy for Self-financing Students

Under the present governmental policy, dictated in part by the apex court, educational institutions are permitted to admit a limited percentage of students to educational programmes in technical and professional fields. There is a need for serious re-thinking in this matter. Liberalising the limits relating to the number of international students, and removal of other constraints presently being faced by international students, are matters that should be addressed on a priority basis.

Strengthening Information and Counselling Services

It is necessary to strengthen the data and information base so that prospective students abroad can obtain information relating to academic programmes available at different universities, eligibility criteria, admission procedures, and tuition fees. Apex organisations should be asked to create web-sites for this purpose and these could be linked to a central education web-site. The Indian embassies and high commissions need to establish suitable counselling units. Such counselling can be undertaken by the nodal aency within the country through e-mail.

Promoting Indian Higher Education Abroad

Indian universities can internationalise their operation by establishing campuses abroad, or by offering distance education programmes through off-shore centres.

Establishment of a campus abroad requires careful planning and assessment of requirements. It entails the finding of suitable partners, securing of government permissions and considerable financial commitment. It may also require the detailing of senior academic staff, from the home campus, for duties abroad. Perhaps private institutions, that have the required flexibility of operations, may be better suited for this type of internationalisation. The Manipal Academy of Higher Education, Manipal and the Birla Institute of Technology and Science, Pilani have already ventured out in this field. Their experience should be valuable.

For most Indian universities 'internationalisation' could involve offering through the distance mode, and with the help of off-shore centres, of academic programmes that are essentially the same as those offered on the home campuses. The UK Open University and Open Learning Australia have successfully internationalised their operations and offered programmes essentially developed for domestic learners. The operational strategy has been described as *Fordist* (Raggat, 1993) for the courses first chosen were foundation courses and undergraduate courses, covering a small range, the learning material for which could be produced on a mass volume basis and offered over a period of time. With low cost of production the Indian universities could well afford a *Neo-Fordist* or *Post-Fordist* strategy aimed at meeting specific requirements. The present courses could be modified to suit the requirements of different regions and cultures (East Africa, Gulf Countries, SE Asia) but with teaching materials being produced in smaller numbers. The recent advances in printing and communication technologies should allow this. The needs of wards of Indian citizens working abroad may require the provision of conventional undergraduate degree programmes. However, it may be better to concentrate on professional programmes aimed at skill-development and updating of knowledge (Powar, 1997). With rapid developments in technology, and the consequent continuous decrease in the half-life periods of equipment, continued education needs to be fostered. Moreover, the emergence of India as a super-power in the area of software technology makes 'virtual classes' through the internet an attractive proposition.

Internationalisation of distance education programmes holds much promise. Needless to add it has to be preceded by comprehensive planning and adequate preparation related to course development, preparation and production of learning materials, delivery mechanisms, student support services and evaluation mechanisms (Powar, 1997).

Institutional Linkages

An important, and perhaps the most common, mechanism for the internationalisation of education is the establishment of linkages between universities in different countries. The idea has been given concrete form by programmes such as the UNITWIN programme of UNESCO, and the ERASMUS and SOCRATES programmes of the European countries. It is noteworthy, for examples, that under ERASMUS more than 1500 institutions have worked together in over 2500 programmes under the 'Interuniversity Cooperation Programs' (de Wit, 1996). The idea is not new as far as Indian universities are concerned and many universities have already entered into Memorandums of Understanding/ Association (MOUs/MOAs) with universities abroad. However most of them relate to research. In many cases it has enabled the foreign universities to enlarge their area of operation (and also their influence), without significant benefit to the Indian institution (though individuals may have benefited marginally). It is also to be noted that many MOUs do not take-off in a meaningful way and end up as dead documents.

It is evident that the development of international links will provide an added dimension to the academic programmes of Indian universities and will also be instrumental in improving their quality and acceptance. As emphasised in the World Declaration on Higher Education (UNESCO, 1998), in the coming decades partnerships and alliances will be key factors in the promotion of higher education. The partnerships will not only help improve quality but will also promote understanding and help overcome cross-cultural barriers. However, to be effective, they have to be on equal basis with both (or all) partners making meaningful contributions. Otherwise 'internationalisation of higher education' may turn out to be 'commercialisation of higher education'. This is a danger that must be avoided.

Need for a Nodal Agency

There is a need to establish a nodal agency within the university system which can coordinate the activities of Indian universities in the area of international education, undertake the vigorous marketing of higher education abroad and, if necessary, also function on their behalf. The University Grants Commission (UGC), on the recommendation of a committee set for the purpose, has recommended (University Grants Commission, 1996) the establishment of a Consortium for International Education (CIE), for which the Association of Indian Universities (AIU) was identified as the nodal agency. The functions identified for the CIE are:

- to identify select universities and institutions of higher learning in respect of their standard, infrastructure facilities and performance, with the view of preparing a directory of centres of excellence (for international education) where international students can be admitted, and to update the directory from year to year,
- to project Indian universities/institutions in other countries and function on their behalf,
- to function as a clearing house for information on courses offered, availability of seats, fees charged, financial-aid available, on-campus and off-campus housing accommodation for individuals and families,
- to publish and distribute guides and handbooks for the promotion of international education programmes in the country,
- to coordinate education and training of international students of the universities/institutions of higher learning in the country,
- to network, liaise, collaborate and interact with relevant institutions, individuals and other agencies, within and outside the country, with the view to facilitating the promotion of international education cooperation programmes,
- to provide help to Indian universities/institutions of higher learning in obtaining approvals of the various ministries of the Government of India in respect of international education cooperation programmes,
- to promote, coordinate, monitor – jointly with the Indian universities/ institutions – the international students affairs,
- to represent Indian universities/institutions at international fairs on Higher Education and to organise similar fairs in India,
- to undertake, with the help of individuals/universities, ethnographic studies on international students with a view to understanding more

about the experiences of individuals, and also to make informed generalisations about specific nationality groups,

- to develop norms and guidelines for ensuring quality in international education, and
- to undertake all other activities that are incidental or, in the view of the Consortium, conducive to the attainment of the main objects of any of them.

In view of financial constraints (the UGC was not in a position to give financial or other assistance) the AIU has started activities, in a limited way, through an '*International Education Cell* (IEC)' within its Student Information Services Division.

Conclusion

India has the second largest higher education system in the world and can do much to meet the global requirements for higher education, especially the requirements of the developing world. There is an urgent need for the country to take effective steps to internationalise its higher education system. This can be done by providing facilities to foreign students to come to India for higher education, and by offering academic programmes overseas. Cooperation and partnership are important. A commitment to quality and competence are obvious pre-requisites for internationalisation. However, the possibilities are immense considering the continuously growing demand for professional and continuing education. Indian universities, both public and private, need to take advantage of the opportunities provided for internationalising of higher education.

References

Altbach, P.G., (1989), The New Internationalization: Foreign Students and Scholars, *Higher Education*, 14(2): 125-136.

de Wit, H., (1996), European Internationalization Programs, *International Higher Education*, 4: 5-6.

de Wit, H., (1999), Changing Rationales for the Internationalization of Higher Education, *International Higher Education,* 15: 2-3.

Lavakare, P.J., Gulati, S.K. and Sukhija, S.S., (1995), Exporting Indian Higher Education: Opportunities and Challenges, *Journal of Higher Education*, 18(1): 105-119.

Powar, K.B., (1997), Globalisation of Distance Learning System: Implications for Developing Countries, *University News,* 35(4): 4-6.

Powar, K.B. and Bhalla, V., (2000), *International Students in Indian Universities*, AIU Status Report 2000/2, AIU, New Delhi.

Powar, K.B., Pandey, S., Panda, S.K. and Bhalla, V., (1997), *International Students in Indian Universities*, AIU, New Delhi.

Raggat, P., (1993), Post-Fordism and Distance Education- A Flexible Strategy for Change, *Open Learning,* 8(1): 21-31.

UNESCO, (1998), *Higher Education in the Twenty-first Century: Vision and Action – Final Report,* UNESCO, Paris.

University Grants Commission, (1996), *Report of the Group on 'Modalities to provide Educational Opportunities to Foreign Students and to Generate Resources for Higher Education',* UGC, New Delhi.

Financing Higher Education

- Government Support for Higher Education
- Role of Private and Public Sectors in Higher Education
- Financing of Higher Education: The Emerging Scenario

13

Government Support for Higher Education*

Introduction

Following a commitment made by the Finance Minister, in his budget speech for 1996-97, the Department of Economic Affairs, Ministry of Finance, Government of India, issued in May 1997, a discussion paper on 'Government Subsidies in India' (Government of India, 1997a). The paper brought out the fact that in 1994-95 the subsidy for services provided by the central and state governments constituted 14.4% of the GDP. Emphasising the need for reducing the overall scale of subsidies by about 50% it made a distinction between 'merit' and 'non-merit' subsidies based on the 'externalities' associated with the goods/services. Education, other than elementary education and agricultural education, has been classified as a non-merit service. The discussions that followed the issue of the paper have highlighted the differences in perception between economists and educationists regarding the extent of governmental support to be given to higher education.

The Discussion Paper

While admitting that subsidies can be a powerful welfare-augmenting instrument of fiscal policy, the discussion paper of the Finance Ministry suggests that subsidies are normally to be advocated when the social benefits of a particular service or commodity are greater than the sum of the private benefits of the consumers. The paper makes a distinction between subsidy for 'merit' services, in which there is a significant gap between the private valuations of the benefits of services and their true social value, and 'non-merit' services for which there is no significant difference between private and social valuations. The paper considers primary (elementary) education and higher education to be respective examples of these two types of services. According to the paper primary

* Reproduced from 'University News', Special Issue on '*Higher Education – A Non Merit Good?: A Symposium*', Vol.36(24), pp.5-19.

education is a 'merit-service' because its benefits "*spread well beyond the immediate recipients*".

According to the discussion paper 'non-merit' subsidies amounted to 10.7% of the GDP at market rates, in 1994-95, while the average all-India recovery rate for these non-merit goods/services was just 10.3%. In the case of education as a whole the recovery rate was less than 1% and even for higher education (university sector) it was only 1.25%. In the same year the combined fiscal deficit of the Centre, States and Union Territories was placed at 7.3% of the GDP. Any reduction in the quantum of non-merit subsidies would have a direct and immediate effect on the fiscal deficit. By increasing the relevant user charge it would be possible to have a more than proportionate increase in cost recovery due to two distinct effects, viz., (i) increase in user prices, and (ii) reduction in quantity demanded. The paper states that in 1996-97 the fiscal deficit of the Centre and States and Union Territories combined was 6.5%. A reduction of the subsidy rate by 50% could shrink this deficit to less than 2% of GDP.

The paper states: "*Most subsidies to higher education accrue predominantly to the better-off sections of society as they have an overwhelming advantage in competing out prospective candidates from the other sections in getting admission to courses that are characterized by scarcity of seats*". In a more specific statement the paper says, "*A significant portion of subsidies in higher education is appropriated by the middle to high income groups, because shortages of seats in this sector are cleared by quality-based clearing in the shape of entrance examination, interview, group discussion etc., where the poorer sections of society are easily competed out*".

The paper concludes that reforms in our present regime of subsidies should focus on, amongst other things, the reduction of overall scale of subsidies and making them as transparent as possible. Further, that it "*may not be unreasonable to set a target of reducing subsidy rate for non-merit subsidies from 90% to 50% in three years, with a further goal of reducing it to 25% in another two years*".

The paper assumes many things. *First,* that the benefits of higher education accrue primarily to recipients (and that society-at-large does not benefit substantially). *Secondly,* that a reduction in the number of recipients would not be harmful to the nation's interests. *Third,* that a substantial increase in user prices is possible. *Fourth,* that the beneficiaries of higher education are predominantly from the middle and higher classes. *Fifth,* that the middle class, including the higher salaried class, will be able to afford unsubsidised or nominally subsidised professional education. These assumptions are to an extent simplistic. Their validity is discussed in later sections of this paper.

There is apprehension in some circles that the views of the Ministry of Finance regarding higher education, as expressed in the discussion paper, are based upon the thinking of the World Bank and its specialists. Tunnermann (1996) writes "*Amongst the specialists of World Bank who started the criticism of higher education was George Psacharopolous, who in several articles stated that resources devoted to higher education were not used efficiently, and, therefore, investments on education must prioritise primary school – where a return/social rate is higher than that corresponding to higher education. As (a) consequence, the policy on higher education must be focused on cost recovery, by means of suppression of gratuity, on the establishment of education credit and greater support to private higher education*".

The arguments of the Finance Ministry are in many ways similar to those presented in the World Bank document '*Higher education: The Lessons of Experience*' (1994). The latter states: "*Indeed it is arguable that higher education should not have the highest priority claim on incremental public resources available for education in many developing countries, especially those that have not yet achieved adequate access, equity and quality at the primary and secondary levels. This is ... because the social rates of return on investments in primary and secondary education usually exceed the returns on higher education....*" (World Bank, 1994, p.3).

Tunnermann (*op. cit.*) points out that this World Bank document has been the subject of strong criticism from academics, analysts and international officials. He summarises some of the criticism as follows:

- "A core problem is that conventional estimations on the return rates do not equate the social benefits of education at any of the levels. This opens the debate to the existence of those benefits in higher education, in functions covering not only teaching activities, but also research and the strengthening of the national identity (nation building).
- The social return rates do not take into consideration the non-private benefits of education emerging from 'positive external factors'. The latter are higher in the case of higher education than for other educational levels, which might put in doubt the legitimacy of a redistribution of the public expenditure allocation in education to the detriment of higher education.

- The aspects relating to the strengthening of cultural identity developed at the universities are not easily quantifiable. They are public goods".

Additionally, there is a need to analyse whether the views of the World Bank, formulated in the context of the smaller developing countries, are relevant to India, a country with a population nearing a billion, having a large industrial infrastructure, the second largest science and technology manpower and the second largest higher education system in the world. Further it is imperative that we take cognizance of the fact that the neglect of the higher education system will make the country vulnerable to inroads from universities from western countries, leading to a stage when we will become dependent upon them for the fulfilment of our manpower requirements in key sectors.

The Role of Higher Education in National Development

The *first assumption* made in the discussion paper, that the benefits of higher education accrue primarily to the recipient, and by implication, that the benefit to the nation is not much, suggests a lack of appreciation of the role of higher education in national development. In fact there is universal appreciation of the fact that higher education provides the competencies that are required in different spheres of human activity ranging from administration to agriculture, business, industry, health, communication, and extending to the arts and culture. The World Bank document referred to in the previous section itself states: *Higher education is of paramount importance for economic and social development. Institutions for higher education have the main responsibility for equipping individuals with the advanced knowledge and skills required for positions of responsibility in government, business and the professions..... .....Estimated social rates of return of 10 per cent or more in many developing countries also indicate that investments in higher education contribute to increases in labour productivity and to higher long-term economic growth, which are essential for poverty alleviation."* (World Bank, 1994). It goes on to add: "*Higher education investments are important for economic growth. They increase individual's productivity and incomes, as indicated by rate-of-return analysis, and they also produce significant external benefits not captured by such analysis, such as long term returns to basic research and to technology development and transfer.*"(World Bank, 1994). In a follow-up document, 'Perspectives and Strategies for Education', the World Bank concludes "*Higher education also contributes to self-sustaining growth through the impact of graduates on the spread of knowledge*"(World Bank, 1995). More importantly this second World Bank document admits that "*Not all the external effects of higher education – such as the benefits from basic research and from technology development and transfer – are fully reflected in the earnings used in calculating those rates of return*".

UNESCO in a policy paper 'Document of Policies for the Change and Development of Higher Education' (UNESCO, 1995) maintains that there is a well-established correlation between investment in higher education and the level of social, economic and cultural development of a country. It expresses concern over the observed trend towards a reduction in State contribution for higher education and its reallocation to earlier educational levels. It maintains, "*State and society must perceive higher education not as a burden on federal budgets but as a long term domestic investment, in order to increase economic competitiveness, cultural development and social cohesion... As a conclusion one could say that the public support to higher education is still essential in order to ensure its educational, social and institutional mission.*" (UNESCO, 1995, para 71).

Access to Higher Education

India has the second largest higher education system comprising 237 universities, nearly 9000 colleges, and about 5.5 million students. In absolute terms five and a half million students appears to be a very high number and is possibly the basis for the second assumption that a decrease in the number of students would not harm the nation's interest, or even that it is desirable. However, it is necessary to keep in view the fact that this number (5.5 million) represents only 6% of Indian people in the age group 18-23 years. The percentage is extremely low compared to 51% in the countries that belong to the Organisation of Economic Cooperation and Development (OECD), and 21% in the middle-income group countries, and the same as that for the low-income group countries. What we require is an increase in the number of students in higher education so that our requirements of manpower are met. Any curtailment can only have disastrous consequences. As the UNESCO document (*op. cit.*) points out "*Access to higher education, and the broad range of services it can render to society, is part and parcel of any sustainable development programme in which high-level human expertise and professional skills are required*" (UNESCO, 1995, para 41).

Significantly, today it is the developed nations that attach the greatest importance to all levels of education, including higher education. Dhanarajan (1998) quotes two examples to illustrate this. In the United Kingdom, the country that gave birth to Thatcherism, the present British

Prime Minister Tony Blair stated in a lecture delivered at Ruskin College that "*...three priorities for (his) government (should his party come to power) would be education, education and education*". Likewise, American President Bill Clinton, in his second inaugural address, called for "*a new land (in which) education will be every citizen's most prized possession...And the doors of higher education will be open for all*". These are sentiments echoed by our leaders, politicians, administrators, social workers, and educationists, when they make impassioned pleas for ensuring access and equity in higher education.

Increase in 'User Charge'

The discussion paper suggests that a reduction in subsidy could be achieved through an increase in user charge, which in the case of education would mean an increase in the tuition fees charged to the students. This leads, by implication, to the third assumption that a substantial increase in user charge is possible, for the envisaged scale of reduction is 40% in the first three years, and a further 25% in the next two years. Admittedly, tuition fees in higher education establishments are extremely low and there is a need for rationalisation. However, the point to be considered is whether a sharp increase in fees is possible, and even if this was done, would it generate any significant amount. Before considering these aspects it would perhaps be useful to review the international situation regarding tuition fees.

At the international level there is great variation in perception regarding tuition fees to be charged from recipients of higher education, and in the amount of fees, as per cent of unit cost, actually charged. At one end of the spectrum are countries like the United States where the fees charged are substantial in absolute terms (with full fees being sometimes charged) while at the other end are countries like France and Germany where higher education is free of cost, for all who deserve it, and where the idea of introducing fees has generated strong protests from students. It is relevant that in a large number of developing countries no fees are (were being) charged, and even in the United States the fees in some State universities are only 15%. Raising the fees to 75% of unit cost in five years is not in keeping with international thinking, nor does it seem possible in the political climate that exists in this country.

Fischer (1990) while discussing increase of tuition fees in the United States noted that there are "*political difficulties on raising tuitions, even when raises are accompanied by increased need-based aid. Opposition will come from across the political spectrum, even from those who view the low-tuition-for-all approach as the surest way to secure subsidies for poor students. It may be too much politically to expect states to pursue alternatives that require large tuition increases*". If a 'capitalist' country like the United States shows hesitancy in raising tuition fees one may only imagine the results in India, which is known to lack political will in such matters. One has to bear in mind that governments have not favoured fee-increase and even the central government had advised the IITs not to implement the fee-rise proposed a couple of years back.

The only state that has made serious attempts to raise fees in non-professional institutions of higher education is Maharashtra. And even in this state there has been some hesitancy in the implementation of recommendations made by the committees constituted by it. The Bhanage Committee, appointed by the State government, in September 1978, in its report submitted in 1979, distinguished between 'user benefits' and 'societal benefits', and recommended the fixation of fees in relation to the cost of education. It further recommended that two-thirds (66.7%) of the cost of education be recovered from the students. It took note of the fact that 50% of the total number of students, including 78.5% of students in rural areas, do not have to pay fees. It further suggested that the fees be reviewed every five years as a matter of principle. The government, however, felt that the suggested formula could cause hardships and fixed the fees at Rs.400/– i.e., 40% of the cost of education. Nearly a decade later, in 1988, it appointed the Powar Committee to again examine the matter and suggest the fees for programmes in the faculties of Arts (including Social Sciences), Science, Commerce and Education. The Committee in its report submitted the same year (Government of Maharashtra, 1988) noted that most young people proceed for higher education only because they are unable to find any kind of employment. It recommended that the fees be fixed at 30% of the cost of education. This implied raising the fees from Rs.400 to Rs.800 annually for undergraduate classes, and from Rs.600 to Rs.1000 for postgraduate classes. Noting that such a large increase could not be implemented in one stage the Committee suggested that as a matter of practice the fees be increased by Rs.100 every year till the amount of 30% of expenditure was reached, and thereafter the fees be increased regularly. The government did not take any action on the report till 1992 (because of lack of political will?) when it decided to raise the fees, in one stage, to the amount recommended. Subsequent agitation by the students made the government reduce the fee enhancement by 50%, but the student organisations did agree to periodic fee increase commensurate with the increase in expenses. However, the government has not thought it appropriate to raise the fees after that. So much for political will.

It may also be pointed out that even periodic increases in fees will not generate any substantial income as a very large number of students receive freeships and scholarships. For example the *Powar Committee Report* points out that, during 1987-88, in the Marathwada University, 95% of undergraduate students in the Arts faculty, 72% in the Science faculty, and 91% in Commerce faculty had their fees reimbursed. The corresponding figures for the University of Bombay, spread over a relatively rich area, were 33% for Arts faculty, 33% for Science faculty and 14% for Commerce faculty. Overall about 60% of undergraduate students in Maharashtra universities enjoyed fee concessions. At the postgraduate level the number was larger, i.e., 71%.

The Beneficiaries of Higher Education

The *fourth* assumption made in the discussion paper is that the beneficiaries of higher education are predominantly students from the middle and upper classes. This may be true for the professional courses, like those of medicine, engineering and management, but not for higher education as a whole. And it must be emphasised that 88% of the students are in the liberal arts programmes, namely, in the arts, social sciences, science and commerce faculties. Moreover, it is a fact that a very large number of students in our mofussil universities are first generation learners. They would never have got an opportunity to enter the portals of a university had it not been for government support to higher education. The data relating to students receiving financial assistance, given in the previous paragraph, clearly show that an appreciable number of students from the less privileged classes are availing of higher education facilities.

In this context it may be pointed out that the 'National Policy on Education, 1986' (Government of India, 1986) envisages education to be:

- a process of empowerment through the development of knowledge, skills and values (Education for Development), and
- an instrument of social change for upward economic and social mobility, through enhancement of qualifications (Education for Equality).

In keeping with this policy efforts have to be made to provide special opportunities to the traditionally under-privileged sections of society, including women, the scheduled castes, the scheduled tribes, other backward classes, and people from the socially backward areas. The results have been encouraging. In the fifty years since independence the ratio between male and female students has dropped from 8.29:1 to 1.69:1. Since 1957 the ratio between general and SC/ST students in professional education has dropped from 11.61:1 to 8.71:1. In the same period the ratio between general and SC/ST students in general higher education has, however, increased marginally from 6.27:1 to 7.16:1 (Powar, 1997). In absolute terms the increase, since 1957, in the number of SC/ST students in both general and professional education has been considerable. In the former category it has increased from about 91,000 to about 6,10,000 and in the latter from nearly 16,000 to over 56,000. It has again to be stressed that this progress has been possible because of government support. Lowering of financial support can only result in slowing down of the movement towards equality.

Affording Higher Education

The fifth assumption made in the discussion paper is that the middle class, including most of the salaried class, can pay for unsubsidised higher education. This is difficult, especially in case of quality professional education. The cost of medical education in a self-financing medical college, not receiving any government subsidy and having a private hospital, was estimated by Christo (1996) to be about Rs.2.25 lakh. After implementation of new scales, and with the normal cost escalation, it would be about Rs.2.75 lakh now. The average cost of medical education at the Manipal Academy of Higher Education, for the years 1993-94 to 1996-97, has been estimated at about Rs.160,000 for the MBBS programme, about Rs.120,000 for the postgraduate degrees and diplomas, about Rs.82,000 for dental undergraduate degree and about Rs.18,000 for the undergraduate nursing degree (Manipal Academy of Higher Education, 1996). Technical education is equally costly. The average annual cost for an engineering degree, for the period 1991-92 to 1994-95, at the University of Roorkee has been estimated at Rs.241,000; and at the IIT, Kanpur at Rs.399,000 (Ray, 1997). The Institutional Unit Cost for Master's programmes, for the year 1993-94, was about Rs.23,000 for Delhi University, Delhi, about Rs.39,000 for Pondicherry University, Pondicherry, about Rs.34,000 for Kurukshetra University, Kurukshetra and about Rs.20,000 for Shivaji University, Kolhapur (Association of Indian Universities, 1995). Paying 50% of the cost for general education, at the Masters level, would be difficult for many middle class families; and professional education would be impossible even for children of the highest paid government personnel. The country cannot allow this to happen. It is evident that government will have to continue to shoulder the major share of responsibility of financing higher education.

Funding Pattern

A global review clearly shows that in the most countries of the world education is almost exclusively financed by the government. In countries of the OECD public source of funding was, in 1991, as high as 99% in Denmark, 98% in the Netherlands and 90% in Canada. Even in the United States it was as high as 78%. In India it was 89%, in Indonesia 62.8% and in Kenya 62.2% (World Bank, 1995). Cost sharing between government and beneficiaries is a relatively new suggestion, and it has not really been put into practice. Tilak (1997) points out that in most societies government is the most important financier of (higher) education. According to the data given by him, in the last decade state finance for the higher education sector in the OECD countries were high. It was 88% in Australia (1988), 89.5% in France (1984), 68.5% in Germany (1986), and 90% in Norway (1987). The contribution was relatively lower in the United States (59.3%) and the United Kingdom (55%). Tilak (*op. cit.*) believes that government financing "*is held not only to be necessary for the development of education, but also as a desirable form of providing education, because markets cannot provide the socially optimum quantities and qualities of education, as markets do not capture externalities*".

In most countries there has been a rethinking on the role of government in financing higher education following the transition of education systems from elite systems to mass systems. Ziderman and Albrecht (1995) point out that as long as education was reserved for elite groups governments were able to meet the full costs without much budgetary strain. With the 'massification' of education governments of most countries find it difficult to spare the required additional resources for education, and hence the proposal for cost recovery. However, it is significant that many Latin American countries increased their expenditure on higher education during the late eighties. Between 1985 and 1990 government financing of higher education, in terms of GDP, has increased from 1.5% to 3.1% in Argentina, from 2.1% to 2.7% in Bolivia, and from 3.8% to 4.6% in Brazil. In Mexico there has been an increase from 3.9% to 5.2% between 1985 and 1992 (Mungaray and Lopez, 1996).

In India, education being on the concurrent list, the expenditure on education is shared by the central and state governments. During 1995-96 the budgeted expenditure for education (all sectors) for the entire country was Rs.36175.66 crore. Out of this Rs.7951.93 crore was for plan expenditure and Rs.28223.73 crore was for non-plan expenditure (Govt. of India, 1997b). The corresponding allotments for higher education were Rs.3648.60 crore, Rs.475.67 crore and Rs.3172.93 crore.

In the case of plan expenditure the share of higher education, with respect to total expenditure on education, is approximately 6%. In the case of non-plan expenditure it is about 11.5%, while for plan and non-plan, both taken together, it is about 10%. The Centre's contribution to plan expenditure on higher education has decreased from 12.79% to 11.46%. Considering the fact that education is on the concurrent list it is reasonable to expect that the Central government should contribute a larger share. However, compared to 1994-95, the centre's contribution decreased in 1995-96, by 4.66% in the case of plan expenditure, and by 4.11% in the case of non-plan expenditure.

The decline in government support commenced in the early eighties. Thus the share of higher education in GNP which was nearly 1% in 1980-81 declined to 0.5% in the early nineties and to less than 0.4% in the late nineties. Likewise as a proportion of total plan expenditure on education the share of higher education decreased from 25% in the Fourth Five-Year Plan (1969-74) to 22% in the Fifth and Sixth Five-Year Plans (1974-79 and 1980-85 respectively), 16% in the Seventh Five-Year Plan (1985-90), 12% in the following 'holiday', and 8% in the Eighth Five-Year Plan (1992-97). However, there has been a small increase in the Ninth Five-Year Plan.

Way back in 1968 the Kothari Commission had recommended that 6% of the GNP be spent on Education (Govt. of India, 1968). This is the figure that has been promised for over a decade now (since the adoption on the National Policy on Education, 1986), but it unfortunately continues to be a mirage. In fact the allotment to education, as a percentage of DNP, has declined slightly in recent years and it today stands at 3.5%. The share of higher education has been falling steadily. It was nearly 1% in 1980-81, declined to nearly half by the early nineties and less than 0.4% of the DNP in the mid-nineties (Tilak, 1997). Hopefully, education will be given its rightful share of 6% by the end of the Ninth Five Year Plan as promised. It is necessary that with this the share of higher education be raised to at least 1%. This would still be less than the share received by higher education in the OECD countries like USA (1.16%), UK (1.04%), Japan (1.04%), the Netherlands (1.79%), Canada (1.98%) and New Zealand (2.53%). The figures in the developing countries of Latin America, as mentioned earlier, are much higher being in the range of 2.7% to 5.2%.

Higher Education and Science and Technology Base

In the fifty years since independence India has developed a science and technology base of which it can be proud. Following the break-up of the

Soviet Union it has the second largest science and technological manpower though this is only about 0.27 per thousand population (compared to about five per thousand obtained in the developed countries). It spends about 0.9% of its GDP on science and technology. In the 1997-98 budget the allotment for science and technology was Rs. 8171 crore. The achievements in the fields of agriculture, spare technology, atomic energy, electronics and communication and even in the basic sciences have been noteworthy. This has been possible because the universities have provided the much needed scientific manpower. However, the situation appears to be changing. Not only is the demand increasing but the source of competent personnel seems to be drying up. It is well known that research projects awarded to teachers in the universities often remain incomplete because suitable (NET qualified) scholars are not available or because there is not enough money for purchase and upkeep of essential equipment. A recent study (Kumar *et al.*, 1998) reveals that there is declining interest amongst graduates for research in different areas of science and technology. This is a contradiction of the assessment made by Maddox (1993) who writes: "*India's science has a great and probably unique asset — the enthusiasm of young people for science and technology*". Kumar *et al.*, (*op. cit.*) point out that between 1991 and 1996 there was only a 0.4% increase in enrolment rate for doctoral and post-doctoral programmes in contrast to the 2.1% increase in population and 5% increase in enrolment to tertiary education. They attribute this to the lack of job opportunities in the academic institutions and brighter avenues in other fields such as marketing. Added reasons are inadequate facilities, in terms of equipment and library, in the universities, and lack of proper environment. This is a disheartening development because skilled scientific and technological manpower will be required in increasingly larger numbers in the fields of agriculture, industry, communications and medicine. As Kasturirangan (1998) points out "*Manpower resources constitute a primary and essential input for a country's socio-economic development process. The goal of economic and social development can only be achieved if there exist adequate supplies of manpower with requisite education and skills*". One may add that this manpower has to be of high quality capable of working in the frontier areas. Neglect of the universities will only make the problem worse. It is necessary to not only enlarge our tertiary education base but also to ensure that the education imparted is of high quality. A few privileged institutions like the IITs, IIMs, IISc and central universities alone cannot fulfill this task. Unless we support a much larger number of universities, and the colleges affiliated to them in substantial measures, our hopes of developing into a major economic power cannot be fulfilled.

Today there is a realisation that the health of our scientific research is not very good, partly because of the neglect of research in the universities that followed the establishment of a chain of national laboratories and research centres. It has to be borne in mind that the field of science and technology is a dynamic one in which obsolescence, both in terms of ideas and equipment, are measured in short periods, often of less than a decade. Freshness of mind, a desire to succeed, vitality and enthusiasm are great assets in this field, and these are qualities to be found largely in the youth. Our largest investments should, therefore, be in the universities that have a regular stream of bright students in need of mature guidance. As Bhide (1990) states: "*To my mind one of the greatest mistakes in our planning process has been the neglect and impoverishment of our universities. In the absence of wherewithal the productivity of the research activity in the university system is low and understandably the universities are unable to promote meaningful industrial and economic growth*". Pleading for a return of the center of gravity of research activity to the university system he adds: "*we must realise that when resources are meager it is prudent to plough them in the universities which have an inherent multiplier effect*".

It is evident that to maintain and develop a research base, that can adequately serve the growing demands of society, the country will have to depend to a very great extent on our universities. These must be adequately supported, and the support cannot be restricted to the funding of some elite institutions. Universities all over the country, and especially those in our mofussil areas, must be supported by the government.

Higher Education for Social Development

As mentioned earlier the National Policy on Education, 1986, visualises education to be a process of empowerment through the development of knowledge, skills and values. Primary and secondary education can fulfil this objective through the creation of awareness and the generation of employment at the lower levels. However, for meaningful contributions that would lead to economic development it is tertiary education that holds promise of substantial contribution. Internationally, in the years between the two World Wars, the concept of elite universities for the privileged was slowly replaced by the concept of egalitarian universities responsible to society and committed to its needs. Dailland (1990) believes that the vigorous growth of socially committed universities reflects a confidence in higher education as a major instrument of social and economic progress.

In the years following independence, and especially in the late sixties and the seventies, Indian higher education underwent rapid growth with the conversion of the elite system of pre-independence days to a mass system. In consonance with this change the University Grants Commission, 1977, adopted 'extension' as the third dimension of higher education. The policy statement issued at that time stated: "*The university system also has a great responsibility to the society as a whole. All universities and colleges should develop close relationships of mutual service and support with their local communities, and all students and teachers must be involved in such programmes as an integral part of their education*" (*cf.* University Grants Commission, 1987).

Admittedly, not all universities have given due importance to extension work in their communities. However, many of them have been active and a few have made outstanding contributions towards generating awareness and assisting in development activities. Work relating to adult literacy, population control, village uplift, prohibition, environmental awareness and a number of other subjects have been undertaken by the universities through the National Service Scheme (NSS). Though the government has been utilising this scheme to push through a number of their socially relevant programmes the colleges and universities have not been given due credit. Planners and economists must appreciate the fact that the universities have been contributing to community development by acting as critic, advisor and helper (Powar, 1990). As critics their function has been to analyse the economic, social, political and cultural developments of the nation, and particularly of their own region. As advisors they have been conducting research on various social problems, and problems relating to agriculture, industry and management, and rendering advice. And as helpers they have undertaken tasks related to various socio-economic programmes through the extension activities described earlier.

Conclusion

The data and arguments presented above suggest that the authors of the discussion paper have erred in making assumptions that are not truly valid, and that they have not assessed the practicability of their recommendations. More importantly, they have not taken into consideration important 'public goods' that are not easily quantifiable. These include the role of higher education in providing the much needed research base, its importance in creating awareness about social problems, and its contributions to community development though programmes implemented through colleges and universities. The discussion paper appears to have been guided by the suggestions made by the World Bank without considering the inconsistencies and contradictions in its reports.

As mentioned earlier India is a large country with a strong base in science and technology. In certain areas its capabilities are equal to the best obtained in the developed countries. It has ambitious plans for industrial and technological expansion. Its major drawback is that the available expert manpower is simply not sufficient to meet the projected demands of the country. And this can be remedied only if our higher education system expands significantly. As Tilak (1997) points out: "*Economic miracles have taken place in some developing countries (e.g. East Asia) mainly due to high rates of growth of their educational systems. A minimum level of 20% enrolment ratio can be viewed as threshold level for a developing country like India to reach a higher level of economic development*". With a 66% enrolment ratio India can hardly expect to meet the requirements of a growing, quality-oriented industry. It is relevant that the United Kingdom started thinking of 'top-up' tuition fees only after its enrolment ratio was about 25%. Curtailing subsidies, as argued earlier, will only lead to a decrease in enrolment, not to the substantial increase that is essential. The danger of foreign universities making inroads into India in large numbers is real and should not be neglected.

Evidently the authors of the discussion paper have not taken cognisance of the recommendations of our own committees that have studied the problem in some detail. The Punnayya Committee (University Grants Commission, 1993), which examined UGC funding of institutions of higher education, states: "*The growth and development of higher education sector has been viewed by Indian policy makers and planners from the very early times as not merely an effort to establish India's cultural identity on the international scene but also as a means to enhance the quality and productive capacity of our manpower. It is perceived also as a crucial input in our efforts to achieve self-reliance and autonomy in many frontal areas of strategic activity..... It would be unfortunate if in the present debate on allocation of resources between sectors of education, this perception of the crucial role of higher education is lost sight of.*"

The Punnayya Committee has recommended, "*Taking into consideration the historical background, the present stage of development and the role of higher education, the availability of alternate sources of funding and the global experience, the Committee unequivocally reiterates that State funding must continue to be an essential and mandatory requirement to support higher education. It is the perception of the Committee that the State must continue to accept the major responsibility for funding the essential maintenance and development requirements of the universities.*"

While maintaining that it is the primary responsibility of the State to provide essential finance for quality higher education we agree that the universities must supplement income through other sources, and also make efforts to curtail unnecessary expenditure. The rationalisation of fees is essential and in this respect the tuition fees have to be gradually raised so that the user contributes about 25% of the academic expenses. Going beyond this percentage would be difficult. Provisions will have to be made for providing assistance to the needy students. It would, however, be necessary to carefully draw up criteria for this purpose to obviate misuse. Support from industry and alumni are other alternatives. Experience however shows that the former has not materialised though the latter holds some promise. For the individual loan scholarships have been advocated. However, experience from the world-over indicates that the recovery rates are low, and "*in some instances loan programmes have been more expensive than continuing with a policy of outright grants.*" (*Albrecht and Ziderman, 1991*). Going by our experience of the national merit loan scholarships, this will, in all probability, hold true for government loans in India. As for loans from banks the present indications are that there are very few takers. Government decisions regarding funding of higher education need to take these facts into account.

University administrators are aware of the fact that there are many avenues where expenditure can be curtailed. The Punnayya Committee (University Grants Commission, 1991) and the Pylee Committee (University Grants Commission, 1997) have both recommended that maintenance grants should be based on 'unit costs'. The Association of Indian Universities has suggested a methodology for the determination of unit costs (Association of Indian Universities, 1995; Powar, 1996) and has recommended that every university undertake this exercise. However, the use of unit cost as a basis for funding must be approached with caution. Imperfect as the system is at present it has to be first tried out over the next two or three years. The Association of Indian Universities has recommended to its member-institutions that they initiate the work of determining unit costs of different types. As pointed out by Powar (1996) "*The universities should consider this exercise as a self-assessment activity for finding out 'where the money goes' – for identifying areas of over-expenditure, as also those that are inadequately supported. A comparison of actual unit cost and optimum unit cost should help initiate a process of adjustment as regards faculty strength, number of support and administrative staff, laboratory and library support, support for research activities, and other expenditures. A caution: funding agencies and grant-giving bodies have to bear in mind that optimum unit costs cannot form the basis for abrupt changes in funding pattern*".

The bottom line is that the government cannot afford to abruptly withdraw support to higher education as proposed in the discussion paper 'Government Subsidies in India' circulated by the Department of Economic Affairs, Ministry of Finance. Such a step will have a detrimental effect on socio-economic development and on national identity. It is necessary that government continues to shoulder the major responsibility as regards funding of higher education.

References

Albrecht, D., and Ziderman, A, (1991) Deferred Cost Recovery for Higher Education; Student Loan Programs in Developing Countries, *World Bank Discussion Papers 137,* The World Bank, Washington D.C.

Association of Indian Universities, (1995), *Unit Cost of Education in Indian Universities*, (Unpublished Report presented to the UGC), AIU, New Delhi.

Bhide, B.G., (1990), Productivity of the System of Higher Education in India, *University News*, 28(48):1-13.

Christo, G.G. (1996). *The Privatisation and Pricing of Professional Education with special reference to Medical Education*, Centre for Policy Research, New Delhi.

Dailland, G. (1990), *Universality, Diversity, Interdependence, IAU-1950-1990: A Commemorative Essay*, IAU, Paris.

Dhanarajan, G., (1998), Reflections on Collaborative and Networked Learning, Keynote Address, International Conference on *Collaborative and Networked Learning*, IGNOU, New Delhi.

Fischer, F.K., (1990), State Financing of Higher Education: A New Look at an Old Problem, *Change*, 22(1):42-56.

Government of India, (1966), *Report of the Education Commission (1964-66): Education and National Development* (Kothari Commission Report), Government of India, New Delhi.

Government of India, (1986), *National Policy on Education, 1986*, Department of Education, Ministry of Human Resource Development, Government of India, New Delhi.

Government of India, (1997a), *Government Subsidies in India: Discussion Paper*, Department of Economic Affairs, Ministry of Finance, Government of India, New Delhi.

Government of India, (1997b), *Analysis of Budgeted Expenditure on Education, 1993-94 to 1995-96*, Department of Education, Ministry of Human Resource Development, Government of India, New Delhi.

Government of Maharashtra, (1988), *Report of the Committee appointed by the Government of Maharashtra to Study and Recommend on the Fee Structure in the*

Faculties of Arts (including social Sciences), Science, Commerce and Education at the Undergraduate and Postgraduate Levels (Powar Committee Report), Department of Education and Employment, the Government of Maharashtra (Unpublished).

Kasturirangan, K.,(1998), Academic Output and Market Demand, *University News*, 36(6):45-49.

Kumar, S., Khilnani, S., and Sehgal, Y.P., (1998), A Declining Trend in Interest of Graduates for Doctoral and Post-Doctoral Training in Different Areas of Science and Technology, *Current Science*, 74:20-24.

Maddox, J., (1993), Science in India:Higher Education with Lower Budgets, *Nature*, 366:617.

Manipal Academy of Higher Education, (1996), *Computation of Cost of Education*, MAHE, Manipal (Unpublished).

Mungaray, A., and Lopez, R., (1996), Introduction to the Latin American Challenges and Perspectives in the Nineties, *Higher Education Policy*, 9(1):3-9.

Powar, K.B., (1990), Concept and Role of a University, *University News*, 28(3):15-17.

Powar, K.B., (1996), Unit Costs in Higher Education, *AIU Occasional Paper*, 96/7, AIU, New Delhi.

Powar, K.B., (1997), *Higher Education in India since Independence: Retrospect and Future Options*, AIU Occasional Paper 97/1, AIU, New Delhi.

Ray, S., (1997), A Case for Subsidies, *The Statesman*, Delhi, 15th October, 1997.

Tilak, J.B.G., (1997), The Dilemma of Reforms in Financing Higher Education in India, *Higher Education Policy*, 10(1):7-21.

Tunnermann, C., (1966), A New Vision of Higher Education, *Higher Education Policy*, 9(1):11-27.

UNESCO, (1994), *Statistical Yearbook*, 1994, UNESCO, Paris.

UNESCO, (1995), UNESCO Policy Paper for Change and Development in Higher Education, Reproduced in *New Frontiers in Education*, 26(3):288-324.

University Grants Commission, (1987), *University System and Extension as a Third Dimension*, UGC, New Delhi.

University Grants Commission, (1993), *UGC Funding of Institutions of Higher Education (Punnayya Committee Report)*, UGC, New Delhi.

University Grants Commission, (1997), *Report on the Recommendations of the Punnayya Committee relating to Unit Cost of Higher Education and Other Issues (Pylee Committee Report)*, UGC, New Delhi.

World Bank, (1994), *Higher Education: The Lessons of Experience*, The World Bank, Washington D.C.

World Bank, (1995), *Priorities and Strategies for Education: World Bank Review*, The World Bank, Washington D.C.

Ziderman, A., and Albrecht, D., (1995), *Financing Universities in Developing Countries*, The Falmer Press, London.

14

Role of Public and Private Sectors in Higher Education*

Introduction

During the twentieth century there has been a progressive transformation of higher education from an elitist system to an egalitarian one. The process of change, often rather inelegantly referred to as 'massification', was initiated in Europe at the turn of the last century when the need arose for educated and skilled manpower to man the newly-developing industries. It acquired visibility in the years following World War I but gained momentum only after World War II as countries of the erstwhile British Empire achieved independence. The elite-to-egalitarian metamorphosis has been particularly remarkable in India. In the fifty-odd years since it gained independence there has been an increase in the number of colleges from 591 to over 9000, of universities from 18 to 260, and of students from 200,000 to over 5.5 million. In spite of this unprecedented growth only about 6% of young people, in the relevant age group of 18 to 23 years, are in the higher education system (Powar, 1997). A continued growth is expected and is, in fact, necessary for a country cannot expect optimum economic returns unless 15-20% of its young people have had the benefits of higher education. As Tilak (1997) points out some East Asian countries have progressed economically mainly due to the high rate of growth of their educational systems. According to him "*A minimum level of 20% enrolment can be viewed as a threshold level for a developing country like India to reach a higher level of economic development*".

The emergence of higher education as a 'mass-system' has put a strain on financial resources, and this in turn has had an adverse impact on quality. Unfortunately, today governments are showing a reluctance to support higher education beyond a particular point. The situation has

* Paper presented at the First Meeting of Vice Chancellors and Directors of India and Nepalese Universities organised by B.P. Koirala India-Nepal Foundation, at Kathmandu on May 24-25, 1998.

become critical and the financial aspects have to be examined by academic administrators, government and society, and there has to be a mutually agreed sharing of responsibility between the public and private sectors.

Role of the Government

With the process of 'massification', the role and financial responsibilities of the government have steadily increased. Thus, since 1950-51 the share of the State (central government, state governments, and local bodies) for all sectors of education, has increased from about 68% to over 90% today. It is unfortunate that this has been accompanied by progressive withdrawal of support from society (11.6% in 1950-51 to about 2% today), and a fall in the share of the students' contribution in the form of tuition fees (from 20.4% in 199051 to little over 5% today) (1950-51 data, Government of India, 1995). By allowing society to withdraw, and by not ensuring that fees for higher education were periodically increased, the governments have put themselves in a dilemma.

The fact of the matter is that higher education is essential for the production of adequately qualified manpower without which national development is not possible. The World Bank in its document 'Higher Education – The Lessons of Experience' (1994) states: "*Higher education is of paramount importance for economic and social development. Institutions for higher education have, the main responsibility for equipping individuals with advanced knowledge and skills required for positions of responsibility in government, business and the professions*". It adds, "*Higher education investments are important for economic growth. They increase individual's productivity and income ...and they also produce significant external benefits*". Likewise, UNESCO in '*Document of Policies for the Change and Development of Higher Education*' (1995), points out "*State and society must perceive higher education, not as a burden on federal budgets, but as a long term domestic investment, in order to increase economic competitiveness, cultural development and social cohesion*".

In recent years governments have given indications that support to higher education will be progressively reduced. For example, the discussion paper on 'Government Subsidies in India' issued by the Ministry of Finance, Government of India (Government of India, 1997) categorises higher education as a 'non-merit service', and suggests that for such services subsidy be reduced by 40 per cent in the first three years; and by a further 25 per cent in the next two. However, considering the importance of higher education in national development this will be a retrograde step. Governments will have to continue to provide the major share of funds required for higher education. Developed countries like France and Germany have accepted almost the entire responsibility for higher education with positive results, and we can only benefit from their example.

Role of the Non-Government (Private) Sector

The private sector was closely associated with the development of higher education in the initial years after the formal university system was set up in 1857. Many colleges, that are now over a hundred years old, were established through the efforts of individuals, social groups or trusts. The Banaras Hindu University, Varanasi, founded in 1916, is a classic example of private initiative, having been established through the efforts of Pt. Madan Mohan Malaviya. Even after independence the trend continued and privately funded educational foundations were responsible for the establishment of, for example, the Birla Institute of Technology, Mesra (1955) and the Birla Institute of Technology and Science, Pilani (1964). However, after independence, as government assumed the responsibility for the expansion of higher education society's support gradually dwindled.

The early 1980's saw the emergence of a large number of societies and educational trusts that established institutions in the professional areas of engineering, medicine and management, especially in the states of Karnataka and Maharashtra. These colleges charge tuition and other fees at a much higher rate than do government institutions. While a few provide quality education most others are deficient in infrastructure. There are approximately 1750 such colleges in India that are affiliated to different universities. These include 510 engineering colleges, 146 medical colleges, 99 dental colleges, 132 homeopathy colleges, 88 pharmacy colleges, and 100 nursing colleges. There are also about 340 institutions for management and 199 computer education colleges that are linked to universities (information from AIU data-base, March 1998). There are, in addition, numerous unaffiliated management institutes that offer postgraduate diplomas. However, the number of such programmes, recognised by the Association of Indian Universities, as being equivalent to MBA, is only ten.

The motivation behind the establishment of these private institutions has not always been the promotion of higher education and many may be considered to be business enterprises. There has also been a parallel establishment of professional institutions that offer career-oriented programmes (for example, in computer education), charging high fees. These programmes are attracting a large number of students even though they do not lead to formal degrees. A Private Universities Bill is under the consideration of Parliament and if enacted could lead to the entry of large industrial houses and businesses into the field of professional higher education.

Many foreign universities, mainly those from the United Kingdom, are now offering degree programmes in collaboration with institutions not affiliated, or in any way associated, with Indian universities. Though the degrees are not officially recognised the programmes attract students who can afford to pay the high tuition fees demanded. This reflects the glamour that is attached to foreign names.

Cost of Higher Education

In recent years some effort has been made to estimate the cost of education at both the graduate and undergraduate levels. For example, in the late eighties the unit cost of undergraduate education in the liberal arts (Arts, Social Science, Science and Commerce faculties) in the State of Maharashtra was estimated to be about Rs.2,600 (Government of Maharashtra, 1988). A more recent study (Association of Indian Universities, 1995) has shown that the unit cost of education, at Masters level for the year 1993-94, at the University of Delhi was about Rs.20,000 in the faculties of Arts, Social Science, Commerce and Management, and about Rs.35,000 in the faculty of Science. At the undergraduate level it could be half to one-third of this. Professional education is much more costly. Christo (1996) estimates the cost of undergraduate medical education in a self-financing medical college, not receiving any government subsidy and having a private hospital, to be about Rs.2,25,000 per annum. The average cost of medical education at the Manipal Academy of Higher Education for the years 1993-94 to 1996-97 has been estimated at about Rs.1,60,000 for M.B.B.S., Rs.82,000 for the undergraduate dental degree and about Rs.18,000 for the undergraduate nursing degree. For postgraduate medical degrees and diplomas it is about Rs.1,20,000 per annum (Manipal Academy of Higher Education, 1996). The average annual cost for an undergraduate engineering degree for the period 1991-92 to 1994-95 at the University of Roorkee has been estimated at Rs.2,41,000; and at the Indian Institute of Technology, Kanpur at Rs.3,99,000 (Ray, 1997). Obviously most students from lower and middle income group families will not be able to afford higher professional education if state support is lowered and they are required to pay even 25% of the cost of education.

Who will Fund Higher Education?

There has been an on-going debate, worldwide, regarding the responsibility for the State towards higher education. The erstwhile 'socialist' states supported higher education to the full. On the other hand in the United States there are both private universities, that expect large contributions from the students, and state universities that subsidise education to the extent of up to 75%. Germany and France have traditionally accepted the responsibility of entirely funding higher education. Even in the United Kingdom the concept of 'top-up' tuition fees emerged only recently, and only after the percentage of young people in the relevant age group crossed 25%.

In the social and economic milieu prevailing in India it will be difficult for the government to disown its responsibilities towards higher education. At the same time the possibility of the government funding higher education, to the extent necessary for maintenance of quality, are remote. Under these conditions the private sector has to assume a more positive and enlarged role. An appropriate mixed model of financing of higher education has, therefore, to be evolved.

Liberal Arts education, as imparted by the traditional universities, will have to be the responsibility principally of the government, with increased contributions from the users (students/parents) and from society (alumni/social trusts). A possible model could be:

- For the government to take care of salaries (both academic and non-academic personnel), maintenance cost of infrastructure, and all developmental costs.
- For the university to meet actual academic costs (other than salaries) from its own resources, including tuition fees. The latter could be raised up to 25% of the unit academic cost.
- For private sector (mainly industry) to take responsibility for developmental costs relating to infrastructure, and to provide facilities for 'hands-on' training.

Research in the universities will have to be financed, to a large extent, through grants from various departments of the government. The private sector (mainly industry) must provide support in the form of grants for equipment and consumables, and for research staff.

In the case of the professional programmes society has shown a willingness to participate, though more as a business opportunity and less as philanthropy. Two parallel forms of technical institutions have emerged: the government-funded institutions and the institutions managed by private trusts. In the case of the latter the 'running expenditure' is met entirely by the private sector with students contributing the major share in the form of tuition fees and other contributions. These trusts, however, look to the government for a good part of their developmental expenditure. The main users of this type of facility are students from the higher income group. The government institutions cater to the needs of all sections of society, though admission through competitive examinations results in the lion's share going to students from the more affluent families.

Till the early nineties technical education in government-run institutions was fully funded by the central and state governments (Raju, 1997). However, though the government still provides the major share of funding the technical institutions, like the Indian Institutes of Technology, are now expected to raise resources through increased tuition fees, consultancy and endowments. Raju (*op. cit.*) has suggested a model in which the 'running budget' would have contributions from the government (35%), student contributions (15%) and institution-generated funds (25%). It is visualised that all capital expenditure will come from government and industry. The model may be possibly over-optimistic about the non-government contribution. However, if the model can be put into practice it will go a long way towards solving the funding problem.

It is clear that in the coming years a working relationship between government and society (read industry) will have to be worked out in which both assume appropriate responsibilities towards higher education. However, as Stassen (1995) succinctly puts it, "*The withdrawal or serious curtailment of government allocations to higher education institutions, before any commitments will have materialized from the private sector, in this domain, may signal the further decline, and eventual non-viability of the Indian higher education system*". It is hoped that the government realises this eventuality and takes appropriate steps to strengthen the existing higher education system. Industry must also realise the danger of a weak and nonviable educational system and come forward to shoulder a larger share of the responsibility. In its own long-term interest industry must contribute in substantial measure.

Finally, to again quote Stassen (*op. cit.*), "*Politicians and academics ...should calculate carefully what will be cheaper and more realistic in the long run: to improve the existing system of higher education, by endowing it with adequate funds and a significant measure of autonomy, or set up a supplementary or complementary system that is, to a certain extent, alien to the culture of the land and will most assuredly draw further resources away from the public institutions*".

References

Christo, G.G., (1996), *The Privatisation and Pricing of Professional Education, with Special Reference to Medical Education,* Centre for Policy Research, New Delhi.

Government of India, (1995), *Budgetary Resources for Education, 1951-52 to 1993-94,* GOI, MHRD, Dept. of Education, New Delhi.

Government of India, (1997), *Government Subsidies in India: Discussion Paper*, Department of Economic Affairs, Ministry of Finance, GOI, New Delhi.

Government of Maharashtra, (1988), *Report of the Committee appointed by the Government of Maharashtra to Study and Recommend on the Fee Structure in the Faculties of Arts (including Social Sciences), Science, Commerce and Education at the Undergraduate and Postgraduate Levels* (Powar Committee Report), Department of Education and Employment, Government of Maharashtra (unpublished).

Manipal Academy of Higher Education, (1996), *Computation of Cost of Education*, MAHE, Manipal (Unpublished).

Powar, K.B., (1997), *Higher Education in India since Independence: Retrospect and Future Options*, AIU Occasional Paper 97/1, AIU, New Delhi.

Raju, V.S., (1996), Discussion on 'Funding and Management in Higher Education', *Australia-India: New Horizons in Education and Training Conference, 1996*, Final Report, p.24.

Ray, S (1997), A Case for Subsidies, *The Statesman*, Delhi, 15th October, 1997.

Stassen, M., (1995), Privatisation of Higher Education – Lessons from the US and Europe, Special Lecture, 70 Session, AIU, Manipal.

Tilak, J.B.G., (1997), The Dilemma of Reforms in Financing Higher Education in India, Higher Education Policy, 10(1):7-21.

UNESCO (1994), *Statistical Yearbook, 1994*, UNESCO, Paris.

UNESCO (1995), UNESCO Policy Paper for Change and Development in Higher Education, Reproduced in *New Frontiers in Education*, 26(3):288-334.

World Bank (1994), *Higher Education: The Lessons of Experience*. The World Bank, Washington, D.C.

World Bank (1995), *Priorities and Strategies for Education: World Bank Review*. The World Bank, Washington, D.C.

15

Financing of Higher Education: Emerging Scenario*

Introduction

In recent years the role of public and private sectors in financing of higher education has been discussed at length (see Powar, 1998). It is evident that in the social and economic milieu that presently prevails it would be difficult for a government to completely disown its responsibility towards higher education. At the same time, the possibility of government funding higher education, to the extent necessary for maintenance of quality, is remote. The private sector would, in the interest of the nation, have to assume a more positive and enlarged role and, therefore, an appropriate mixed-model of financing of education is necessary. The role of the main stakeholders – the government, the students, and private management – need to be clarified.

The Changing Pattern of Financing

Liberal arts education which at one time received considerable support from society is today in India almost fully financed by the Government. Since independence, the government's share of the expenditure has increased from about 45% to over 90%. Correspondingly, the share of the community has decreased from 14% to about 2%. The students' own contribution, in the form of tuition fees, has come down from about 25% to about 5%. The government itself is responsible for this. In its enthusiasm to promote higher education in the 1960's and 1970's it took an additional responsibilities, and allowed society to withdraw. At the same time, as a populist measure, it did not increase fees. Now, with the realisation that primary education needs extensive support, the axe has fallen on higher education.

Professional education is a little better placed with society showing a willingness to participate, albeit more as a business venture and less as

* Paper presented at the Second Meeting of the Vice Chancellor and Directors of India and Nepalese Universities organised by B.P. Koirala India-Nepal Foundation at Birla Institute of Technology and Science, Pilani on April 1-3, 1999.

philanthropy. There are two types of professional academic institutions – the government-funded institutions and the institutions managed by private trusts. Governments in India, central and state, have been relatively more liberal in financing professional institutions of engineering and technology, and some engineering institutions are fully funded by the central government. It is only recently that these institutions have been asked to raise resources through consultancy work and increased fees. Institutions in the private sector depend largely on tuition fees and other contributions from students. Their management, however, look for government support for developmental expenditure.

Government funding of higher education has steadily decreased over the last two decades though the total expenditure on higher education has increased significantly. The decline in government support commenced in the early eighties. Thus the share of higher education in GNP which was nearly 1% in 1980-81 declined to 0.5% in the early nineties and to less than 0.4% in the late nineties. Likewise as a proportion of total plan expenditure on education the share of higher education decreased from 25% in the Fourth Five-Year Plan (1969-74) to 22% in Fifth and Sixth Five-Year Plans (1974-79 and 1980-85), 16% in the Seventh Five-Year Plan (1985-90), 12% in the following 'holiday', and 8% in the Eighth Five-Year Plan (1992-97). However, there has been a small increase in the Ninth Five-Year Plan.

Possible Models of Financing

In India about 88% of the undergraduate students are in liberal arts education. With little possibility of the private sector entering this area of higher education in a large way the major responsibility still lies with the government. Under the circumstances a possible model for liberal arts education (Powar, 1998) could be:

- For the government to take care of salaries (both academic and non-academic personnel), maintenance cost on infrastructure, and some developmental costs.
- For the universities/institutions to meet actual academic costs (other than salaries from its own resources), including tuition fees. The latter could be raised up to 25% of the unit academic cost (see Powar, 1996). Examination and other miscellaneous fees can contribute significantly.
- Society be asked to take the responsibility of contributing at least 50% of development costs.

- Private trusts be given permission to start professional institutions only on the condition that they support, fully or to a major extent, a liberal arts institution in the same region.

For professional institutions (like the IITs) financed by the government a model suggested by Raju (1996) could be tried out. In his model, expenditure on the 'running budget' will have contributions from government (35%), students' contributions (15%) and institution-generated funds (25%). It implies that consultancy is an essential function of the institution. This in turn would require the faculty to contribute to teaching, research and consultancy work in approximately equal measure. The model may possibly be over-optimistic with regard to non-governmental contributions.

For professional institutions managed by private trust a business-based model has to be accepted with the provision that the 'profit' would be marginal and would be utilised for developmental activities. The income of these institutions, that are primarily at undergraduate level, has to be essentially from student fees though small amounts can be earned from consultancy. Permission to allow foreign students on differential fee basis, is essential for budgets that promote quality maintenance.

Raising fees through Foreign Students

The free-market philosophy requires a student to pay for the full cost of his education (and perhaps a little more). If implemented it would put quality education beyond the reach of most students. Hence, it is necessary that an effective mechanism of cross-subsidy be evolved. The free-seat/payment-seat concept, proposed by the apex court, does not really work. A student from a poor family can conceivably be 51st in the merit list and, therefore, will have to subsidise a student from an effluent background who has managed the 50th position because of a relaxed home-environment. The pragmatic way would be to adopt the policy of the Manipal Academy of Higher Education which has equal tuition fees for all with cross-subsidisation coming from foreign students who pay higher fees. It is, however, necessary that the government allow the professional institutions to admit a higher percentage of foreign students than the 10% permitted at present. The calculations made by a Committee of Expert (Manipal Academy of Higher Education, 1997) show that for the MBBS programme the cost, per year per student, would be about Rs.1,35,000 if 10% NRI/foreign students are admitted on a full-course fee of US $ 50,000/- per student. The fee charged to Indian students could be reduced to about Rs.80,000/- by admitting 25% NRI/foreign students; and to about Rs.50,000/- by admitting 33% foreign students.

Admitting a fair proportion of NRI/foreign students would be a good solution, for it would also bring foreign-exchange contribution to local economy, and encourage cross-cultural exchange. If the chances of admission of Indian students are not to be reduced then the 10-15% of seats for international students could be supernumerary.

Other Sources of Funding

It is clear that in the coming years government support for higher education will be limited. Social and political conditions place a limit on the amount that can be realised by ways of fees. Hence universities will have to look for other sources of revenue. These include consultancy, sponsored research, corporate support and alumni contributions.

Universities in India are consistently being advised to undertake consultancy work to augment resources. But this is easier said than done. For various reasons it has not been possible to develop university-industry cooperation. Most Indian universities do not have the wherewithal for industrial consultancy or are not located in industrial areas. They can (and do) undertake material characterisation and testing services which can yield small incomes. Major consultancy income is possible only for the engineering and technological institutions.

Universities with well-developed research facilities are capable of attracting funding in the form of sponsored research, especially in the emerging areas of science and technology like biotechnology, genetics and software development. The money, however, is mostly for infrastructure development with only a limited percentage for administrative expenses. Corporate support is becoming increasingly important but then again is obtained only by the already developed universities and is available only for specified purposes.

Alumni support promises to be an important source of funding. Past students are often able to help their *alma mater*. However, there is a need to develop an active alumni association. Though one-time large donations are often obtained, and should be sought for, sizeable funds can be collected by requesting alumni to give smaller grants annually.

Financing Strategies in the Private Sector

Educational trusts, having connections with business houses and politicians, have entered the professional higher education system in a big way; and some of these have lived upto the promise of providing relevant and quality education. However, they also face financial problems because of inefficiencies (and resulting high unit costs) that are characteristic of the sub-continent. The success of these private enterprises in higher education may well depend upon the ability to contain costs, increase productivity and undertake entrepreneurial activities. Some measures that could be effective are:

- Cut salary-expenditure by contracting out non-academic services like security, learning and maintenance, and gardening services,
- Undertake detailed unit cost studies to identify areas of large revenue loss and take measures to eliminate them,
- Withdraw subsidies on such services as canteen, guest house and hostels (in fact these could profitably be leased out on contract),
- Make maximum use of infrastructure and facilities by introducing short-term, vocationally-oriented programmes, generally offered by non-university institutions,
- Increase the size of small programmes to make them cost effective, or eliminate them if there is insufficient demand,
- Undertake market surveys to anticipate demands for new programmes and introduce these in advance of other institutions,
- Network with other institutions and share faculty and facilities, and
- Introduce continuing education programmes through the distance mode, or through practice schools located with industry.

Financing the Students

With the real cost of quality higher education increasing rapidly there is a need to ensure that it does not go beyond the reach of the merited student of average, or less than average, means. There should be provision for freeships, scholarships and loans. Currently government-backed loan programmes involving low interest rates, are available in about 50 developing and industrialised countries, and are supposed to assist students to pay their living expenses. The loan programmes work best when awarded in conjunction with tuition-exemption. However, an analysis of such governmental loan programmes shows that loan recovery is poor and administrative costs high. In some cases, loan programmes have been more expensive than continuing with a programme of outright grants (Albrecht and Ziderman, 1991). Loans offered by commercial banks are not very popular in India, and because of high interest rates they can generally be availed of only by the relevantly affluent – a class that does not really need the facility. In order to be effective loan programmes should be available for only the most needy and merited students.

The government may consider implementing deferred-fee payment system in which fees are recovered only after the student starts earning. However, in the conditions prevailing in India fee recovery would be difficult and costly. A more pragmatic alternative would be to levy a 'graduate-tax' on the employer. This would increase government revenue, that could be spent on higher education, but will be of no utility to the institution.

Conclusion

It is necessary for governments and management of educational institutions to evolve strategies that will ensure survival at the minimum level and at the optimum level to enable them to undertake developmental activities. The secret lies in keeping low the trajectory path of costs, and elevating the trajectory path of income. Unfortunately, this is not always possible. Government loans and social practices do allow the implementation of cost effective measures like cutting staff or increasing workloads. Hence, the only alternative is to elevate the income trajectory through new endowments/grants, increased tuition fees and increased productivity. Increased managerial competence leading to cost-reduction is now necessary in the new climate of free market economy.

References

Albrecht, D. and Ziderman, A, (1991), Deferred Cost Recovery for Higher Education, *World Bank Discussion Papers, No.137.*

Powar, K.B., (1996), *Unit Costs in Higher Education*, AIU Occasional Paper 96/1, AIU, New Delhi.

Powar, K.B., (1998), Role of Public and Private Sectors in Higher Education. *Paper presented at the First Meeting of Vice Chancellors and Directors of India and Nepalese Universities* Kathmandu.

Manipal Academy of Higher Education, (1997), *Report of the Committee of Experts,* Manipal Academy of Higher Education, Manipal.

Raju, V.S., (1996), Discussion on *Funding and Management in Higher Education*, Australia-India: New Horizons in Education and Training Conference, 1996, Final Report, p.24.

In Search of Quality

- Accreditation: Concept and Practices
- Quality in Higher Education
- Performance Indicators and Benchmarking in Higher Education

16

Accreditation: Concept and Practices*

Introduction

Accreditation, as commonly understood, is the recognition accorded to an institution that meets standards, or satisfies criteria, laid down by a competent agency, association or organisation. Its essential purpose is to recognise, ensure and promote quality in education, especially at the post-secondary level. It was devised in the United States nearly ninety years ago, and developed in that country into a unique mechanism for self-regulation of colleges and universities. It has evolved from a relatively simple attempt to find agreed standards, for distinguishing a college from a secondary school, to a complex system involving sponsors, practitioners and users (Young, 1983b). Accreditation is today accepted, the world over, as being the most effective means of quality assurance in higher education. Definitions of accreditation have generally emphasised the role of external agencies and of external evaluation. Thus, according to Zook and Haggerty (1936), accreditation is *"the recognition accorded to an educational institution...... by some agency or organisation which sets up standards or requirements that must be complied with in order to secure approval"*. Selden (1960) describes it as *"the process whereby an organisation or agency recognises a college or university or program of study as having met certain predetermined qualifications and standards"*. And the U.S. Department of Health, Education and Welfare (1968) considers it to be *"the voluntary process whereby an agency or association grants public recognition to a school, college, university or specialised program of study that meets certain established qualifications and educational standards, as determined through initial and periodic evaluations"*.

* Reproduced (with modifications) from K.B. Powar (1996), *Accreditation in Higher Education: An Indian Perspective*, Viva Books, New Delhi.

Keeping in view the self-regulatory character of the American accreditation system the Council on Postsecondary Accreditation (COPA) has defined accreditation as "*a process by which an institution of post-secondary education evaluates its educational activity, in whole or in part, and seeks an independent judgement to confirm that it is substantially achieving its objectives, and is generally equal in quality to comparable institutions or specialised units* (Binder, 1983)". Lenn (1987) points out that in the United States a significant portion of the voluntary nature of accreditation was lost when the U.S. Congress adopted, in 1952, the Serviceman's Readjustment Act tying accreditation to eligibility for federal grants. She defines accreditation as *"a communal, self-regulatory process by which non-governmental voluntary associations recognise educational institutions or programs that have been found to meet or exceed stated criteria of educational quality and assist in the further development of the institutions or programs"*.

Two other terms that are commonly used in relation to educational programmes are *Licensure* and *Certification.* Licensure has been defined (National Commission on Accrediting, 1971) as *"the process by which an agency or government grants permission to persons meeting predetermined qualifications to engage in a particular occupation and/or use a particular title"*. Certification is *"the process by which a nongovernmental association grants recognition to an individual who has met certain predetermined qualifications specified by the association and who voluntarily seeks such recognition"*. Thus while accreditation relates to an institution or programme, licensure or certification applies to individuals.

The contrasting emphasis in the above definitions, on external evaluation on the one hand, and self-regulation on the other, may pose a dilemma to countries that are in the process of adopting the accreditation system especially the developing countries and nations without democratic traditions. A self-regulatory mechanism can be evolved only over a period of time and requires strong traditions of critical self-appraisal, a sense of quality consciousness and widespread public awareness. It also requires an efficient administrative structure. In a country like India, characterised by diversity in all sectors, where there are a large number of institutions offering education of a spectrum of standards, and where employment opportunities are strongly linked with degrees, the self-regulatory mechanism is not likely to be effective. In fact, looking at the unplanned manner in which new institutions are being started external controls appear to be essential.

The Purpose of Accreditation

The system of accreditation of colleges, and other institutions of higher learning, has its genesis in the attempt to establish the equivalence of examinations and programmes in the United States. Young (1983a) records that on 3-4 August, 1906 a meeting of a joint committee of the Association of State Universities was convened in Williamstown, Massachusetts *"to present a plan..... for establishing, preserving and interpreting in common sense the standards of admission to colleges ...... in order to accommodate migrating students and to secure just understanding and administration of standards".* The committee recommended the establishment of a permanent commission for this purpose. The original purpose was, thus, that of formulating educational norms and deciding minimum standards. However, in keeping with the mood of a restless, yet motivated, society there was a progressive change in the understanding of the purpose of accreditation. In 1929 the North Central Association adopted the principle that an institution would be evaluated not in terms of arbitrary standards but in terms of its own objectives or purposes. This proved to be a decision of great significance so far as the American system of accreditation is concerned. Over a period of time the concept of self-study, self-evaluation and self-improvement became an integral part of the country's accreditation process. The emphasis shifted from ensuring minimum standards to improving quality through self-regulatory methods.

With the process of globalisation having set in, accreditation has acquired a new dimension. International cooperation in the field of education is increasing and soon it may be a common feature for a student to undertake courses, in different universities, in different countries. For the purpose of giving equivalence to degrees and diplomas, and for transfer of credits, internationally accepted standards will have to be evolved.

In terms of a global perspective accreditation has basically three main purposes. First, to formulate educational norms, conduct assessments and recognise institutions that come up to certain minimum standards; second, to assure quality and help improve standards through self-regulatory and external-control mechanisms; and third, to keep students, public and prospective employers informed of the quality of education being imparted by educational institutions.

The accreditation system provides useful service not only to the students and the public but also to the institutions themselves. To the student it provides a certification that the institution or programme being considered by him has been evaluated and found satisfactory; to the public, including potential employers, it gives the assurance that the institution under review is performing in conformity with public expectations; and for the institution concerned, besides enhancing its reputation and strengthening its case for financial support, it provides a stimulus for self-evaluation and self-improvement. More significantly, accreditation has generated, amongst institutions and systems, a healthy competition for providing quality education.

Types of Accreditation Systems

Accreditation systems (and bodies) are of two main types — institutional and specialised. *Institutional accreditation* is conducted by national and regional accreditation agencies and it looks at the institution as a total operating unit. It focuses attention on the general characteristics of the institute: its objectives, infrastructure, faculty and resources. Of major concern are questions of programme integrity, administrative and academic control, quality assurance, availability of resources and supervisory accountability (Lenn, 1987). Institutional accreditation bodies generally promote improvement by encouraging self-evaluation, identifying areas of weakness, providing advice through visiting teams and conducting periodic reviews.

Specialised (or professional) accreditation relates to specific, profession-related programmes and is also referred to as programme accreditation. The accreditation bodies are often associations or councils of professions like medicine or law or engineering. The principal objective is to ensure that the quality of education and training meets the minimum requirements of the profession. The accreditation requirements are clearly defined and emphasise the infrastructure, the facilities, and the personnel required for satisfactory professional preparation. Evaluation is invariably external and conducted by visiting teams comprising of members of the profession. The visiting team may ensure standards by prescribing additional accreditation requirements and advising on other matters.

The Characteristics of Accreditation

Though no longer unique to the United States accreditation is still essentially an American phenomenon. The American system of accreditation is a non-governmental, largely voluntary and self-regulatory process which adapts a system of self-evaluation and peer review. It respects, even encourages, institutional diversity; protects its autonomy; and, more importantly, gives a period to institutions for introspection on strengths and weaknesses. In evaluating institutional quality and effectiveness, accreditation agencies rely on inputs, interactions and outcomes (Wolff, 1993). Accreditation is an integral part of the American educational system and is today being implemented through about 80 non-governmental agencies including regional associations of colleges and universities. It is recognised as being one of the central means through which quality is assured in American post-secondary education. It must, however, be remembered that the characteristics of the system were shaped in the period between the two World Wars by the demands of an ambitious and progressive, fast-developing society, and subsequently nurtured by the ideals of innovation, autonomy and quality. The characteristics of the American system may not all be suited to countries with different traditions and socio-political environments.

The non-governmental nature of the American accreditation system is related to the fact that under the United States' Constitution the national government has not been assigned the responsibility of regulating education. Government control, however, does come in through the practice of licensing of institutions of higher education by the governments of states. This involves governmental review to assure minimum standards. After this initial licensing, most governments rely on the process of accreditation for review and improvement of quality beyond the minimum licensing requirement (Wolff, 1993). In France, the Law of 1968, which was revised in 1984, established a system that assured complete university autonomy. But there is a government-appointed autonomous body with responsibility for quality assurance in higher education. This body does not have formal sanction over institutions but its findings are taken into account by the government for funding purposes (Lenn, 1993). In the United Kingdom, the Education Reforms Act of 1988 replaced the University Grants Committee by the University Funding Council (UFC) as the body through which the funds of the government would come to the universities. The UFC has the authority to attach, to payments, terms and conditions it thinks fit (Tasker and Packham, 1990). In other countries, governments have assigned to themselves strong steering roles in the development of higher education (Vroeijenstijn, 1993). Therefore, though the accrediting agencies themselves may be non-governmental, they can be (and are) used by governments to exert controls.

It is generally accepted that accreditation should be a voluntary process and that no institution should be legally required to be accredited. In the United States there is a strong tradition of voluntary accreditation and all respected institutions of higher education have voluntarily obtained accreditation, it being accepted as an indicator of assured quality and integrity of institutional operations (Wolff, 1993). The voluntary nature of activities generally encourages innovation and experimentation, and provides alternatives to government actions. It is accepted as a matter of principle that accreditation should be sought rather than be forced upon an institution.

The American system of accreditation is self-regulatory and strongly stresses self-assessment as the prime mechanism in the accreditation process. It believes that external review should only be a means of confirming that the activities of an institution are in conformity with its objectives, and that its progress is satisfactory. In most other countries external peer review is regarded to be essential for evaluating performance and for monitoring progress. In a country like India, where the number of institutions is very large, and where there is a considerable disparity in standards, external review needs to be a crucial, if not the deciding, factor in the accreditation process.

The Accreditation Procedure

The procedure of accreditation is essentially a procedure of quality assessment and can be both complex and difficult. It raises some basic questions like: 'Can quality of teaching and research be quantified?', 'Is it possible to formulate a set of criteria and standards of quality of education?', 'Can external evaluators really understand the ethos of an institution?' or even 'Can peers be trusted?' (Vroeijenstijn, 1993). Assuming that the answers are positive it will be necessary (Vlasceanu, 1993) to:

First, identify the domain of evaluation. This could be an institution, or one of its units (e.g. a Department), or an activity (teaching or research) undertaken by the institution or unit,

Second, specify the criteria (e.g. examination results, research output or unit cost) to be used in the process of assessment, and

Third, define for each criterion standards indicating both minimum acceptability and desirability.

The accreditation procedure clearly requires both internal and external actions. The internal action is basically the preparation of documents and other material detailing facts that substantiate the claim that minimum conditions required for accreditation have been fulfilled, and that the institution is working in accordance with its objectives. The external action is an on-site review, by peers from outside the institution, of the performance of the institution or the effectiveness of a programme. The final decision on accreditation is taken by the accreditation agency after reviewing all information and reports. The accrediting body usually examines the objectives of the institution, its plans, organisation structure, programmes of teaching and research, faculty, student facilities and support services, and special activities. After accreditation is granted the institutions are revisited and re-evaluated periodically to ensure that minimum standards are maintained.

Accrediting/Evaluating Agencies: A Global Review

In the United States of America there are more than 100 voluntary organisations that call themselves accrediting bodies. Out of these about 80 are recognised as such by the Council of Postsecondary Accreditation (COPA). There are six regional associations of schools and colleges which grant general accreditation to institutions of higher education. These are: Middle States Association of Colleges and Secondary Schools, New York; New England Association of Colleges and Secondary Schools, Boston; North Central Association of Colleges and Secondary Schools, Chicago; Northwest Association of Secondary and Higher Schools, Seattle; Southern Association of Colleges and Schools, Atlanta; and Western Association of Schools and Colleges, Oakland. In addition about twenty professional organisations grant specialised accreditation. These include the American Association of Collegiate Schools of Business, Engineers' Council for Professional Development, American Bar Association and the American Medical Education through its Liaison Committee on Medical Education. There is also a National Committee on Accrediting. It is an educational association established by the colleges and universities of the United States, in 1949, to improve, coordinate and monitor accreditation. The Commission has no legal authority and is independent of the state and federal governments. It influences accreditation by listing the accrediting agencies that it recommends its 1300 member institutions consider dealing with. It thus influences the working of the accreditation agencies bringing about improvements in their procedures and standards.

In the United Kingdom there are no accreditation agencies *per se.* Educational evaluation is, however, done by the Advisory Board of Research Council, the Council of National Academic Awards and the Committee of Vice Chancellors and Principals. A Higher Education Quality Council (HEQC) was set up in 1992 and it functions as the Quality Audit Unit for U.K. higher education. Its core functions are: testing universities' and colleges' systems for assuring quality, scrutinising what institutions are saying about their academic provision, helping institutions in determining the extent to which they are achieving their objectives, identifying areas in which institutions may have difficulty in maintaining or enhancing quality, and advising parent bodies and third parties on quality issues on higher education. Within the HEQC two groups, the Quality Assurance Group (QAG) and the Quality Enhancement Group (QEG) have been set up. The QAG is responsible for scrutinising an institution's quality assurance mechanisms, with the view of ensuring public accountability for maintenance and improvement of academic quality and standard. The QEG supports the objective of quality maintenance and enhancement through a varied range of activities. In August, 1997 the quality functions of MEQC were taken over by a new agency the Quality Assurance Agency for Higher Education (QAA).

In Australia, Academic Standards Panels have been constituted in some disciplines to oversee under-graduate programmes. In New Zealand, in order to carry out course approval and accreditation functions, the New Zealand Vice Chancellors' Committee has set up a Committee on University Academic Programmes. The universities have also set up an Academic Audit Unit. In Nigeria, the National Universities' Commission has prescribed minimum standards in a number of disciplines and accreditation is granted to under-graduate programmes in 31 Nigerian universities on the basis of self-study forms and panel visits (Lenn, 1993).

In France, the work of evaluation is done by the autonomous National Evaluation Committee (Comite' National d'Evaluation). Set up in 1984, the committee takes into account requests for evaluation that may be made by the Ministry or individual institutions. It reports directly to the President of the Republic (Sirinelli, 1993, p14).

The Russian Federation adopted, in 1992, a Law on Education that laid down procedures for licensing, attestation and accreditation, for the control of evaluation of educational institutions. It provides for accreditation to be undertaken by various Russian and international non-governmental educational, scientific and industrial structures, or by non-governmental accreditation agencies established by them, (Prokopchuk, 1993)

Japan has accepted, in principle, that all institutions must use a process of self-evaluation in the creation of all new programmes and is working on a process of internal institutional evaluation. In China, an Academic Degree Committee examines, through specialised sub-groups, curriculum structure, faculty and research activity to determine the disciplines in which universities have a right to offer degrees (Lenn, 1993).

Accreditation: The Indian Situation

During the past two decades there have been discussions in India regarding the formulation and functioning of an appropriate mechanism of accreditation. The 'Programme of Action' related to 'the National Policy on Education, 1986', called for the development of "*a mechanism for accreditation and assessment for maintaining and raising the quality of institutions of higher education*". (Government of India, 1986). A National Assessment and Accreditation Council (NAAC) was established in 1994, with headquarters at Bangalore and it presently undertakes institutional evaluation, though there is also a provision for departmental evaluation. The principal objectives of this Council are to:

- grade institutions of higher education and their programmes,
- stimulate the academic environment in these institutions,
- help the institutions in realising their academic objectives, and
- promote changes, innovations and reforms necessary for the above purposes, and encourage innovations, self-evaluation and accountability in higher education.

In the case of professional education the establishment and recognition of institutions is presently regulated by different professional associations including the All India Council for Technical Education (AICTE), the Medical Council of India (MCI), Indian Nursing Council (INC), Dental Council of India (DCI), Pharmacy Council of India (PCI), Council of Architecture, and Bar Council of India (BCI). However, these do not undertake accreditation. The All India Council for Technical Education (AICTE) became a statutory body in 1987 and was assigned the responsibility of setting up a National Board of Accreditation (NBA) for periodic evaluation of programmes of institutions under it. The NBA was established in October, 1994 and it undertakes programme accreditation.

At NAAC, the process of assessment and accreditation is undertaken in three stages: first, the preparation of a self-study report by the institution undergoing assessment; second, the validation of the report through a peer-team visit; and third, a review of the peer team's evaluation, and the final decision regarding accreditation by NAAC.

NAAC follows a two-tier assessment system. At Level 1 the institution is first classified as 'Accredited' or 'Not-Accredited'. At Level 2 the accredited institutions are graded into five categories, improving quality being indicated by an increasing number of stars as superscript to the letter A (indicating accredited). Thus A* indicates the threshold level of quality and A***** the best quality.

For the purpose of grading seven parameters are considered. These are: Curricula Aspects; Teaching-learning and Evaluation; Research, Consultancy and Extension, Infrastructure and Learning Resources; Student Support and Progression; Organisation and Management; and Healthy Practices. For the three types of institutions, namely colleges, universities and autonomous colleges, different weightages have been assigned to each of these parameters. From parameter-wise judgement of the peer team, and after taking into consideration the assigned weightages, a composite Institutional Score (IS) is calculated. The IS is then used for grading the institution on a five-point scale (A***** the highest and A* the lowest) (see Powar, 2001). Till the end of December 2000, NAAC had assessed 22 universities and 123 colleges.

The procedure followed by NBA is essentially similar to that at NAAC and involves submission of information and data on a proforma provided by NBA, visit of peer-team and consideration of its report, first by a sectoral committee and then by NBA. The decision is finally reported to the AICTE. The assessment is based on the following criteria: Mission, Goals and Organisation; Financial and Physical Resources, and their Utilisation; Human Resources – Faculty and Staff; Human Resources – Students; Teaching-learning Processes; Supplementary Processes; Industry-Institution Interaction; and Research and Development. The assessment is on a four-point scale – A (Excellent/very good), B (Good), C (Satisfactory) and NA (Not Accredited). In case of both NAAC and NBA accreditation is valid for five years.

Accreditation in India is in its infancy. The implementation of this laudable concept is being examined (Powar, 2001). Hopefully, mid-term corrections will be made. The success of accreditation is important from the viewpoint of maintenance of standards.

References

Binder, L.W., (1983), Accreditation: Misuses and Misconceptions, in, Young, K.E. *et al.*, (Editors), *Understanding Accreditation,* Jossey-Bass Publishers, San Francisco, p. 1-15.

Government of India, (1986), *National Policy on Education; Programme of Action,* GOI-MHRD, New Delhi, p. 20-24.

Lenn, M.L., (1987), Accreditation, Certification and Licensure, *New Directions for Higher Education,* 15(1):49-63.

Lenn, M.L., (1993), Quality Assurance in Higher Education: A Global Tour of Practices and Resources, *Higher Education in Europe,* 18(3):71-80.

National Commission on Accrediting, (1971), *Study of Accreditation of Allied Health Education Programs*, N.C.A., Washington, D.C.

Powar, K.B., (2001), Grading of Institutions by NAAC: A Meta-evaluation, *University News*, 39(21): 4-6.

Prokopchuk, A., (1993), The Control and Evaluation of Higher Education Institutions, *Higher Education in Europe*, 18(3):134-136.

Selden, W.K., (1960), *Accreditation: A Struggle over Standards in Higher Education*, Harper and Row, New York.

Sirinelli, M., (1993), quoted in, Overview of the International high-level Consultation on Policy Issues of Quality Assessment and Institutional Accreditation in Higher Education, *Higher Education in Europe*, 18(3):8-17.

Tasker, M.E. and Packham, D.E., (1990), Freedom, Funding and the Future of Universities, *Studies in Higher Education*, 15(2):181-195.

U. S. Department of Health, Education and Welfare, (1968), *Nationally recognised Agencies and Associations*, U.S. Dept. H.E. and W., Washington D.C.

Vlasceanu, L., (1993), Quality Assessment: Issues and Policy Implications, *Higher Education in Europe*, 18(3):27-41.

Vroeijenstijn, A.L., (1993), Some Questions and Answers with regard to External Quality Assessment, *Higher Education in Europe*, 18(3):49-66.

Wolff, R.A., (1993), The Accreditation of Higher Education Institutions in the United States, *Higher Education in Europe*, 18(3): 91-99.

Young, K.E., (1983a), Prologue: The Changing Scope of Accreditation, in, Young K.E. *et al.* (Editors), *Understanding Accreditation*, Jossey-Bass Publishers, San Francisco, pp. 1-15.

Young, K.E., (1983b), What Accreditation Is, in, Young K.E. *et al.* (Editors), *Understanding Accreditation*, Jossey-Bass Publishers, San Francisco, pp. 17-18.

Zook, G.F. and Haggerty, M.E., (1993), *The Evaluation of Higher Institutions, Vol. 1: Principles of Accrediting Higher Institutions*, University of Chicago Press, Chicago.

17

Quality in Higher Education*

Introduction

In higher education the quality movement was initiated in the eighties of the last century, gained momentum during the nineties and today, with the internationalisation of higher education, has become an integral component of all higher education systems. While in some countries it has just been introduced, in others it has reached a stage of maturity (Meade, 2001). For the latter to happen in any country it is necessary that the need for quality assurance be nationally recognised, quality-related policies introduced, monitoring agencies established and quality-assessment procedures standardised.

What is Quality in Higher Education

Germane to a realistic approach to the problem of quality assurance is a proper appreciation of the term 'quality' when used with reference to higher education. This calls for some thought because quality is an elusive attribute, an attribute of values, which cannot be easily measured or quantified. Many stakeholders would find it difficult to precisely define quality. The Webster's Dictionary describes it, amongst other things, as 'a degree of excellence' and 'superiority in kind'. In reality it is a relative concept that means different things to different people (Sallis, 1993; Green and Harvey, 1993; Green, 1994). In the field of education, while discussing quality, the focus of students may be on the facilities provided, of teachers on the teaching/learning process, of management and parents on the scores or grades achieved, and of prospective employers on the nature of the output.

Green and Harvey (1993) have identified five different approaches to the viewing of quality in the field of higher education. According to them quality may be viewed :

* Modified version of Introduction to the *Volume 'Effectiveness and Quality in Higher Education'* (Selections from University News - 4), 1999, published by the Association of Indian Universities.

- in terms of the exceptional (highest standards),
- in terms of consistency (without defects and getting it right the first time),
- as fitness for purpose,
- as value for money, and
- as a transformative (transformation of the participants).

The concept of quality has been drawn from industry. Not very long ago education and industry functioned independently of each other and displayed very contrasting ethos and values. This is no longer true as in recent years the two have moved towards each other, borrowing ideas and practices. Thus, as pointed out by Taskar and Packham (1993), in industry the Fordist values of hierarchy, power and control are being replaced by the post-Fordist values of autonomy, cooperation and sharing of responsibilities — values generally associated with the world of academia. On the other hand, educational institutions are adopting corporate patterns of organisation, including strategic planning, delineation of responsibility and accountability. It is, therefore, not surprising that the concepts of standards and quality used in industry are being considered for application in the field of education. The British standard BS 5750, its International equivalent ISO 9000, and Indian equivalent IS 14000, have attracted attention in educational circles. The definition of quality as used in these and related standards, is therefore, important. Quality is defined in them as *"the totality of features and characteristics of a product or service that bear on its ability to satisfy stated or implied needs"* (Bureau of Indian Standards, 1988). In the present social and economic milieu this definition of quality will appeal to many in the field of education, and especially to those students who join universities only to acquire professional skill and training that will establish them in the labour market. It may, however, be argued that in the field of education the assessment of quality of education cannot be only student-oriented for it is mainly society that pays for the operation of the educational system. The views of other constituents of society, therefore, also have to be considered (Henderikx, 1992). Perhaps, because of this the definition of quality adopted by most educationists is that of 'fitness for purpose' — the ability to meet the stated purpose for which the service was offered. As a corollary one can add that unless the objectives of an institution, or a programme, are clearly defined it would be difficult to assess if quality is being maintained.

Universities have always been considered as the home of scholarship and of academic pursuits of the highest order. Yet, the concern for quality is a recent phenomenon. It comes with the realisation in most segments of society that higher education, through the knowledge and skills it imparts, provides the means for upward economic and social mobility. Educational institutions have realised that in the present-day, highly competitive, environment students can be attracted to them only by providing the best in terms of facilities and inputs. Moreover, government bodies responsible for funding are asking the universities to demonstrate their commitment to quality before approving major financial assistance. Above all, in most societies education is loosing its traditional aura and the resulting de-mystification has generated an expectation that, like other forms of services, education also must be responsible to the society that supports it (Deshpande, 1994). It is significant that the demand for quality in education is coming from all concerned. Naudeau (1992) notes that "*Call for quality and excellence have origins within the institution whether coming from students, faculty, administrators, or service personnel. They also come from alumni, interest groups, the community, the media and governmental bodies, in many ways, shapes and forms*". Evidently the highest priority has to be given to quality assurance in education.

Quality-related Terminology

Along with the concept of quality, education has adopted from industry a variety of terms like quality control, quality assessment, quality audit and quality assurance. Unfortunately, in the literature on quality - issues in higher education these terms have often used with overlapping connotations, and sometimes the same term has been used with different meanings. It is, therefore, desirable to review the sense in which these terms are used.

Quality Control is the oldest of the quality concepts. It involves the detection and elimination of components or final products that are not of the visualised or expected standard. In education, however, it indicates an operational process concerned with the organisation, imparting and evaluation of teaching activities in order to ensure 'fitness for purpose' optimal utilisation of resources and attainment of identified goals. In a white paper of the British government, presented in 1991, 'quality control' has been used to describe internal procedures for quality maintenance and enhancement (Green, 1994).

Quality Assessment is the evaluation of teaching and research quality in a specific subject (Calder, 1994). It is often used, in an extended sense, for the evaluation of an institution, or part of it, for overall performance using both internal and external procedures. In the United

Kingdom the aim of quality assessment is to assess the social relevance of an institution's programmes and the worth of its products in terms of societal goals.

Quality Audit is concerned with processes and procedures. As defined in BS 7229 and IS 13999 it is the *"systematic and independent examination to determine whether quality activities and related results comply with planned arrangements and whether these arrangements are implemented effectively and are suitable to achieve objectives"* (Bureau of Indian Standards, 1988; British Standards Institution, 1989). Quality audit is not concerned with the appropriateness of the objectives or with the results obtained. In the British white paper referred to earlier quality audit refers to external scrutiny of documents and procedures.

Quality Assurance has been defined by Green and Harvey (1993) as *"the mechanisms and procedures designed to reassure the various 'stakeholders' in higher education that institutions accord a high priority to implementing policies designed to maintain and enhance institutional effectiveness"*. Vroeijenstijn (1995) describes it *as "systematic, structured and continuous attention to quality in terms of quality maintenance and quality improvement*". The International Network of Quality Assurance Agencies in Higher Education is of the view that "*.... quality assurance may relate to a programme, an institution or a whole higher education system. In each case quality is all of those attitudes, objects, actions, and procedures which, through their existence and use, and together with quality control activities, ensure that appropriate academic standards are maintained and enhanced in and by each programme. Quality assurance extends to making the process and standards known to the educational community and public at large*" (Lenn, 1993). Stated more simply quality assurance is the achievement of desired standards through application of agreed procedures (Calder, 1994). Quality assurance is a dynamic process involving continuous monitoring of performance and corrective actions when necessary. As Warren *et. al.*, (1994) succinctly put it *"at a general conceptual level quality assurance in both higher and distance education refers to a continuous process that is proactive rather than reactive process, and that, though involving all actors and many facets of the institution, it is integrative"*.

Quality Policy and Quality Management are two other terms that have gained currency. Quality policy refers to *"The overall policy intentions and direction of an Organisation as regards quality, as formally expressed by top management"*, and quality management is *"that aspect of the overall management function that determines and implements the quality policy"* (Bureau of Indian Standards, 1988).

Quality, Autonomy and Accountability

There is a strong feeling amongst the members of the academic community that quality of higher education and research can be assured only if it is granted complete autonomy in academic and administrative matters. It must, however, be realised that no institution can enjoy full autonomy, that autonomy carries with it accountability, and that quality has to be striven for under the conditions that prevail. It is, perhaps, necessary to examine the relationship between autonomy and accountability further for the two are obviously mutually complementary.

Autonomy may be described as the power to act without external control. It may be viewed as an organisational or managerial requirement for the fulfilment of responsibilities. An individual or an organisation cannot be held responsible for lack of performance if it has not been given the requisite freedom to act. If a university is to be held responsible for the quality of its education, or the preparedness of its product (students), then it has to be given autonomy regarding essential matters like selection of staff, content of curricula, minimum standards to be achieved, and apportioning and utilisation of funds allotted to it.

The quality of education imparted by an institution is greatly dependent on the performance of its teachers. While discussing the aspect of their performance an issue raised is that of 'academic freedom'. Tight (1988) points out that "*academic freedom refers to the freedom of individual academics to study, teach, research and publish without being subject to or causing undue interference*". It does not confer upon the academic community unfettered rights of action and behaviour. It is a privilege that carries with it the responsibility of ensuring that it is used primarily for the improvement of the quality of education, the good of the parent institution and the welfare of the academic community.

Accountability, according to Berdahl (1990), is the requirement to demonstrate reasonable actions to some external constituency or agency. In the case of the universities and other institutions of higher learning this external constituency is, broadly speaking, 'society' and more specifically 'government'. Accountability has two aspects — moral and legal or contractual (Wagner, 1989). Moral accountability is based upon a sense of responsibility, a feeling that one is responsible to one's clients (students and parents), to colleagues and to oneself. Legal accountability is being responsible to ones employer only in terms of fulfilment of terms of employment. It is possible to satisfy legal responsibility and yet not live up to moral responsibility. For maintenance of quality it is necessary to devise an accountability evaluation system which shifts the emphasis from legal accountability to moral accountability. The accountability procedure should not result in a feeling of failure but should generate a feeling of responsibility.

The Management Context

The success of any quality assurance initiative is greatly dependent on the managerial factor. It is essential that the top management be totally committed to the concept, be able to visualise future actions in their totality, and design appropriate procedures. This means that the mission of an institution should be clearly defined, its long-term and short-term objectives precisely identified, the strategies for achieving these carefully planned, the financial requirements of different programmes assessed, adequate budgetary controls exercised, and interpersonnel relationships maintained at an optimum level. Self-evaluation is usually the starting point with the main objective being to identify areas of weakness. However, as Williams (1993), commenting on Dill's six basic themes, notes "*quality improvement comes not from inspection but from design, that is the establishment of procedures which make it impossible for bad quality to be undetected and encourage the primary aim of continuous quality improvement*".

The Japanese concept of Total Quality Management (TQM) is being sought to be applied to educational institutions worldwide. Though a number of success stories have been cited it is too early to say whether it works in higher education. TQM is a philosophy of continuous improvement — hence, also referred to as Continuous Quality Improvement (CQI) — which can provide, educational institutions with appropriate tools for meeting the wants and expectations of their customers (Sallis, 1993). The basic principle of TQM is that the interest of the customer comes first. It stresses management by fact, continuous innovation, improvement and change. Placing a premium on human relationship it presupposes an understanding leadership that provides a suitable work environment, encourages the staff and recognises achievement. The TQM approach emphasises that in every organisation there is considerable dormant potential in its personnel, and that this should be given an opportunity to express itself. An important procedural aspect is that of benchmarking — "*the systematic search for best practice*" (Marchese, 1993).

Crawford (1991) has visualised the various stages in the implementation of TQM. He believes that "*It starts with a **Vision** of how the institution would like to be, primarily in its human aspects touching staff and their outside world, what would constitute greatness for it as a university .. ? It must then define its **Mission** to be compatible with its Vision. It (then) sets its broad **Objectives**. Objectives have to be transformed into specific,* *attainable, measurable* ***Goals*** *that are motivating for individuals and offer a payoff to the institution. The customer's requirements, e.g. those of the student or research sponsor, are broken down into elements and detailed processes are designed for satisfying them. Necessary materials, facilities, and standards to be met, must be specified at this stage....* ***Plans*** *to bring together human, physical and financial resources must be developed iteratively taking account of the* ***Resources*** *that can be secured to permit* ***Implementation*** *of the resulting plans. Quality assurance measures are built in during the iterative process*".

The implementation of TQM in educational institutions is not likely to be easy for as Crawford (op. cit.) points out "*To develop a powerful quality ethos requires not only cultural change but also staff development to appropriate levels of education and training*". He adds "*Experience suggests that development of TQM culture will meet with initial apathy or rejection, and take up to five years*". Chaston (1994), in a study to ascertain whether British universities were in a position to consider implementing TQM, came to the conclusion that they have a number of initial barriers that will have to be overcome before implementation of TQM becomes a feasible option. The Indian situation is not likely to be better. The implementation of TQM is likely to be more successful in institutions that are to be started, and those which are young, or have very specific objectives, like the technical universities and the open universities. Considerable efforts may be required in the established, multi-faculty, conventional universities to implement TQM for most of them do not have well-defined mission statements and are enmeshed in bureaucratic tradition.

Assessment of Quality

It is accepted that for implementing programmes of quality assurance it is necessary to first assess the functioning, performance and current standard of an institution and that this has to be done against its mission, goals and objectives. However there has been a debate (perhaps now ending) on the manner in which the assessment is to be conducted – through internal mechanisms (self-assessment) or by external review (external audit).

Many academics, placing stress on academic freedom and autonomy of institutions, believe that assessment of quality should be done through self-evalution. It is argued that every institution has its own goals and objectives, and that the ethos of an institution is best understood by its constituents. Members of an external visiting team, however objective, may not be able to appreciate, during the course of a short visit, the goals, traditions and manner of functioning of an institution. An example of the strong conviction of some academics is the assertion by Brown (2000) that *"only those who design and deliver programmes and assess and examine students are in a position, through quality control, to assure the quality of what they do and no one else can do it for them"*. Internal assessment is, however, a difficult exercise. Successful internal assessment pre-supposes that minds are open and receptive to ideas. It requires the involvement of all major stakeholders, i.e. faculty, students and management, and close interaction between them. It is necessary to review all programmes dispassionately and take note of new developments. Self-assessment can be fruitful only in an institution that has a culture in which continuous quality enhancement occupies a central place. Japan is one of the few countries that had traditionally relied upon self-evaluation (along with continuous self-monitoring) for maintaining quality. The practice of self-evaluation is widely practised by the national, local public and private universities (Tachi and Yonezawa, 2001). However, it too has moved towards external evaluation by establishing a central evaluation agency called the National Institute for Academic Degrees.

Quality assessment through external review is now a standard practice in practically all developed, and many developing countries, and most of them have established quality audit or accreditation agencies for this purpose. In practically all countries assessment of institutions is carried out periodically through well-laid down and formalised procedures. This generally involves an inspection of the infrastructure, facilities and programmes of the institution by a peer-team that essentially validates a self-study report submitted by the institution. The peer-team report on the status of an institution or programme usually highlights the positive aspects, points out deficiencies, and makes recommendations for improvement. Successful validation results in a certification, commonly referred to as accreditation.

External review is often viewed as a mechanism by which government attempts to control the functioning of higher education institutions by making it the basis for allocation of funds. Meade (2001) points out that the focus on external audit has engendered in institutions a culture of compliance, rather than one of continuous quality enhancement. He, however, states that external audits have had a significant positive impact on higher education as they have prompted higher education institutions to develop better quality review and quality enhancement processes.

Evidently, both self-assessment and external review have important roles to play in the quality assurance movement. There is consequently the need to achieve the right balance between the two (Benadusi, 1999; Kekale, 2000). Academic institutions need to take the self-assessment exercise seriously, and set up internal quality monitoring and enhancement units. The external review teams on their part should attach considerable significance to the self-study reports submitted by the institution under review.

An issue that has come to the forefront in India is that of the unit of assessment. The National Assessment and Accreditation Council (NAAC), the premier assessment agency for higher education institutions in India, has opted for the assessment of the institution (university or college) as a whole. This has largely been dictated by the fact that there are over 260 universities and about 11,500 colleges to be assessed, and full efforts have to be made to achieve some unrealistic goals of government agencies. Experience shows that institutional evaluation follows popular perception, which is generally based on reputation acquired over a number of years and does not always reflect the present situation. The usefulness of such an evaluation is questionable, especially in the case of the universities that have a large number of departments undertaking post-graduate teaching and research. The limited number of peer-team members cannot do justice to the large number of disciplines that have to be evaluated. And inferior departments are shielded, attracting students on the basis of the overall grade of the institution. The cause of students and parents would be better served if assessment in the non-professional disciplines at the university (post-graduate teaching and research) level is undertaken with the department or school as the unit of assessment, and at the college (under-graduate teaching) level with the faculty as the unit. In the professional disciplines the National Board of Accreditation (NBA), under the All India Council for Technical Education, is undertaking programme evaluation and this needs to be continued.

Indian Initiatives for Quality Improvement

Since independence, in 1947, concerted efforts are being made in India for improvement of quality of higher education. Various measures have been outlined in policy documents including, for example, the Report of the Education Commission (1964-66), the National Policy on Education (1986), and the Programme of Action (1992) that emanated from it (Government of India, 1966, 1986, 1992). The responsibility of assuring quality is basically that of the University Grants Commission

(UGC). Its objective, under the UGC Act of 1956, is to take "*all such steps as it may think fit for the promotion and coordination of university education and for determination and maintenance of standards in teaching, examination and research in the universities*". In keeping with this objective the UGC has formulated and issued, from time to time, guidelines and regulation for:

- minimum infrastructure facilities to be fulfilled before a university is declared fit for central assistance,
- minimum infrastructure facilities to be fulfilled before the grant of affiliation to a college by a university,
- essential qualifications for the appointment of lecturers, readers and professors,
- workload of teachers, duration of courses, and minimum number of teaching days for first degree programmes,
- schedule of academic events, and
- evaluation and assessment of performance of teachers.

In order to bring about a qualitative improvement in teaching at the under-graduate level the UGC introduced in 1974-75, the College Science Improvement Programme (COSIP) and the College Humanities and Social Sciences Improvement Programme (COHSSIP). A scheme for Autonomous Colleges has also been introduced under which about 120 selected colleges, that have a reputation for academic excellence, have been granted freedom to develop their courses and syllabi and evolve methods of evaluation and conduct of examinations. The UGC, through Curriculum Development Centres established for the purpose, have developed model curricula in 28 subjects and these were recommended, in the early nineties, to the universities for adoption. A second cycle of revision of model curricula is underway.

In order to promote excellence in research the UGC has devised a Special Assistance Programme (SAP) under which selected departments in the faculties of science, humanities, social sciences, engineering and technology are given financial support at three levels, namely in the form of Departmental Research Support (DRS) or by upgradation to Departments of Special Assistance (DSA) or Centres of Advanced Studies (CAS). The UGC also assists selected Science and Technology Departments in universities for procuring sophisticated and costly equipment under a scheme formulated by the Committee for Strengthening of Infrastructure in Science and Technology (COSIST). The UGC has also established seven autonomous Inter-University

Centres for providing common facilities, services and programmes in frontier areas. These centres are the Nuclear Science Centre, New Delhi; Inter University Centre for Astronomy and Astrophysics, Pune; Inter University Centre for Atomic Energy, Indore; M.S.T. Radar Centre, Tirupati; Crystal Growth Centre, Madras; Consortium for Educational Communication, New Delhi; and Information and Library Network, Ahmedabad.

In 1994 two important quality monitoring agencies were established. These are the National Assessment and Accreditation Council (NAAC) under the University Grants Commission, and the National Board of Accreditation (NBA) under the All India Council for Technical Education. The responsibility for promotion and coordination of the open university and distance education system, and for determination of its standards, has been assigned to Distance Education Council of the Indira Gandhi National Open University (DEC-IGNOU). The responsibility of maintaining standards in different professional programmes rests with different statutory councils that have been established through Acts of Parliament. These include the All India Council for Technical Education (AICTE), Bar Council of India (BCI), Medical Council of India (MCI), Pharmacy Council of India (PCI), Indian Nursing Council (INC), Dentists' Council of India (DCI), Central Council for Homeopathy (CCH), Central Council for Indian Medicine (CCIM), Veterinary Council of India (VCI) and Rehabilitation Council of India (RCI).

Envoi

The success of any quality assurance initiative is greatly dependent on the managerial factor. It is essential that the top management be totally committed to the concept, be able to visualise future actions in their totality, and design appropriate procedures. This means that the mission of an institution should be clearly defined, its long-term and short-term objectives precisely identified, the strategies for achieving these carefully planned, the financial requirements of different programmes assessed, adequate budgetary controls exercised, and inter-personnel relationships maintained at an optimum level. Self-evaluation is usually the starting point with the main objective being to identify areas of strength and weakness. However, as Williams (1993) notes: *"Quality improvement comes not from inspection but from design, that is the establishment of procedures that make it impossible for bad quality to be undetected and encourage the primary aim of continuous quality improvement".*

It is often argued that for the successful implementation of quality assurance measures the concept of Total Quality Management (TQM) should be applied in educational institutions, worldwide. However, the application of TQM techniques is not likely to be easy in higher education institutions for an essential requirement would be significant cultural change - from the present collegial culture to the enterprise culture of business (see Powar, 2001). The study by Chaston (1994), relating to possible implementation of TQM in the British universities, has shown that a number of initial barriers that will have to be overcome before implementation of TQM becomes a feasible option. The situation in India is not different. Significantly, Ewell (1999) has emphasised the fact that ideas and concepts borrowed from an alien sector rarely succeed. All innovations related to quality assurance must, therefore, have their roots in the traditional collegial culture that prevails in most universities of the world.

References

Berdahl, R., (1990), Academic Freedom, Autonomy and Accountability in British Universities, *Studies in Higher Education*, 15(2): 169 - 180.

Benadusi, L., (1997), 'Editorial', *European Journal of Education*, 32(2): 107-110.

British Standards Institution, (1989), BS 7229 *Quality Systems Auditing*, B.S. I., London.

Brown, R., (2000), The New UK Quality Framework, *Higher Education Quarterly*, 54(4): 323-342.

Bureau of Indian Standards, (1988), *IS 13999-Quality System Vocabulary, IS-14000 Quality Systems: Guidelines for Selection and Use of Standards on Quality Systems*, BIS, New Delhi.

Calder, J., (1994), *Programme Evaluation and Quality*, Kogan Page, London.

Chaston, I., (1994), Are British Universities in a position to consider implementing Total Quality Management, *Higher Education Quarterly*, 48; 1 1 8-134.

Crawford, F., (1991), *Total Quality Management*, Occasional Paper C VCP, London.

Deshpande, P.M., (1994), Quality Assurance in Higher Education: Issues and Trends, in Deshpande, P.M. and Mugridge, I., (Editors), *Perspectives on Distance Education: Quality Assurance in Higher Education*, COL, Vancouver, 83-105.

Ewell, P.T., (1999), Imitation as Art: Borrowing Management Techniques in Higher Education, *Change*, 31(6): 10-15.

Government of India, (1966), *Report on the Education Commission (1964-66): Education and National Development*, GOI, New Delhi.

Government of India, (1986), *National Policy on Education*, 1986, GOI, New Delhi.

Government of India, (1992), *Programme of Action, National Policy on Education*, 1986, GOI, Reprinted by UGC, New Delhi.

Green, D, and Harvey, L., (1993), Quality assurance in western Europe: Trends, practices and issues, in Santa, T.W., Anderson, C.L. and Berendt, B., (Editors), Proc. Fifth

International Conference on *Assessing Quality in Higher Education*, Indiana University-Purdue University, Indianapolis.

Green, D., (1994), *What is Quality in Higher Education ?.* S.R.H.E and Open University Press, Buckingham.

Henderikx, P., (1992), *Management and Promotion of Distance Education*, Open Education, 7: 34-41.

Kekale, J., (2000), Quality Assessment in Diverse Disciplinary Settings, *Higher Education,* 40(4): 465-488.

Lenn, M.P., (1993), Quality Assurance in Higher Education: A Tour of Practice and Resources. *Higher Education in Europe*, 18: 71-80.

Marchese, T., (1993), TQM: A Time for Ideas, *Change*, 25(3): 10-13.

Meade, P., (2001), Consolidating Enhancement in Higher Education, in *Quality Assurance in Higher Education: Quality, Standards and Recognition, 2001 INQUAAHE, Bangalore* : 1-20.

Naudeau, G.G., (1992), *The Use of Quality and Excellence Indicators in Post-Secondary Education*, Canadian Society.for the Study of Higher Education, Ottawa.

Powar, K.B., (2001), *Management of Universities,* AIU Occasional Paper 2001/1, AIU, New Delhi.

Sallis, E., (1993), *Total Quality Management in Education*, Kogan Page,London.

Tachi, A. and Younezawa, A., (2001), New Quality Assurance System in Japan: What should be done by the National Institute for Academic Degrees?, in *Quality Assurance in Higher Education: Quality Standards and Recognition, 2001 INQUAAHE, Bangalore,* : 202- 210.

Taskar, M. and Packham, D., (1993), Industry and Higher Education: A question of Values, *Studies in Higher Education*, 18:122-136.

Tight, M., (1988), What is Academic Freedom?, in Tight, M. (Editor*), Academic Freedom and Responsibility*, p 114-132 Open University Press, Milton Keynes.

Vroeijenstijn, A.I., (1995), *Improvement and Accountability: Navigating between Sxylla and Charybdis,* Jessica Kinglsley, London.

Wagner, R.B., (1989), *Accountability in Education: A Philosophical Enquiry*, Routledge, London.

Warren, J., McManus, K. and Nnazor, R., (1994), Quality Assurance and Distance Education: A Review of Literature, in Deshpande, P.M. and Mugddge, 1. (Editors), *Perspectives on Distance Education: Quality Assurance in Higher Education*, COL, Vancouver.

Williams, G., (1993), Total Quality Management in Higher Education: Panacea or Placebo, *Higher Education,* 25(3): 229-237.

18

Performance Indicators and Benchmarking in Higher Education

Introduction

Quality Assurance in Higher Education calls for the development of dependable performance indicators and for the adoption of benchmarks that are acceptable to stakeholders nationally, and preferably, globally. This latter is desirable as today, quality assurance has become a global issue with many countries calling for international standards in higher education, and for benchmarking. In this paper the basic issues related to the significance of performance indicators and benchmarking are discussed.

Performance Indicators

The criteria used for evaluating the work of an individual or institution, or for adjudging the effectiveness of a programme, are often referred to as 'performance indicators'. Following the publication of the Jarratt Report, in 1985, by the Committee of Vice Chancellors and Principals, UK, considerable interest has been generated, world over, on the use of performance indicators in higher education. A very large number of such indicators have been identified, and as many as 264 have been listed by Bottrill and Borden (1994) (One presumes that since then there has been a significant number of additions to the list). However, the validity, reliability and utility of many of them have been questioned. Evidently, performance indicators cannot be universal in their applicability and must, therefore, be chosen with care keeping in view the goals and objectives of the institution, the ethos of the educational system of which it is a part, and the available data-base.

Concept

The idea of performance indicators in higher education is borrowed from economics where the efficacy of a system or institution is related to its productivity in terms of efficiency and returns. As Ramsden (1991) puts it: "*The idea of performance indicators derives from economic models of the education system as a process within a wider economic system which converts inputs (such as academics' salaries) into outputs (such as research papers)*". They may, therefore, broadly be described as quantifiable variables that may be used as tools in decision-making.

In a survey undertaken by the Organisation for Economic Cooperation and Development (OECD) in the mid-1980s performance indicators are defined as "*numerical value(s) used to measure something which is difficult to quantify (and) which can be derived in different ways. They provide measurement for assessing the quantitative and qualitative performance of systems*" (Cuenin, 1987). Later the Morris Report (1990) improved upon this definition and stated that "*Performance indicators are statistics, ratios, costs and other forms of information which illuminate or measure progress in achieving the mission and corresponding aims and objectives of the government (or agency) or of a university (or other institution)*". Kells (1992) attempting to balance subjective and objective information proposes the following definition: "*Performance indicators are factual or opinion information gathered from existing data bases or de novo, about the functioning of organisations or their constituent units and for various purposes (monitoring, decision support, comparing, evaluating, improving). They serve as signals to institutions or governments to explore the reasons for deviation from normative or expected levels of activity or achievement in relation to goals or standards*".

In recent years a distinction has been made between performance indicators and statistics, or more specifically, management statistics. The latter terms cover the basic 'descriptions' of an institution (university) or of a system (higher education system). It has to be emphasised that while an indicator is a statistic not all statistics are indicators that reflect performance. To provide information about performance of an institution or system the indicator must have a reference point, or benchmark, against which to judge the statistic (Freeman, 1995). As Sizer *et al*. (1992) point out: "*Indicators differ from statistics in that they are signals of guides rather than absolute measures and, more important in this context, they acquire their significance from the process of 'operationalising' the theoretical aspects of quality, effectiveness and efficiency*".

The development of performance indicators has its roots in the dissatisfaction of the UK government, in the early eighties, regarding the effectiveness of its universities. This was first manifested in the form of a green paper (Department of Education and Science, 1985) on *The Development of Higher Education into the 1990s*, which pressed for improved contribution from the educational sector in national economic development. It demanded that higher education should be more responsive to the requirements of the economy, should try to obtain increased private funding and should not be heavily dependent on public funds, should display greater selectivity in the allocation of research funding, and should be more cost conscious managing its resources efficiently and effectively. A Steering Committee set up by the Committee of Vice Chancellors and Principals, to examine the efficiency and effectiveness of universities, in its report (the Jarratt Report, 1985) recommended that reliable and consistent performance indicators needed to be developed. It suggested that *"a range of performance indicators should be developed covering both inputs and outputs and designed for use both within individual institutions and for making comparisons within institutions"*.

The concept of performance indicators is today accepted universally but for different reasons. In the United Kingdom it came as a response to market forces that demanded better products from universities. In Australia performance indicators were developed so that education institutions could respond more positively to government priorities. In the Netherlands quality assessment, through performance indicators, was used to impose fiscal responsiveness and discipline. And in the United States its use facilitated the securing of greater autonomy from state legislatures (Gaither *et. al*, 1994).

Performance indicators, if they are to be used to measure the accountability of an academic institution, must comply with certain basic conditions. As emphasised by Sizer (1979), they must be, relevant, verifiable, free-from-bias, quantifiable, economically feasible, and acceptable in the institution being evaluated. It may be added that the performance indicators must be capable of being upgraded and easily comprehendable. Further they must take into account the goals of the institution. Ball and Halwachi (1987) point out "*the use of such indicators must be accompanied by a clear statement of goals, the relative importance of each goal and an indication of how each indicator measures the goal in question*". Some workers, e.g., Birch *et.al.* (1979), suggest a 'value-added approach' for assessing performance. This would require the evaluation of the capability of a student twice – initially at entry-point and later on the completion of studies; and then assessing improvement. Johnes and Taylor (1990) emphasise that while comparing performances of universities it is necessary to take into account both inputs and outputs. They state, "*Instead of comparing each university's outputs with (say) the average for all universities, each university's outputs should be compared with the outputs that we would expect each university to produce given its particular mix of inputs*". Regression analysis undertaken by them shows that it is equally important to take input variations into consideration when calculating research output.

A Working Group set up in the United Kingdom, jointly organised by the University Grants Commission and the Committee of Vice Chancellors and Principals, recommended the development of a range of quantitative performance indicators that would be of use to the universities (Committee of Vice Chancellors and Principals, 1988). The indicators should:

- relate to the objectives of the universities, especially teaching and research,
- be specific, quantifiable and standardised so as to enable comparisons within and between institutions,
- be simple so as to aid understanding of activities,
- be acceptable, credible and free of bias, and
- provide information about the activities and operations of the institution.

Subsequently, the Higher Education Funding Councils in the UK jointly established, in 1993, a Joint Performance Indicators Working Group to develop performance indicators that could be consistently and equitably interpreted. The report of this working group recommended institution indicators in the broad areas of teaching and learning, research, estate management and financial health; and also macro indicators related to student participation and output, research and financial aspects. (Committee of Vice Chancellors and Principals, 1995). The Working Group suggested that the performance indicators should be flexible, problem-oriented and policy-relevant, and quantitative rather than qualitative. Further, they should utilise simple and reliable statistics that are constructed from information and data available from existing sources.

Types of Performance Indicators

The Jarratt Committee proposed the development of three types of performance indicators: internal, external and operational. *Internal indicators* are those that are based on information relating to the institution such as number of applications for admission, graduation rates, examination results, and attraction of research grants. *External indicators* are concerned with the external performance of the institution such as acceptability of graduates for employment, publications by staff, honours conferred on the faculty, and overall reputation as judged by external reviews. *Operational indicators* include variables such as student/staff ratio, unit cost of education, class sizes, and availability of library and computing facilities.

The UGC/CVCP Working Group (Committee of Vice Chancellors and Principals, 1988) identified three broad types of indicators:

- *Input indicators* that relate to the resources and factors employed to produce an institution's outputs (financial resources, physical facilities, student and staff profiles),
- *Process indicators* that relate to the ways in which resources and factors are combined and used in order to produce an institution's output (management of teaching, research and services), and
- *Output indicators* that describe the outputs produced by institutions (products of teaching, research and services).

To these may be added the *Outcome Indicators* of Kaufmann (1988) which are the effects of outputs in society (employment rates, life expectancy).The majority of indicators in use relate to inputs and processes and regrettably there are much fewer indicators based on outputs or outcomes.

Kells (1992) recognises two types of indicators, namely those used by government, and by institutions. *Indicators for government* include nationally defined measures of institutional responses to government goals and policies (equality of access, reservations). *Indicators for institutions* include institutional management indicators (workload, student enrollment, financial trends) and teaching, research and service indicators (examination results, publication and citation analysis, finished product quality). In keeping with this classification, in the United Kingdom, a distinction is made *between Macro-performance* indicators that are indicators of the higher education system as a whole, and *Institution performance indicators* that may be applied to individual institutions.

Chandrashekhara Rao (1997) has identified, specifically for the distance education system, three types of performance indictors, namely micro-, macro- and mega- indicators. *Micro-indicators* are those that relate or to specific operations within a sub-system that have a bearing on overall performance. An example is the method of identification of courses and programmes in the process of learning materials development. *Macro-indicators* include those areas of performance that are of aggregate nature like entry-exit performance of students. *Mega-indicators* are those areas of performance in which an open university, as a special sub-system, interacts with the social system as a whole. Examples are the ratio of formal education programme to non-formal educational packages, and the nature and extent of the institute's interface with industry.

The Use of Performance Indicators

The basic purpose of a performance indicator obviously is to evaluate the performance of a system, institution or organisational structure. In the case of academic institutions it is to be used, internally, for enhancing the quality of teaching, research or social service provided by the institution. To the outsider it can provide important evidence regarding the health and functioning of the institution.

Sizer *et.al.* (1992), while investigation government-institution relationship, have identified five core functions for performance indicators. These are:

Monitoring: Registering developments in the system on the basis of information in existing databases.

Evaluation: Commenting on the degree of goal achievement.

Dialogue: Facilitating the improvement of mutual administrative relationships.

Rationalisation: Assisting in the accomplishment of a coherent policy-making process.

Resource Allocation: Providing parameters for resource allocation models.

Within the framework of the above functions performance indicators may be used for various purposes, namely:

- As a measure of accountability.
- For comparison of performances of similar institutions, or of individuals performing similar functions.
- For improving effectiveness of management by providing information regarding a range of activities.
- For staff development by providing faculty with appropriate feedback designed to help them to improve performance.
- For creating awareness amongst students by providing information about systems, programmes and performances.

- For image building and marketing of programmes, and for influencing government policy.
- As a basis for allocation of resources.

In most countries the academic community, long used to unquestioned freedom of thought and action, has not taken kindly to performance indicators. The initial reaction has been one of suspicion. While many are willing to accept performance indicators for the purposes of self-evaluation and policy formulation they are afraid that it may be used for controlling academic institutions and curtailing grants. Davis (1996) sums up the situation thus: "*Where performance indicators become most controversial is where the emphasis shifts from their use as one of many inputs into effective decision-making to using them as a ranking devise to allocate esteem and funding differentially*".

Constraints

The development of performance indicators, for assessing the performance of academic institutions, has been supported by governments and funding agencies in the belief that such evaluations are in the interest of students, citizens and management. Reservations have, however, been covertly expressed by many educationists regarding their use for decision making related to policy and funding. There is a fear that universities may be encouraged to report only simple, readily available quantitative measures (that are of benefit to them) instead of complex, qualitative assessments of the quality of higher education that are based upon professional judgement. There is a possibility that universities may be tempted to distort the educational experience they offer in order to return high scores on performance indicators (Morrison *et.al.*, 1995). Fears have also been expressed regarding the relevance, accuracy and efficacy of many measures that have been, or are likely to be, employed. This only suggests that performance indicators have to be carefully chosen and the trust of academic institutions ensured. It must be emphasised that performance indicators are not an end in themselves, but only tools of evaluation. Much depends on how they are utilised. Strictly from the point of view of quality assurance and quality enhancement it has been suggested (Banta and Borden, 1994; Cave *et. al.,* 1997) should largely be used with reference to future actions rather than past performance.

Performance Indicators for Indian Institutions

Keeping in view the need to assess the quality of teaching and research in different educational institutions in India a shortlist of performance indicators that are most relevant in the Indian context is presented below. While drawing up this list the factors taken into account are cost, availability of information, general acceptability and comparability. These are:

A For Evaluation of Teaching:

- Implementation of academic calendar
- Examination results
- Curricula quality
- Student/Alumnus evaluation
- First destination of graduates

B For Evaluation of Research:

- Publications and citations
- Research projects
- Peer review
- Awards, honours and patents

C For Evaluation of Administration:

- Faculty and staff profiles
- Unit costs – academic and administrative
- Generation of funds
- Utilisation of grants
- Administrative efficiency

Benchmarking

'Benchmarking' is a term derived from management that has been loosely used and understood, and variously defined. The definition generally adopted in the world of business and management is that given by the American Productivity and Quality Center (1993) namely that *"Benchmarking is the process of continuously comparing and measuring an organisation with business leaders anywhere in the world to gain information which will help the organisation to take action to improve its performance"*. Price (1994) described it as *"the open and collaborative evaluation of services and processes with the aim of emulating best available practice"*. Evaluating benchmarking in terms of educational requirements Fielden (1997) described it as *"a self-improvement tool for organizations which allows them to compare themselves with others, to identify their comparative strengths and weaknesses, and learn how to improve".* Schofield (1998) while describing the processes that characterise benchmarking stated: *"Benchmarking is a means of making comparisons of performance, usually with a view to establish 'good' - or more ambitiously 'best' – practice methods, and as such it is also used to diagnose problems in performance and to identify areas of strength".* He points out that in the literature relating to quality assurance and enhancement 'benchmarking' has come to acquire a meaning somewhat removed from 'benchmark' which is generally considered to be a standard against which an item and be measured or judged. It is, perhaps, for this reason that benchmarking does not always refer to 'the best'. Bolton (2000), quoting three different definitions of benchmarking, points out that in higher education it is used in at least three contexts. He writes: *"... benchmarking is being used – confusingly – to refer to comparisons with levels of performance which are respectively world class, successful and at the threshold, that is the minimum acceptable".* The present tendency is to use benchmarking with reference to comparison, not necessarily comparison with the best.

Schofield (1998) has reviewed the development and present status of benchmarking in the developed world (United Kingdom, North America, Australia and Europe). He has cited conceptual and practical difficulties but is of the view that it has clear potential as an effective approach to quality management within higher education. Benchmarking, as Farquhar (1998), points out involves two facets. First, the systematic generation of management information that can produce performance indicators and lead to the identification of benchmarks. Second, the identification of 'best practices' and their adaptation for continuous improvement of quality. While the first is common the second has been taken up seriously by only a few institutions.

Types of Benchmarking

In higher education benchmarking has taken up different forms. Alstete (1995) has identified four types:

- *Internal benchmarking* in which comparison is made between different units (departments, faculties, colleges) within the same university, without comparing with external standards, principally to identify and emulate good/best practices.
- *External competitive benchmarking* where a comparison of performance in key area is made on the basis of information from other institutions that are seen as competitors.

- *External collaborative benchmarking* in which comparisons are made with larger groups of institutions which are not regarded as competitors, and using a methodology that is relatively open amd collaborative.
- *External trans-industry (best-in-class) benchmarking* which involves looking across multiple industries/ institutions in search of new and innovative practices.

Benchmarking Procedures

Benchmarking is not simply the compilation of information on an organisation and comparing it against standards or norms. It is a fairly complicated exercise and involves, first the examination and understanding of the internal work procedures of an organisation or institution, next the searching for 'best practices' in other similar institutions, and finally the adaptation of these practices for quality improvement. As described by Epper (1999), *"Benchmarking is a humbling experience. It requires us to look deeply at ourselves, to recognise our weaknesses, and to look elsewhere for examples of how to do things better"*.

Schofield (1998) has enumerated five methodologies used in benchmarking: These are:

- *Benchmarking by ideal-type standards* in which a model, based on idealised best-practices, is created and institutions are assessed on the basis of the extent to which they fit the model.
- *Activity-based benchmarking* in which a selected number of typical or representative activities are analysed and compared with similar activities in other institutions.
- *Vertical benchmarking* in which the costs, workloads, productivity in a defined functional area (example the work of student admission department) are quantified.
- *Horizontal benchmarking* in which the cost, workloads, productivity and performance of a single process that cuts across one or more functional area (example all aspects of student admission irrespective of location) are analysed.
- *Benchmarking through comparative performance indicators* (example league tables) undertaken by outside interests that influence public opinions and judgement.

Epper (1999) has drawn attention to the *Consortium Benchmarking Methodology* developed by the American Productivity and Quality Center in which a group of institutions, sharing a common interest, work together with corporate sponsors to identify best practices. The decisions are based on collective inputs of institutions, sponsors, a subject expert and APQC facilitators.

Benchmarking for Recognition of Qualifications

Increased student mobility and greater employment opportunities at the international level have brought into focus the need for formalising a system that would facilitate the recognition of academic qualifications. Randall (2001) has drawn attention to the fact that students are not only concerned about the quality of learning opportunities provided but also about the recognition, by governments, professional bodies and potential employers in the market, of the qualifications gained by them. Benchmarking provides the mechanism by which this can be done.

Conventionally, degrees have been recognised (and equivalence granted) essentially on the basis of the duration of the programme and the prescribed curricula. Within a country, and even regionally, the practice of mutual recognition of degrees is followed. In India, for example, the degrees of different universities are recognised mutually on the basis of a resolution of the Association of Indian Universities first adopted in 1956 and reiterated in 1993, that specifies that *"the examination of one university be recognised by another, on reciprocal basis, provided that the entrance qualifications, duration of the course and the general standard of attainment are similar to those prescribed by the recognising university"*. (Association of Indian Universities, 1993).

With the globalisation of higher education the system of mutual recognition is finding acceptance, especially in the professional fields. An example is the Washington Accord, signatories to which are professional associations or statutory bodies with government recognition. The Accord has adopted the principle of benchmarking for it specifies that the criteria, policies and procedures used by the signatories in accrediting engineering programmes should be comparable, and also provides for mutual monitoring and information exchange.

The second half of the twentieth century saw the 'massification' of higher education in practically all countries of the world, A large number of new institutions were established, many with sub-standard infrastructure and facilities. Quality was a major casualty in the developing countries, and within every country there is today great variation in standards. Duration of a programme and the curricula are, in many cases, no longer valid criteria for grant of equivalence to degrees, especially those in the non-professional subjects. New benchmarks may be necessary, and these should preferably based on output in terms of the learning process. The attributes prescribed for the Bachelors, Masters and Doctoral degrees in the National Qualifications Framework descriptor in the new U.K. Quality Framework (see Randall, 2001) provide starting point in the development of new benchmarks for liberal higher education.

The rapid expansion of distance education, following unprecedented developments in information and communication technologies, has given rise to new problems. Universities of the developed world are offering a variety of 'off-shore degrees' on-line – for a price. As Altbach (1999) points out *"quality control in the educational market place is spotty"*. At least a few of the 'off-shore degrees' are 'off-the-shelf degrees'. International distance education is an area that needs to be controlled and regulated. Benchmarking and the establishment of benchmarks needs to be undertaken on a priority basis.

Conclusion

Quality assurance cannot be achieved by assessment alone. It calls for introspection and systematic planning. The present standards have to be adjudged and compared with those prevailing in the better (if not first-rate) institutions. For this carefully chosen performance indicators need to be used and benchmarking resorted to.

References

Alstete, J.W., (1995), *Benchmarking in Higher Education: Adapting Best Practices to Improve Quality,* ASHE-ERIC-HE Report No 5, the George Washington University, Washington.

Altbach, P.G., (1999), The Perils of Internationalizing Higher Education: An Asian Perspective, *International Higher Education, 15(Spring)*: 4-5.

American Productivity and Quality Center, (1993), *The Benchmarking Management Guide,* APQC, Portland, Oregon.

Association of Indian Universities, (1993), Resolution of General Body, *Proceedings, 65th Annual Meeting, University of Delhi, Delhi,* AIU, New Delhi.

Ball, R., and Halwachi, J., (1987), Performance Indicators in Higher Education, *Higher Education,* 16: 393-403.

Banta, T., and Borden, V., (1994), Performance Indicators for Accountability and Improvement, in Borden, V. and Banta, T. (Editors), *Using Performance Indicators to Guide Strategic Decision Making,* Jossey Bass, San Francisco.

Birch, D., Calvert, J., and Sizer, J., (1979) Case Study of some Performance Indicators in Higher Education in the U.K., *International Journal of Institutional Management in Higher Education,* 10: 133-142.

Bolton, A., (2000), *Managing the Academic Unit,* Open University Press, Buckingham.

Bottrill, K., and Borden, V., (1994), Performance Indicators: History, Definitions and Methods, in Borden, V. and Banta, T. (Editors), *Using Performance Indicators to Guide Strategic Decision Making,* Jossey-Bass, San Francisco.

Cave, M., Hanney, S., Henkel, M. and Kogan, M., (1997), *The Use of Performance Indicators in Higher Education (Third Edition),* Jessica Kingsley Publishers, London.

Chandrashekhara Rao (1997), Performance Indicators in Distance Education: A look at Levels of Analysis, *Staff and Educational Development International,* 1: 143-150.

Committee of Vice Chancellors and Principals, (1988), *University Management Statistics and Performance Indicators in the UK,* CVCP, U.K. London.

Committee of Vice Chancellors and Principals, (1995), *Higher Education Management Statistics: A Future Strategy;* CVCP, U.K. London.

Cuenin, S., (1987). The Use of Performance Indicators in Universities: An International Survey, *International Journal of Institutional Management in Higher Education,* 11: 149-162.

Davis, D., (1996), *The Real World of Performance Indicators,* CHEMS, London.

Department of Education and Science, (1985), *The Development of Higher Education into the 1990s,* HMSO, Cmnd 9524, London.

Epper, R.M., (1999), Applying Benchmarking to Higher Education, *Change,* 31(6): 24-31.

Farquhar, R.H., (1998), Higher Education Benchmarking in Canada and the United States of America, in Schofield, A., (Editor), *Benchmarking in Higher Education: An International Review,* CHEMS, London.

Fielden, J., (1997), *Benchmarking University Performance,* CHEMS, London.

Freeman, T.M., (1995), Performance Indicators and Assessment in the State University of New York System, *New Directions for Higher Education*, 23(3): 25-49.

Gaither, G., Nedwek, B.P., and Neal, J.E. (1994) *Measuring Up: The Promises and Pitfalls & Performance Indicators in Higher Education.* The George Washington University, Washington.

Jarratt Report, (1985), *Report of the Steering Committee for Efficiency Studies in the Universities,* CVCP, U.K. London.

Johnes, J., and Taylor, J., (1990), *Performance Indicators in Higher Education,* SRHE and Open University Press, Buckingham.

Kaufmann, R., (1988), Preparing Useful Performance Indicators, *Training and Development Journal, September Issue*: 80-83.

Kells (1992), Performance Indicators for Higher Education: A Critical Review with Recommendations, World Bank, Document No. PHREE/92/56.

Morris Report, (1990), Performance Indicators: *Report of a Committee of Inquiry*, PCFE, London.

Morrison, H.G., Magennis, S.P., and Carcy, L.G., (1995), Performance Indicators and League Table, *Higher Education Quarterly*, 49(2): 128-145.

Price, I., (1994), *A Plain Person's Guide to Benchmarking, Sheffield Hallam University, (Unpublished)*, (*cf.* Schofield, A., 1998).

Ramsden, P., (1991), A Performance Indicator of Teaching Quality in Higher Education, *Studies in Higher Education*, 16(2): 129-150.

Randall, J., (2001), Defining Standards: developing a Global Currency for Higher Education Qualifications, in *Quality Assurance in Higher Education: Quality, Standards and Recognition, 2001 INQUAAHE, Bangalore* : 46-56.

Schofield, A., (1998), Benchmarking: An Overview of Approaches and Issues in Implementation, in Scofield, A., (Editor), *Benchmarking in Higher Education : An International Review,* CHEMS, London.

Sizer, J., (1979), Assessing Institution Performance: An overview, *European Journal of Institute Management*, 3 : 59-75.

Sizer, J., Spee, A and Bormans, R., (1992), The Role of Performance Indicators in Higher Education, *Higher Education,* 24: 133-155.

Distance Education

- Distance Education: Concepts and Models
- Distance Education in India
- Globalisation of the Distance Learning System: Implications for India

19

Distance Education: Concepts and Models

Introduction

Moore (1990) defines distance education, or distance learning as "*all deliberate and planned learning that is directed or facilitated in a structured manner by an instructor ....separated in space and/or time from the learners*". Also referred to as non-traditional education, it includes all forms of education other than the traditional classroom type in which the teacher and taught are in a face-to-face situation. Thus, programmes variously designated as postal tuition, correspondence course, independent study fall within the ambit of distance education. Distance Education has its genesis in the need to provide instruction to those who are not in a position to avail of traditional oral type of instruction because of low income, age or involvement in an occupation. Almost invariably the users of the distance education mode are relatively older people, their age-range varying from young adults to the elderly. Distance learning has taken systematic teaching-learning process to persons living in isolated areas where facilities for the traditional form of classroom teaching cannot be developed. Further, as distance learning addresses the needs of specific target groups, there is a great variation in the range of programmes offered. Consequently, the basic characteristics of distance education are spatial separation of the teacher from the learner, an age-heterogeneous learner group, easy availability, and diversity in the nature of programmes offered.

Keegan (1993) points out that distance education is characterised by:

- The quasi-permanent separation of teacher and learner throughout the length of the learning process.
- The influence of an institution in both the planning and preparation of learning material, and in the provision of student support service.

* Keynote paper presented at the National Seminar *on* '*Quality Assurance in Distance Higher Education*' organised by the Association of Indian Universities, Indira Gandhi National Open University, and University of Delhi at New Delhi on November 17-19, 1998.

- The use of the technical media bringing together teacher and student.
- The provision of two-way communication in some form.
- Individualised teaching and not teaching in groups (as informal education).

Open education is a term that has been used interchangeably with distance education. It has been described as "*arrangements to enable people to learn at the time, place and space which satisfies their circumstances and requirements*" (Manpower Services Commission, 1984). While distance education refers to the process of learning in which there is spatial, and usually temporal, distance between the teacher and learner, on the other hand open education (or open learning) refers to the process of making learning available to a learner at a place and time of his/her choice, and at a rate suitable to the learner. The term 'open education' also implies open access to learning regardless of previous qualifications or age of the learner. A third term which is being increasingly used is flexible learning. The National Council for Educational Technology defines it as "*a means of making it possible for learners to gain access to education and training provision tailored to their needs and aspirations*". Lockwood (1998) points out that with reference to learning systems 'flexible' has the same meaning as 'open', only that the former term emphasises the individual nature of the programme. The layman need not do much hair-splitting as far as terminology is concerned.

While discussing distance education in the Indian context Kulandai Swamy (1992) refers to it as the third stage in the evolution of education; the first stage being represented by the Gurukul system of ancient India, and the second stage by the conventional classroom system. He believes that the distance education system symbolises the transition of education from the stage of craft to that of technology. Characterised by flexibility, high productivity and the capability to readily respond to market demands, it is an instrument that can satisfy the requirements of equity and universal education.

The Role of Educational Technology

Educational technology (ET) means different things to different people. To the lay person it usually means the use of technology in education. For specialists in the field of education the term connotes the technology of education. The professional view of ET is that it is an instructional system design that comprises both 'technology in education' and 'technology of education'; while the former involves the design of instructional devices by applying physical sciences and engineering technology, the latter includes the creation of technology of learning by applying behavioural sciences (Lumsdaine, 1964). Distance education is obviously concerned with both aspects.

Teaching Aids and Instructional Technologies

At the beginning of the twentieth century conventional classroom teaching consisted of lectures supplemented by the use of blackboard and chalk, and of books. Distance education in its earliest form utilised only the print media. Subsequently, in the period between the two World Wars, projectors of different types and audio cassettes were added as teaching aids in formal (traditional) education, and the latter made its entry in non-formal (distance) education also. A little later video films were added to the repertoire of teaching aids. The advent of the *'techniques of the air'* (broadcasts and telecasts) marked a clear divergence in the pathways of formal and non-formal education. The years following World War II saw rapid developments in the field of communication technology opening up new pathways in both formal and non-formal education, especially in the latter. The development of computer-based technologies has revolutionised teaching and learning process. Today, as we stand on the threshold of the second millennium the advent of virtual classrooms and video desktop (two-way audio and video) promises interesting possibilities, including the remerger of the formal and informal streams.

Garrison (1989) has recognised three generations of distance learning, namely, correspondence courses, audio tele-conferencing and advanced computer-based options. James and Gardner (1995) have added a fourth generation — the options of the future. Corresponding to these generations of distance education we today recognise in distance learning the following generations of teaching aids and teaching technologies:

Generation 1: Teaching aids used in distance education through correspondence, viz., print materials, audio- and video-cassettes.

Generation 2: Technology used in distance education 'through the air', viz., broadcast and telecast, talk-back TV, interactive TV, and tele-conferencing (audio- and video-).

Generation 3: Computer-based technologies used in both formal and distance education, viz., software packages, CD-ROM, multi-media, E-Mail and Internet.

Generation 4: Technologies of the immediate future, viz., video-desktop (two-way audio-, video-), virtual classrooms.

Communication technologies in distance education may be grouped into three types (Takwale 1996):

Mass communication technologies - Radio broadcasts, TV telecasts, audio and video cassettes, audio and video tele-conferencing.

Personalised communication technologies - telephones, PC, fax, e-mail and internet.

Knowledge technologies - multi-media (integrated media) learning packages, knowledge packages, and teaching machines (virtual teachers).

It can be safely assumed that by 2025 broad-band multimedia network services will be available in all countries at public access points like institutions, if not in every home.

Strategies of Teaching-Learning

The Elton Model (Elton, 1977) on ET visualises three strategies for the teaching-learning process. These are mass communication, individualised learning (which in the case of distance education can be referred to as independent study) and group learning. All of these are currently in use.

Mass communication involves the transmission of information and knowledge by an individual to a group, or groups, of varying size/s. In the classroom situation, where the number of students is manageable, the teaching-learning process is facilitated by the use of relatively simple teaching aids like blackboard and chalk, books, visual aids like overhead and slide projectors, and audio-visual aids like films and video-cassettes. Because of developments in communication technology it is now possible to impart instructions to much larger number of students. The use of Closed Circuit Television (CCTV), for example, allows a lecture to be simultaneously delivered to different groups of students sitting at different places. The development of satellite technology has now made it possible to reach thousands of students in scattered locations through telecasts.

Individualised learning has its genesis in the pioneering work of behavioural psychology conducted by Skinner (e.g. see Skinner, 1968) in the 1950's. It led to the development of programmed learning materials that can be given to the individual learner, in small, logically structured frames. The structured materials that need individual learning needs may be in the form of print material, audio tapes, video cassettes, film strips and computer programmes. With the development of information storage devices like CD-ROM, the availability of multi-media and the incoming of Internet, individualised learning has the potential of becoming the most popular learning strategy, in both formal and informal education.

Group learning, which was put into practice in the early 1980's, involves the interaction of students with each other in a group situation. The dynamics of group learning shifts emphasis from hardware and software to techniques like tutorials, controlled group discussions, and simulation. As such technology is not important in group learning. However, tele-conferencing may become important at some point of time in the near future.

Models of Distance Education

Distance Education requires the development of programmed learning materials that can be given to the learner in small, logically-structured packages. It is learner-centred and makes use of a great variety of pedagogical forms and delivery techniques. It largely calls for independent study but group learning is also possible. The different pathways of distance education have been grouped by Miller (1995) under different models — the Correspondence Course Model, the Telecourse Model, the Open University Model, and the Distributed Classroom Model. The following discussion is based on his review.

The *Correspondence Course Model* is the oldest and most stable model of distance education. Though practised in medieval England and Germany its modern usage dates back to the 1890's when Dr. William Rainey Harper of the University of Chicago adapted it for implementing a continuing higher education programme for Chautauqua (Froke, 1995). As pointed out by Cantelon (1995) the Chautauqua movement brought continuing education to millions of Americans long before anyone used distance education. Dr. Harper may, therefore, be regarded as being the father of modern distance education and the Chautauqua programme the prototype of the Correspondence Course Model. Harper, however, saw for his adaptation only a limited role, for he wrote: *"Only those persons are encouraged to study by correspondence, or, indeed, (be) admitted to such study, who because of age, poverty, occupation, situation or some other good reason cannot avail themselves of oral instructions. Away, therefore, with all baseless and foolish prejudice in this matter. The correspondence system would not, if it could, supplant oral instruction, or be regarded as its substitute. There is a field for each which the other cannot fill. Let each do its proper work*" (Harper, 1890, quoted by Froke

1995). Unfortunately, Harper's perception still finds support, amongst most laypersons and also some educationists, in many parts of the world, including India. It is accepted as a substitute form of education for the under-privileged and the deprived, but not as an equal alternative to the traditional lecture form.

The printed word has been the dominant medium of delivery in correspondence programmes and will probably continue to be so in the foreseeable future (Verduin and Clark, 1991). In India, nine Open Universities and 61 Correspondence Course Institutes (CCIs) attached to dual mode universities offer correspondence programmes almost exclusively through the print mode. The syllabi of the programmes offered is the same as that of regular courses offered in classrooms, with the lectures being replaced by written (printed) texts that may incorporate visuals. Interaction between teacher and student is through written answers submitted as a response to tests administered periodically. Some CCIs are, however, now making efforts to supplement the printed material with audio and video cassettes. The CCIs offer a wide range of programmes, ranging from undergraduate and postgraduate degree courses to diplomas and certificates in professional areas. The Directorate of Distance Education attached to the Annamalai University, for example, offers bachelors and masters degree programmes in Arts, Science, Commerce, Management, Education and Law, as also diplomas in such diverse areas like construction management, industrial hygiene and sugar and fertilizer technologies (Association of Indian Universities, 1998).

The *Telecourse Model* was developed in the United States, primarily for the community colleges, when in the late 1960's and 1970's they faced considerable enrolment pressures and it was realised that there was the need to grant access to education to the poor and disadvantaged classes (Miller, *op. cit.*). As implemented then it consisted of a series of video lessons that were supplemented by a text and a study guide. With development of technique and technology the video lessons are now in the form of high quality documentaries broadcast to fit the schedules of general audience. The telecourses have greatly promoted adult and continuing education in the United States. A national service initiated by the Public Broadcasting Service is now available and as pointed out by Miller *(op. cit.)* a new dimension has been added to the treatment of subject matter.

In India, the telecourse model has not been utilised for imparting regular higher education courses leading to degrees or diplomas. However, programmes relating to both general themes and specific topics are being telecast on all weekdays on the national television network, Doordarshan. These are the Countrywide Classroom (CWCR) and the Open Channel of Indira Gandhi National Open University (IGNOU), the target group being the undergraduate students. Individual programmes are of 18-30 minutes' duration. About 80% of the programmes are produced in India and the remaining 20% imported keeping in view their high quality and relevance. For producing programmes of desired quality and content the University Grants Commission (UGC) has established seven Education Media Research Centres (EMRCs), and seven Audio Visual Research Centres (AVRCs). It has also set up a Mass Communication Research Centre (MCRC) and a Consortium for Educational Communication (CEC) for adapting and distributing programmes. The CEC handled about 500 programmes during 1992-93.

The *Open University Model* has been designed keeping in view the need to widen access, especially for disadvantaged groups, to quality higher education by providing a flexible and cost-effective system of instruction. It is generally accepted that the open university movement took concrete form with the establishment of the Open University at Milton Keynes, UK, in 1970. However, the oldest open university is the University of South Africa, which started teaching at a distance in 1946 (Holmberg, 1995), and the idea of a 'University of the Air' originated in Japan in the 1960's. It stemmed from a university lecture programme series of the Nippon Hoso Kyokais (NHK) conducted with the cooperation of 16 private universities of Japan. The idea was apparently shared by Mr. Yoshinori Maeda, President of NHK with Mr. Harold Wilson, then Leader of the Opposition in the British Parliament, who, evidently impressed by the concept, made the starting of such a 'University of the Air' a part of the 1963 election campaign pledge; and on winning went on to make it a part of government policy in 1964 (Gokhale, 1986). The nomenclature 'Open University' was suggested by the Planning Committee set up for establishing the university in its report of 1969. The use of the adjective 'open' is possibly enigmatic and, certainly, imprecise. It conveys a liberal attitude and, therefore, by implication, flexibility. In the words of MacKenzie *et al.* (1975) 'open' carries "*suggestions of the lessening or removal of restrictions, of exclusions and of privilege; of demolishing or lowering established barriers between subject areas; of enlarging and enriching the areas of activity and experience graded as educational*". Further, it symbolizes "*a shift in the relationship between teacher and pupil towards that of student and adviser*". Open universities and open learning, therefore, stand for access and equity, interdisciplinarity, versatility, informality and student centrelines.

Unlike in the case of the two models described previously, in the open university programmes the course curriculum does not replicate the curriculum used for traditional programmes but is specially designed by course teams to meet the requirements of students learning at a distance. The approach towards course development is characteristically interdisciplinary. The delivery is through different delivery media including print, audio and video cassettes, telecasts, interactive TV, tele-conferencing, computer software and E-Mail. Extra support is provided to learners through Student Support Services (SSS) like study centres, counselling sessions, and evaluation of Students' Assignment Responses (SAR). There is formative as also final evaluation.

In the case of open universities in India the presentation of the subject matter is largely through specially developed print material, but also through a limited number of audio and video cassettes, and a few supporting telecasts. The contact between students and tutors is through written correspondence and face-to-face sessions at study centres. The evaluation is based on SARs and end-of-session examinations and the grading is on a five-point scale, except in the case of one university where a four-point scale is employed.

The *Distributed Classroom Model* has its genesis in the need to offer popular courses to a large number of students sitting in different classrooms using close-circuit television. Initiated in the 1950's, in the United States as a one-way system, the model received impetus in the early 1990's with the introduction of interactive, compressed, video tele-communication systems (Miller, *op.cit.*). It facilitates distance learning for groups at off-campus locations in a live situation. However, the time and pace of study is under the control of the educational institution. This model is rarely utilized in India, the problem of large numbers being attended to through the formation of different 'divisions'— the same course being taught in different classrooms, usually by different teachers.

Distance Education Systems

Rumble (1986), while discussing the planning and management of distance education, describes three types of distance education systems (DES), viz., institute-centred, person-centred and society-based.

In the *Institute-centred DES* there is a predominance of systematic models of education. The institutional mission focuses on the cost-effectiveness and cost-efficiency of the system. Academics become consultants to the institution for material design and development. All other functionaries in the institution are assigned key functions with accountability and individual responsibility.

In the *Person-centred DES* the programmes are more individualised and negotiable as the aim is to serve the individual learner. Individualised learning is personally negotiated and is followed up by tutors/counsellors.

In the *Society-based DES* learning materials are developed in accordance with the needs of the community. These are used in community situations where the teacher strives to involve the entire community in the study of the learning materials. The teacher functions as a facilitator for the identification of learning goals, learning materials, evaluation mechanisms and the like.

A recent clarification of open (distance) learning systems, proposed by Freeman (1997), identifies six systems based on: (i) whether the system is campus-based, organisation-based or individual-based; and (ii) whether it is institution-paced or self-paced. These systems are:

- *Campus-based, paced DES* which has the characteristics of the formal system, like semester, lectures, time-table, yet at the same time requires individual responsibility for learning. An example is the computer programming course at the University of Sunderland, UK.
- *Organisation-based, paced DES* in which training and continuing education is based on the work at hand, and not on the employees, need. The in-company flexible learning schemes of the Open College, UK are cited as the best examples of the system.
- *Individual-based, paced DES* in which institution provides guidance and all teaching-learning materials. The programme is offered at a pace dictated by the institutes, preparedness. Deadlines are prescribed for all activities that are followed by the learners who wish to complete the academic programme within the stipulated time. Examples are the programmes of Open Universities.
- *Campus-based, self-paced DES* is characterised by considerable tutor-learner contact and interaction. Both tutoring and assessment are based on the needs of the individual learner. There is also interaction between the learners. An example is the basic IT course at the University of Lincolnshire and Humberside, UK.
- *Organisation-based, self-paced DES* which is in many ways similar to the campus-based, self-paced DES. Here, learning takes place at

the work place with the line-manager performing the role of tutor. The CBT course of the National Westminister Bank, UK is a good example of this system.

- *The Individual-based, self-paced DES* where the institution allows sufficient flexibility to the learner which enables them to proceed at their own pace. In the absence of regular tutor-learner contact, individual learners may be at different points in the learning continuum. Examples are the correspondence courses of the National Extension College, UK.

Epilogue

Since its establishment more than hundred years ago, in the form of correspondence courses, distance education has come a long way. It is developing very rapidly, and assuming new forms. The latest version - online education - promises to play a very important role in the immediate future, even threatening to partially replace conventional education.

References

Association of Indian Universities, (1998), *Handbook on Distance Education*, AIU, New Delhi.

Cantelon, J.E., (1995), The Evolution and Advantages of Distance Education, in Rossman, M.H. and Rossman, M.E. (Editors), 'Facilitating Distance Education', *New Directions for Adult and Continuing Education*, 67: 3-10.

Elton, R.B., (1977), Education Technology — Today and Tommorow, in Hill, P. and Gilbert, J. (Editors), *Aspects of Educational Technology, XI*, Kogan Page, London.

Freeman, R., (1997) *Managing Open Systems*, Kogan Page, London.

Froke, M.D., (1995), Antecedents to Distance Education and Continuing Education: Time to Fix Them, in Rossman, M.H. and Rossman, M.E. (Editors), 'Facilitating Distance Education', *New Directions for Adult and Continuing Education,* 67: 61-70.

Garrison, D.R., (1989), Distance Education, in Merriam, S.B. and Cunningham, P.M. (Editors), *Handbook of Adult and Continuing Education*, Jossey-Bass, San Francisco.

Gokhale, L.N., (1986), *The Use of ETV in India and Japan*, Mudra, Pune.

Holmberg, Borje (1995), Theory and Practice of Distance Education, (Second Edition) London, Routledge.

James, W.B. and Gardner, D.L., (1995), Learning Styles: Implications for Distance Learning, in Rossman, M.H. and Rossman, M.E.(Editors), 'Facilitating Distance Education', *New Directions for Adult and Continuing Education*, 67: 19-31.

Keegan, D., (1993), Reintegration of the Teaching Act, in Keegan, D., (Editor), *Theoretical Principles of Distance Education,* Routledge, London.

Kulandai Swamy, V.C., (1992), Distance Education in the Indian Context, *Indian Journal of Open Learning,* 1(1): 1-4.

Lockwood, F., (1998), *The Design and Production of Self Instructional Materials*, Kogan Page, London.

Lumsdaine, A.A., (1964), Educational Technology, Programmed Learning and Instructional Science, in Hilgard, F.R. (Editor), *Theories of Learning and Instruction*, Univ. of Chicago Press, Chicago, Ill.

Mackenzie, N., (1975), Open Learning: Systems and Problems in Post Secondary Education Unesco Press, Paris. (498 pages).

Manpower Services Commission, (1984), *A New Training Initiative*, MSC, Sheffield.

Miller, G.E., (1995), The Undergraduate Curriculum and Distance Education, in Rossman, M.H. and Rossman, M.E. (Editors), 'Facilitating Distance Education', *New Directions for Adult and Continuing Education,* 67: 41-49.

Moore, M.G., (1990), Correspondence Study, in Galbraith, M.W. (Editor), *Adult Training Methods*, Krieger, Malabar, Fla.

Rumble, G. (1986), *Planning and Management of Distance Education*, Croom Halin, London

Skinner, B.F. (1968), *The Technology of Teaching,* Appleton-Century-Crofts, New York.

Takwale, R.G., (1996), New Paradigm for a Networked System of Higher Education, Preprint, *Symposium on Vision 21: Paradigm Shift in Tertiary Education*, OLI, Hong Kong.

Verduin, J.R. and Clark, T.A., (1991), *Distance Education: The Foundations of Effective Practice,* Jossey-Bass, San Francisco.

Wabberley, R. and Haffenden, I, (1987), 'Skills Training and Responsive Management' in Thorpe, M. and Grugeon, D. (Editors) *Open Learning for Adults*, Longman, Harlow.

20

Distance Education in India*

Introduction

Our present understanding of the role of distance education in promoting higher education in India is reflected in the report of the CABE Committee on distance education appointed to advice on the direction and growth and development of the open university system in India (Government of India, 1994). The report has listed the major objectives of distance education as:

- To provide an alternate, cost-effective, non-formal channel for tertiary education.
- To supplement the conventional university system and to reduce the pressure on it.
- To provide 'second chance' education to those who have had to discontinue their formal education or could not join regular colleges or universities owing to social, economic and other considerations.
- To democratise higher education by providing access to large segments of the population, in particular the disadvantaged groups such as those living in remote and rural areas, including working people like women and other adults, who wish to acquire and upgrade their knowledge and/or skills.
- To strengthen and diversify the degree, certificate and diploma courses related to employment, and necessary for building the economy of the country, on the basis of its natural and human resources.
- To provide continuing and life-long education to enrich the lives of the people.

* Updated version of paper presented at the National Seminar *on 'Quality Assurance in Distance Higher Education'* organised by the Association of Indian Universities, Indira Gandhi National Open University and University of Delhi, at New Delhi on November 17-19, 1998.

- To provide an innovative system of university-level education, which is flexible and open in terms of method and pace of learning, combination of courses, eligibility for enrolment, age of entry, conduct of examination and operation of the programmes with a view to promoting learning and encouraging excellence in new fields of knowledge.

In India higher education is imparted through the distance mode by two types of institutions — the correspondence course institutes attached to the conventional universities, and the open universities. The first were established largely to meet the rapidly increased demand for higher education in the years immediately following independence; the second to provide a flexible and open form of education in which the quality of education could be ensured through an optimum use of technology. Today, both forms of distance education are firmly established. While their growth is to be encouraged more crucial is the ensuring of the quality of programmes offered by them.

Correspondence Course Institutes (CCIs)

Distance education in India, in formalised form, has its genesis in a recommendation of the Central Advisory Board of Education (CABE), made in 1961, that a detailed study of correspondence courses be conducted. A committee set up under the chairmanship of Dr. D.S. Kothari to examine the matter recommended the starting of correspondence courses because of their flexibility, economic viability and innovativeness. The University Grants Commission decided to encourage part-time and own-time education, and the University of Delhi, Delhi was asked to undertake a pilot project by instituting correspondence courses. Accordingly the university established, in 1962, its School of Correspondence Courses and Continuing Education (Singh *et al.*, 1994). The Education Commission appointed by the Government of India in 1964, to advise it on the adoption of general principles and policies for the development of education in all its aspects, strongly advocated the promotion of correspondence education. In its report (Government of India, 1966) it recommended that *"opportunities for part-time education through evening colleges and own-time education through programmes like Correspondence Courses should be extended as widely as possible and these programmes should also include courses in Science and Technology".*

Punjabi University, Patiala was the second university in India to launch correspondence courses, in 1968, through its Directorate of Correspondence Courses (DCC), and the first university to introduce regional medium of instruction. In subsequent years the number of CCIs increased rapidly and in 1999-2000. there were 64 CCIs attached to different dual-mode universities (Association of Indian Universities, 2000). These collectively offer a great variety of post-graduate, under-graduate, diploma and certificate programmes and cater to the needs of about 810,000 students. Three of these CCIs, namely those at Annamalai, Madurai and Delhi universities, enrol more than 50,000 students each.

The only comprehensive study undertaken on the CCIs in India is the one by Singh *et al.* (1994). Analysing the data, for 1989-90, for 29 institutions they conclude:

- The male:female ratio of students was approximately 60:40; 42% of those enrolled were employed, 39% came from rural areas, and 12.3% were from the reserved categories (SC, ST, BC).
- The number of faculty members employed in the CCIs varied considerably; from only three at SNDT University, Mumbai and Barkatullah University, Bhopal to 95 at University of Delhi, Delhi. The majority of the faculty did not have any qualification in distance education, except for their on-the-job experience, and they are not encouraged to undertake research in distance education. However, there was good interaction between the CCIs and the teaching departments in the universities regarding curriculum development, development of course material and the conduct of Personal Contact Programmes (PCP).
- In the case of most CCIs the courses were framed by the Boards of Studies and Academic Council of the universities, on which the CCIs had representation.
- In the majority of the CCIs the lessons were written by the teachers of the CCIs working in course teams; content editing was done by faculty members and course leaders; and language editing by faculty members/ course leaders/ editors.
- Print material was the principal media for communication. This was supplemented by some audio and video cassettes. A few CCIs organised radio programmes.
- Less than half of the CCIs had study centres, and their number varied from one to twenty (at Delhi). Most of the CCIs engaged their own teachers, and teachers from colleges for teaching/ counselling. The attendance of students at the centres varied from 5% to 82%.

The findings of Singh et al. (op. cit.) are rather discouraging. They state: "*Unfortunately, most of the CCIs in India have confined their instructional package only to the printed course material which in many cases is neither self-instructional nor in any known distance education format*", and "*The weakest feature of the CCIs are the lack of proper staff development programmes, poor quality of course material and the lack of student support services..... Study centres set up by some of them are mere apologies as they hardly serve any purpose*". One must, however, add that this indictment is not across the board. The overall assessment of Singh et al. is that "*Some of the CCIs enjoy good reputation, some are regarded as just satisfactory but some which do not have proper infrastructure do not enjoy much credibility*".

The reasons for the indifferent performances of most of the CCIs are apparent:

- The primary objective of establishing most of the CCIs was to broaden access. They were seen as a means to make higher education available to the less merited students who could not secure admission to colleges - largely because of poor performance in the qualifying examination. It was as if the CCIs themselves accepted a 'poor-cousin' status.
- Initially the teachers were drawn from the conventional stream and they had no training in the distance education system, and were therefore largely unaware of its special requirements.
- The programmes offered were the same as those in the conventional system, and the course materials were adaptations of those available to the students of the formal system. Little effort was put in to make them self-instructional.
- The instructional packages consisted only of print material, and not much has been done to take advantage of new technologies made available by advancements in communication technology.
- At a later stage some of the universities started regarding the CCIs as resource generating centres and registered students in large numbers without ensuring that there was a corresponding increase in infrastructure and faculty. In many institutes there were no student support services, in others only in name. Quality was the first casualty. This aspect is highlighted by the controversy relating to the B.Ed. programmes, with large enrolments, started by some CCIs in dual mode universities.

In order to overcome the evident weaknesses in the CCIs, Singh *et al.* (*op. cit.*) have made several suggestions. On the academic side there is a need for the CCIs to adopt distance-education teaching-learning methodologies. This includes making the course materials self-instructional, putting them in distance-education format, introducing electronic media as supplement to print material, providing well-equipped study centres, making arrangements for face-to-face counselling, having an efficient delivery system, and providing for assessment of assignments. Special stress has been placed on staff development, improvement in the quality of course materials, establishing efficient student support services, networking and, above all, on the provision of liberal funding.

Taking into consideration the deficiencies in the present CCIs, the University Grants Commission (UGC) has accepted the need to change the functioning of the CCIs to the distance education mode. For this special efforts will have to made for, amongst other things, staff development, computerisation of operational processes, adopting multi-media teaching-learning methodology, bringing about qualitative improvement in teaching material, providing adequate student support services with emphasis on study centres, library facilities and personal contact programmes, and the diversification of academic programmes to include vocational, technical and professional programmes. This is to be achieved with the assistance of the Distance Education Council (DEC) and Staff Training and Research Institute of Distance Education (STRIDE) of Indira Gandhi National Open University (IGNOU). In order to facilitate this, with the beginning of the Ninth Five Year Plan, the CCIs stand transferred from the purview of UGC to IGNOU.

For the transformation from the correspondence to distance mode DEC has formulated a policy (Takwale, 1996) that envisages:

- Transforming the present print material into an appropriate mix of print and non-print material that can be used on network.
- Establishing a network for academic, administrative and information services to the learners. The principal partners in the network will develop local area networks for internal functioning.
- Changing the present linear structure of programmes, where a limited set of courses lead to a degree, to a structure in which there is a spectrum of modules, with assigned credits, pre-requisites and co-requisites, from which a learner can make his choice, and on gathering the required number of credits, earn his degree.

Critical to the success of this endeavour is the adoption of new communication technologies, and the development of high quality programmes.

Open Universities (OUs)

By the end of the sixties the idea of starting an open university in India was being discussed. A working group constituted in 1971 under the chairmanship of Shri G. Parthasarthy recommended that the Government of India should establish an Open University so that students from the remotest parts of the country could have access to education and obtain degrees equivalent to those awarded by the universities located in urban centres. Significantly the group also made a specific recommendation regarding the preparation of reading materials of high standard and written keeping in view the requirement of students not having the benefits of teachers (Government of India, 1975). However, not much progress was achieved. In 1982 the UGC pointed out the need to establish a National Open University. While the Central Government deliberated over the issue the Government of Andhra Pradesh appointed in 1982 an expert committee to consider the matter, and in the same year established the first Indian open university, the Andhra Pradesh Open University, at Hyderabad (Government of Andhra Pradesh, 1982). It was subsequently redesignated as the Dr B. R. Ambedkar Open University (BRAOU). The encouraging start of the Andhra Pradesh Open University gave an impetus to the idea of having an open learning system for the country. It led to the establishment, in 1985, of the Indira Gandhi National Open University (IGNOU) at New Delhi. This national university has, in addition to teaching, the added responsibility of promotion of distance education, of coordination and maintenance of standards, and of providing financial assistance to state open universities (Government of India, 1985). These latter objectives are to be achieved through a Distance Education Council (DEC). Subsequently eight other open universities have been established. These are the Kota Open University (KOU), Rajasthan (1987), Nalanda Open University (NOU), Bihar (1887), Yashwantrao Chavan Maharashtra Open University (YCMOU), Maharashtra (1989), Madhya Pradesh Bhoj (Open) University (MPBOU), Madhya Pradesh (1991), Babasaheb Ambedkar Open University (BAOU); Gujarat (1994); Karnataka State Open University (KSOU), Karnataka (1996), Netaji Subhas Open University (NSOU), West Bengal (1997) and the U.P. Rajarshi Tandon Open University (UPRTOU), Uttar Pradesh. The total cumulative enrolment for the ten universities as on January 1, 2001 was about 17.85 lakhs (1.78 million). However, the registered students were about 6.18 lakhs. The universities together offer 288 programmes with 1920 courses of different levels, have 3027 full-time academic staff and engage about 38,000 academic counsellors. They have 96 regional centres and 3111 study centres. Table 20.1 summarises information regarding the open universities in India.

Table 20.1: Statistical Data on Open Universities

	BRAOU Andhra	IGNOU Central	KOU Rajasthan	NOU Bihar	YCMOU Maharashtra	MPBOU Madhya Pradesh	BAOU Gujarat	KSOU Karnataka	NSOU West Bengal	UPRTOU Uttar Pradesh	Total
Established	1982	1985	1987	1987	1989	1991	1994	1996	1997	1998	
Programmes on offer	23	60	22	8	60	30	11	29	3	41	287
Courses on Offer	307	640	195	9	236	49	96	244	18	126	1920
Students Registred	106748	287366	8980	1221	113500	55360	8575	32658	2798	1089	618295
Students on Roll	450000	646651	13000	1644	486651	108549	33892	40690	2798	1089	1784964
Regional Centres	21	44	6		10	9	2	4			96
Learner Support Centres	137	624	40	5	1451	667	61	52	36	38	3111
Academic Staff	98	295	23	1	60	36	39	66	40	1	631
Administrative Staff	340	856	294	23	173	33	46	25	41	26	2396
Technical Staff	35	238	5	1	30	33	46	25	41	26	2396
Academic Counsellors	4837	20364	541	28	4521	3200	776	2812	733	214	38026

Source : `Open Universities in India' Distance Education Council, Indira Gandhi National Open University (DEC), January 1, 2001

The Indira Gandhi National Open University has a pivotal role to play in the development of open/distance education in India. Apart from its teaching function it has been assigned responsibilities relating to distance education that are in many ways similar to those of the UGC for higher education in general. The IGNOU Act, 1985 prescribes three other functions, namely:

- Promotion of the open and distance education systems.
- Coordination and determination of standards of teaching, evaluation and research in these systems.
- Allocation and disbursal of grants to distance education institutions for performance of their functions.

In keeping with these responsibilities IGNOU has been interacting with state governments and advising them as regards the establishment and development of distance education in the states. It has formulated a programme for sharing of learning materials developed at IGNOU and other open universities. It is working towards the development of a network that will facilitate immediate sharing of information of all types. The Distance Education Council has developed guidelines for extending support to state open universities, identified a common pool of courses and programmes that could be shared by the open universities and has started giving grants for research in open and distance education. It has also established a quality assurance panel and is developing criteria and tools for evaluation of performance and consequent accreditation.

Organisational Structure and Learners

In the case of the CCIs the present universities have full control over the institute's functioning, and over its finances. The statutory bodies, composed largely of teachers from the formal stream, have the final say in all academic matters, and it is usually difficult to start, in the CCIs, programmes that are not already existing in the university. It is difficult for the CCI faculty to introduce curriculum reform. The difficulties are compounded by the fact that most CCIs are under-staffed. In quite a few cases there is only one teacher per discipline/subject.

Many universities treat the CCIs as sources of income, and it is known that in some cases upto half of the expenditure of the parent university is met from the income generated by the CCI through registration and tuition fees. Only a small percentage of fees collected is spent on the CCI. It is, therefore, not surprising that the quality of correspondence education has been low in terms of course lessons, teacher's input, student support and student learning. If the performance of the CCI students is to improve it is necessary to give its faculty greater academic freedom, and if necessary constitute separate academic statutory bodies like Boards of Studies, and allocate a much larger quantity of funds. It is heartening that recently the institutes have been given faculty status and department status, and constituent college status, as in the formal stream, with reasonable financial, administrative and academic autonomy.

The organisational structures of open universities are broader, diversified, and conform to the industrial system of education. The universities enjoy considerable autonomy, occasional state and central government interferences notwithstanding. The Vice-Chancellor is assisted by a Board of Management, planning board, academic council and finance committee. Four organisational units are usually obtained in OUs via academic schools, service divisions, administration, and regional support services division (further comprising regional centres and study centres). In IGNOU, for instance, while regional centres are occupied by permanent staff, the services of study centre staff are hired from the mainstream college/university/hospital/industry and the like. Regional centres liaison between study centres and headquarters, and actual student counselling takes place at study centres.

The academics in open universities enjoy reasonably higher autonomy in formulating, designing, developing, implementing and evaluating academic programmes, though within the boundary of institutional mission, national development priorities and available resources. There is considerable variation in academic staffing of open universities, and between academic and administrative staff of each open university (where the strength of the latter has been increasing, however, faster than that of the former).

Conclusion

The data presented above suggests that for India both the Correspondence Course Model and the Open University Model are equally important and have positive roles to play in the immediate future. Presently 7% of persons in the age group 17-23 years are in higher education. This is well below the percentage obtained in developed and many developing countries. As India's economic base widens many more young people will aspire for higher education. Moreover many adults are now seeking avenues for upgrading of skills or simply acquiring degrees in the liberal arts. The demand for higher education will increase greatly and formal education will not be in a position to meet the demand. Distance education presently caters to the needs of 18-

20% of persons seeking the benefits of higher education. Its contribution will have to increase to at least 30% if the demand is to be fully met.

At this juncture serious thought has to be given to the financial viability of the institutions of distance education. Out of the ten open universities that exist, only five are fully operational and a sixth has made considerable progress. The other four have still to make a meaningful impact, largely because development has been restricted by financial constraints. This poses the question as to whether the other states should establish new universities if they are not sure of providing 'adequate' (which in effect means substantial) support? Or would it be more pragmatic to build upon the already existing CCIs? The number of learners that are expected to enrol, their location, and their access to the latest communication technology should be deciding factors.

There has to be an understanding first between the OUs and the CCIs, and next between IGNOU and the state universities, regarding the domain of activity and the sharing of responsibilities. Though a precise separation of target groups cannot by prescribed the CCIs may be assigned the task of looking to the needs of persons in the 17-23 age group, who are unable to secure admission to regular institutions of learning; and the open universities could cater to the more diverse requirements of the more mature adults already employed. This in itself means that the open universities should cater largely to the needs of the employed and concentrate on professional programmes, especially programmes that fulfil the needs of people residing in rural areas. Incidentally, IGNOU has taken the lead in offering a number of professional programmes in management, engineering and computer education. YCMOU has implemented a number of certificate programmes in engineering and agriculture (including horticulture). BRAOU and YCMOU have initiated research programmes leading to the Ph.D. degree.

An issue that needs to be looked into immediately is that of overlapping of territory over which the different open universities operate. It would be preferable that a state university restricts its enrolment to students residing within the state. Further, the state universities should concentrate on programmes offered in the language of the state, though it could also have programmes in English and Hindi. In the long run the open universities need to concentrate on the development of course curricula and learning materials. These could be made available to the CCIs for possible adaptation and/or adoption. As the larger states establish and develop their own open universities the IGNOU could possible devote greater attention to its promotional role, leaving imparting of education in the more common areas to the state universities and the CCIs. One can visualise it developing into a national resource centre for distance education producing a variety of programmes and learning materials for use of different distance education agencies.

References

Association of Indian Universities, (2000), *Handbook on Distance Education*, AIU, New Delhi.

Distance Education Council, (2001), *Open Universities in India*, DEC-IGNOU, New Delhi.

Government of Andhra Pradesh, (1982), *Towards an Open Learning System*, Report of the Committee on the Establishment of an Open University, GOAP, Hyderabad,

Government of India, (1966), *Report of the Working on the Education Commission (1964-66): Education and National Development*, GOI, New Delhi.

Government of India, (1975), *Report of the Working Group on Open University*, Ministry of Education and Social Welfare, GOI, New Delhi.

Government of India, (1985), *Indira Gandhi National Open University Act, 1985*, GOI, Department of Education, Ministry of Human Resource Development, New Delhi.

Government of India, (1994), *Report of the CABE Committee on Distance Education*, Department of Education, Ministry of Human Resource Development, GOI, New Delhi.

Singh, Bakhshish, Mullick, S. and Chaudhary, N., (1994), *Correspondence/Distance Education in India*, Research Report, Indira Gandhi National Open University, New Delhi.

Takwale, R.G., (1996), IGNOU's Challenges of Quality, Quantity. and Equity, *University News*, 34(22), 7- 15.

21

Globalisation of Distance Learning System: Implications for Developing Countries*

Introduction

With unprecedented developments in communication technology, and with an increase in the demand for quality education, higher education has transgressed national boundaries. There has been an expansion of distance and flexible education and the situation offers a unique opportunity to Indian universities to internationalise their operations, with a focus on countries having a large Indian expatriate population. The requirements of a 'globalisation programme', in the context of changing paradigms in education, need to be taken into consideration.

Changing Paradigms

Change is all pervasive and inevitable, only the nature of change and the rate at which it takes place varies with time, space and field of operation. In the realm of higher education changes have traditionally been slow, mainly because of its elitist nature and the 'ivory tower' existence of its institutions. However, in the years following World War II, higher education systems, the world over, have undergone transformation from elite systems to mass-systems. At the same time, there have been remarkable developments in communication technology. Consequently changes are more rapid and more radical. The following changes, that are of the nature of paradigm shifts, are especially relevant.

- The existing model of higher education, requiring *selective learning over a specified period* is being replaced by a model of *lifetime learning for all*. This has become necessary because of the changing nature of jobs which now require continuous renewal and updating of knowledge and skills (UNESCO, 1995).

* Keynote Address delivered at the National Seminar on '*Globalisation of Distance/ Open Learning System: Possibilities and Problems for Developing Countries*' organised by the Indira Gandhi National Open University, December 15-16, 1996.

- Throughout the world Higher Education is undergoing a paradigm shift from an *instruction-centred college/university* model to a *learner-centred integrated network* model, based on access to learning, resources and on student initiative (ICDE, 1996).
- Distance Education, which is commonly regarded to be an industrialised form of education, has evolved from a *Fordist to neo-Fordist* and *post-Fordist* forms of production (Farnes, 1993; Raggat, 1993; Rumble, 1995 a, b, c; Peters, 1996).

A natural consequence of the acceptance by society of the 'lifelong learning for all' concept has been expansion of distance/open learning. This is exemplified by developments in the western world, especially in the United States. In this country, as revealed by a survey conducted by the National Center for Educational Statistics in 1995, forty per cent of the adult population takes adult education courses. Thus, while considerable expansion in distance/open learning education programmes may be expected, these will largely relate to updating of skills, and to knowledge enhancement. Courses leading to degrees may probably not develop to the same extent, though open education institutions are expected to take over some load from the institutions of formal education.

The developments in computer based information technologies have promoted learner-centred learning in both formal and distance/open systems. In the western countries computer-aided learning (CAL) is common, with the site of learning being not only the premises of educational institution but also workplaces and homes. The impact of the CAL on distance/open learning is, however, dependent on computer availability and the extent of computer literacy.

Technologies in Distance Education

Based on the teaching aids used and the technologies adopted, different distance learning models have been recognised (Garrison, 1989; James and Gardner, 1995). These are:

Generation 1: Using 'mailable' materials including print materials, and audio- and video-cassettes.

Generation 2: Education 'through the air' using broadcasts and telecasts, talkback TV, interactive TV, and tele-conferencing (audio and video).

Generation 3: Computer-based education using software packages, CD-ROM, Multimedia and internet.

Generation 4: Technologies of the immediate future, viz., video desktop (2-way audio video) and virtual classrooms.

The mere existence of a technology in a country is not enough. It is difficult to use the technology for distance education unless it is integrated in the lifestyle of the public at large. Even in advanced countries like the United States, Japan, United Kingdom and France the promises held out by TV and computer technologies have not been fulfilled (Pottiez, 1994). TV broadcast is often presented as having vast possibilities, even as a panacea for problems relating to mass education and training. The accumulating evidence from all over the world, however, suggests that one-way broadcast television is one of the least effective media of learning, though it is useful for raising awareness and spreading information (Foks, 1995). Hence, it would be pragmatic to largely restrict programmes to be developed for developing countries to print materials and audio- and video-cassettes.

Most developing countries do not have reliable delivery systems. The Indian open universities and correspondence course institutions predominantly make use of the print media delivered through government postal services. This is not the most effective mechanism of delivery. Attempts to internationalise education must take this fact into consideration.

Globalisation

Globalisation, simply put, is the 'space-time compression' (Evans, 1995) which brings together nations, cultures and economies, and at the same time increases their inter-dependency. The process has been promoted by speeding up of transport and of communication, and by increase in economic activity. Globalisation does not necessarily result in homogenisation but, on the contrary, may lead to the strengthening of ethnic identities – both local and regional (Edwards, 1994). This is a fact that needs to be kept in view.

An essence of globalisation is collaboration with mutual respect. Successful collaborative efforts require active participation from both sides. A programme based on offering by one side and passive acceptance by the other can have limited success. Inputs from the receiving countries arc desirable while adapting programmes. Validation by them of the course content in relation to their own identities and backgrounds is necessary. It is also necessary that the receiving countries be actively involved in the setting up (and franchising) of student support services (as counselling centres).

The U.K. Open University and Open Learning Australia have successfully internationalised their operations and marketed programmes essentially developed for domestic learners. The production strategy of the Open University has been described as Fordist (Raggat, 1993) primarily because the university operated a mass volume system with a relatively small range of courses and print-runs sufficient for four years. Even after this period some courses have been extended. Moreover, the courses first chosen were foundation courses and undergraduate courses leading to a first degree.

The strategy that needs to be adopted in the case of developing countries has to be *neo-Fordist* or *post-Fordist*. The established courses of IGNOU could be modified to suit the requirements of different regions and cultures (East Africa, Gulf Countries, South East Asia) and be produced in smaller numbers. Recent advances in printing technology should allow for cost-effective production. It may also be a good idea to concentrate on professional programmes aimed at skill-development and updating of knowledge, though in some specific situations degree-oriented undergraduate programmes may also be popular.

Suggestions

Internationalisation of Distance education programmes should be undertaken only after comprehensive planning and adequate preparation. The following aspects may be kept in view:

A *While Planning Programmes and Developing Learning Materials:*

i) Market research and needs assessment be undertaken to determine what type of programmes are required.

ii) In case of most developing countries the requirement is for professional courses that aim at enhancing skills (Management, Electronics, Computer-Science, Nursing).

iii) Countries with large number of non-resident Indians on short time assignments may have market for first-degree programmes.

iv) Inputs regarding objectives, content of courses and instructional aids be obtained from academics/experts and potential employers in user countries.

v) Course structure needs to be detailed out before development. There is the desirability of having a large number of modules and units covering (a) core aspects, and (b) aspects relevant to a region/ culture. It should be possible to substitute (b) in accordance with the requirements.

vi) Various models of course design and development have to be carefully considered on the basis of appropriateness, effectiveness and economy.

B *In Production of Materials:*

i) Course materials should reflect quality of production and must be attractively packaged.

ii) There should be flexibility in production procedure to ensure meeting of specialised needs.

C *In Conducting Programmes:*

i) Ensure that assignments are graded promptly and academic enquiries receive individualised response.

D *While Finalising Delivery Mechanisms:*

i) Materials need to be despatched promptly as per predetermined schedule.

ii) The delivery service must be effective. Students must have, at all times, an adequate supply of study material.

E *Regarding Student Support Services:*

i) It is encouraging if provisions are made for scholarships.

ii) Franchising of counselling centres is made after careful scrutiny and taking into consideration physical facilities, availability of academic support and objectives of collaborating agency/institution.

F *In Administrative Matters:*

i) A well thought-out marketing strategy needs to be developed.

ii) There should be an easy registration system and enquiries need to be replied to promptly, with a personal touch.

iii) Examinations must be conducted efficiently and results declared promptly.

Finally, as Lambert (1996) succinctly states "*Everything that the school provides the student... should reflect high quality, competence, taste and an obvious commitment to service*".

References

Edwards, R., (1994), From a Distance? Globalisation, Space-Time Compression and Distance Education, *Open Learning,* 9(3):9-17.

Evans, T., (1995), Globalisation, Post-Fordism, and Open and Distance Education, *Distance Education,* 16(2):256-269.

Farnes, N. (1993), Modes of Production: Fordism and Distance Education, *Open Learning,* 8(1):10-20.

Foks, J., (1995), Technology and Learning, *Open Learning through Distance Education,*1(3):1, 10-11.

Garrisson, D.R., (1989), 'Distance Education' in Merriam, S.B and Cunningham, P.M (Editors), *Handbook of Adult and Continuing Education*, Jossey-Bass, San Francisco.

James, W.B. and Gardner, D.L., (1995), 'Learning Styles, Implications for Distance Learning' in Rossmann, M.H. and Rossmann, M.E. (Editors), *Facilitating Distance Education, New Directions for Adult and Continuing Education,* 67:19-31.

ICDE, (1996), The Educational Shift: Implications for ICDE and the Distance Learning Community, *Report of the Task Force of the International Council for Distance Education Standing Committee of Presidents,* pp. 22.

Lambert, M.P., (1996), The Distance Education and Training Council: At the Cutting Edge, *Quality Assurance in Education,* 4(4):26-28.

Peters, O., (1996), 'Distance Education and Industrial Production: A Comparative Interpretation in Outline' in Sewart, T., Keegan, D., and Holmbert, B. (Editors), *Distance Education:International Perspection,* Croom Holm, Bechenham Kent, pp. 95-113.

Pottiez, J.M., (1994), Distance Education and the New Technologies: A New Adventure in Knowledge and Communication in Husen, Torsten (Editors), *The Role of the University: A Global Perspective,* UNESCO, Paris, pp.185-202.

Raggat, P.,(1993), Post-Fordism and Distance Education – A Flexible Strategy for Change, *Open Learning*, 8(1):21-31.

Rumble, G., (1995a), Labour Market Theories and Distance Education I: Industrialisation and Distance Education, *Open Learning,* 10(1):10-20.

Rumble, G., (1995b), Labour Market Theories and Distance Education II: How Fordist is Distance Education? *Open Learning,* 10(2):12-28.

Rumble, G., (1995c), Labour Market Theories and Distance Education III: Post-Fordism – The Way Forward, *Open Learning,* 10(3):25-42.

UNESCO (1995), *Document of Policies for the Change and Development of Higher Education,* UNESCO, Tokyo.